Advertising Management : Theory and Practice

ADVERTISING MANAGEMENT: THEORY AND PRACTICE

By

Dr. Mahendra Kumar Padhy

Assistant Professor

Deptt. of Mass Communication and Journalism

Babasaheb Bhimrao Ambedkar University

(A Central University)

Govt. of India

Lucknow

UNIVERSITY SCIENCE PRESS

(An Imprint of Laxmi Publications Pvt. Ltd.)

BANGALORE • CHENNAI • COCHIN • GUWAHATI • HYDERABAD
JALANDHAR • KOLKATA • LUCKNOW • MUMBAI • PATNA
RANCHI • NEW DELHI

Published by :

UNIVERSITY SCIENCE PRESS

(An Imprint of Laxmi Publications Pvt. Ltd.)

113, Golden House, Daryaganj,

New Delhi-110002

Phone: 011-43 53 25 00

Fax : 011-43 53 25 28

www.laxmipublications.com

info@laxmipublications.com

First Edition : 2011

OFFICES

Bangalore	080-26 75 69 30	**Chennai**	044-24 34 47 26
Cochin	0484-237 70 04, 405 13 03	**Guwahati**	0361-251 36 69, 251 38 81
Hyderabad	040-24 65 23 33	**Jalandhar**	0181-222 12 72
Kolkata	033-22 27 43 84	**Lucknow**	0522-220 99 16
Mumbai	022-24 91 54 15, 24 92 78 69	**Patna**	0612-230 00 97
Ranchi	0651-221 47 64		

UAM–9618–175–ADVERTIS MGMT : THEO PRAC–PAD C—

Typeset at: Monu Printographics, Delhi

Contents

Chapters | *Pages*

1. Introduction **1–18**

1.1 Introduction 1
1.2 Methodology 6
1.3 Review of Literature 7
1.4 The Research Problem 12
1.5 Scope and Objectives of the Study 13
1.6 Hypotheses 13
1.7 Sample Design 13
1.8 Classification and Tabulation of Data 14
1.9 Analysis and Interpretation of Data 14
1.10 Definition of Concepts 14
1.11 Experiences of the Investigator 15
1.12 The Questionnaire 15
1.13 Statistical Techniques Used 16
1.14 Data Collection 17
1.15 Chapter Division 17
1.16 Limitations of the Study 17

2. Advertising: A Conceptual Framework **19–58**

2.1 Introduction 19
2.2 Nature and Scope of Advertising 20
2.3 Definitions 21
2.4 Historical Perspective 24
2.5 Effect of Urban Growth on Advertising 25
2.6 Advertising: Its Role and Importance in the Modern Business World 25
2.7 Defining Advertising Goals for Measured Advertising Results (DAGMAR) 26
2.8 Advertising in Marketing Mix 28
2.9 Market Segmentation 32
2.10 Advertising Process 33
2.11 Effectiveness of Advertising 36

	2.12 Media Selection for Advertising	39
	2.13 Need and Importance of Media Planning	40
	2.14 Media Selection	42
	2.15 Media Research	44
	2.16 Print Media and Advertising	45
	2.17 Broadcast Media and Advertising	47
	2.18 Creativity in Advertising	48
	2.19 Creativity in Communication	49
	2.20 Advertising Appeals	50
	2.21 Creating and Producing an Advertisement	53
	Summary	58
3.	**Socio-Economic Implications of Advertising**	**59–70**
	3.1 Introduction	59
	3.2 Economic Effects of Advertising	59
	3.3 Explicit Role of Advertising	61
	3.4 Indirect Role of Advertising	64
	3.5 Critical Analysis of Advertising	65
	3.6 Social Issues in Advertising	66
	3.7 Controversial Effects of Advertising	68
	3.8 Concluding Comments	69
4.	**Advertising: Truth, Ethics and Social Responsibility**	**71–77**
	4.1 Introduction	71
	4.2 Ethics and Morality	71
	4.3 Advertising and Social Responsibility	72
	4.4 Obligation to Value System and Lifestyle	74
	4.5 Legal Aspects of Advertising	75
	Summary	77
5.	**Advertising and Consumer Behaviour Research**	**78–112**
	5.1 Introduction	78
	5.2 Consumer Behaviour	78
	5.3 Consumer Research	82
	5.4 Motivation and Consumer Behaviour	84
	5.5 Social Class Lifestyle and its Influence on Consumer Behaviour	86
	5.6 Decision Process	89
	5.7 Types of Purchase Decision Behaviour	91
	5.8 Model of Buyer Behaviour	91

5.9 Post-Purchase Behaviour 93
5.10 Marketing Research 94
5.11 The Rational Consumer 97
5.12 Presentation of Consumer Behaviour in Models 99
5.13 Interdisciplinary Contributions to Marketing Thought 102
5.14 Models of Buyer Behaviour 104
5.15 Cultural Context of Consumer Behaviour 107
5.16 Consumer Behaviour and Advertising 107
Summary 111
6. Advertising and Lifestyle Communication **113–148**
6.1 Introduction 113
6.2 Lifestyle and Communication 114
6.3 Values and Lifestyle Survey 115
6.4 Social Class Lifestyles 116
6.5 Social Class and Income Related to Lifestyle Patterns 117
6.6 Lifestyle Marketing 118
6.7 Lifestyle and Psychographic Segmentation 120
6.8 Effects of Advertising on Lifestyles 125
6.9 Communication and Attitude Change 128
6.10 Types of Communication 131
6.11 Barriers to Communication 132
6.12 Mass Communication 134
6.13 Advertising and Communication 136
6.14 Advertising Communication System 138
6.15 Advertising Exposure Model 140
6.16 Mass Communication Research 141
6.17 Attitude Modification 143
6.18 Behavioural Change 144
6.19 Comprehension and Recall Tests 144
6.20 Attitude Change 144
Summary 146
7. Impact of Advertising on Consumer Behaviour **149–185**
7.1 Introduction 149
7.2 Magazine/Newspaper Readership 149
7.3 Television Watching Pattern 150
7.4 Popular Programmes in Television 151

7.5	Exposure to Advertisement	152
7.6	Viewing Pattern of Television/Magazine/Newspaper Advertising	152
7.7	Usefulness of Advertising	153
7.8	Truthfulness in Advertising	153
7.9	Influencing Buying Decision	154
7.10	Nature of Advertisement	154
7.11	Preferable Medium of Advertising	155
7.12	Advertising in Shaping Brand Image	156
7.13	Advertising Resulting in Incremental Cost of Products and Services	157
7.14	Informative Value of Television Advertising	158
7.15	Influence of Television on Consumer Behaviour and Lifestyle	159
7.16	Television Advertising and Purchase Behaviour	159
7.17	Television Advertising and Brand Switching	160
7.18	Cell Phone User	160
7.19	Frequency of Internet Chatting	163
7.20	Feeling towards Internet Chatting	164
7.21	Browsing Porno Web-site on Internet/Reading Pornographic Magazine	165
7.22	Computer Use	166
7.23	Tele Shopping/Online Shopping	167
7.24	Readymade Dress Buying	167
7.25	Purchase of Car and Motorbike	168
7.26	Consumption of Cold Drinks and Fast Food	169
7.27	Drinking Water Preference	170
7.28	Participation in Social Drink	170
7.29	Invitation for Drink	171
7.30	Participation in Disco Dancing	171
7.31	Appearance of Girls with Tight Jeans and Skimpy Dresses	173
7.32	Beauty Contest	175
7.33	Condom Advertisement on AIDS	176
7.34	Advertisement of Sanitary Napkins	177
7.35	Products/Services without Advertisement	178
7.36	Advertisement and its Impact on Younger Generation	178
7.37	An Opinion on Break Time for Advertisement	179
7.38	Celebrity Endorsement of Products and Consumer Preference	180
7.39	Influencing Factor for Leading Modern Lifestyle	180
7.40	Development of a Model for Consumer Behaviour	182
	Summary	184

8. Lifestyle Communications Through Print and Electronic Advertisements **186–206**

Part–A : Print Presentation of Lifestyle

8.1 Introduction 186

Summary 195

Part–B : Electronic Presentation of Lifestyle

8.2 Introduction 196

Summary 205

9. Advertising in the Age of Economic Liberalization **207–215**

9.1 Introduction 207

9.2 Branding Strategies in India 209

9.3 Advertising Management in a Global Scene 213

10. Conclusions, Major Findings and Recommendations **216–219**

10.1 Introduction 216

10.2 Major Findings of the Study 216

10.3 Testing of Hypotheses 218

10.4 Practical Utility of the Research Study 219

10.5 Future Extension of the Study 219

Case Studies **220–225**

Appendices

Appendix—I : Bibliography 226–232

Appendix—II : Product and Service Advertisements 233–246

Appendix—III : Questionnaire 247–252

Abbreviations **253**

Index **255–260**

Preface

The world is full of expressions—natural and man-made. Nature is creative and man tries to follow her and thus originates civilisation with its inventions, art, craft, and knowledge, which are communicated from generation to generation and within the existing community. This art or science of communication has also its inventiveness and creativity, particularly in the field of advertising.

Advertising comes to people mostly uninvited, touching their subconscious. It soothes the burden of life and often takes them to a joyous dreamland. Although a business proposition, it mystifies, astounds, delights, tickles and amazes the purely logical in a bid to motivate people in a desired way.

Advertising has witnessed a rapid growth during the past few decades. Behind the glamour and glitter of advertising world, there is planning, organising, staffing, directing and controlling of a number of tasks—creative as well as non-creative which contribute to the attainment of the marketing objectives of the sponsoring organisations. Advertising is an art as well as a science and therefore its study has to be based on two approaches; a graphical and structural approach and a managerial approach, which are blended together to generate a result oriented advertisement copy or advertisement campaign.

The objective of advertising is not only confined to moulding consumer's choice of brands/ services, but also at creating awareness about products and services among the consumers. From the marketer's point of view, the effect of advertisement upon the consumers is of crucial importance because the survival or the exit of their operations depend a lot on how well the message reaches the target consumers and how well it is received.

As the research study is based on Advertising and Lifestyle Communication: An Assessment of Media Impact on Consumer Behaviour, this can be better understood only when consumer behaviour itself is well understood.

Consumer behaviour research is a very important aspect of marketing research since consumers' together only forms the market. To effectively perform the business activities that direct the flow of goods and services from producer to the ultimate consumer or user, the needs, motives and desires of the consumer must be understood well. These are the areas, which form the bulk of the domain of consumer behaviour research. These are the factors of 'Attitude', 'Attention', 'Brand', 'Comprehension', 'Intention' and 'Action', which are so important in measuring the effectiveness of advertising, are studied in depth through various sophisticated models in consumer behaviour research. In fact, advertising or for that matter any marketing activity can be more effectively practised when there already exists an abundance of knowledge in the buyer behaviour process.

Consumer behaviour is defined as the acts of individuals directly involved in obtaining and using economic goods and services, including the decision process that precede and determine these acts.

Lifestyle is related to consumer's values and personality that represent internal states or characteristics. Lifestyles are manifestations or actual patterns of behaviour. In particular, they are represented by a consumer's activities, interests, and opinions (AIOs). What one does in one's spare time is often a good indicator of one's lifestyle. Lifestyle research in this project work is more specific on product usage and patterns. This enables marketers to gain a better understanding of how their product fits into the consumer's general patterns of behaviour. Advertising messages and promotions are often designed to appeal to certain lifestyles. Often marketers can develop new products and service ideas by uncovering unfulfilled needs of certain lifestyle segments. General lifestyle items that correlate well with product usage might well explain characteristics of the markets' activity, interest and opinions to the seller. Such findings could give the marketer some direction for product, promotion channel and pricing decisions.

Against such a backdrop, the present research study is an attempt to examine media impact on consumer behaviour, and also to study and assess how advertising communicates lifestyles to the ultimate consumers. It is advertising that communicates lifestyles through projection of different celebrities and top-class models. The research study is an attempt to assess the role of media in moulding consumers' behaviour.

—Author

Acknowledgement

I am immensely indebted to my guide, Prof.(Dr.) Dasarathi Mishra, Professor of Journalism and Mass Communication, Berhampur University, Berhampur, for his able guidance, inspiring suggestion and meticulous care, without which this book would not have been completed. I find no words to express my heartfelt gratitude to him for his gracious commitment to my research work.

I am deeply grateful to Prof. Sunil Kant Behera, Head, Department of Mass Communication, Berhampur University, Berhampur for his encouragement and timely support.

I express my deep sense of gratitude to Prof. N.C. Sahu, and Prof.N.B. Pradhan, Dept. of Economics for their valuable suggestions.

I record my deep sense of gratitude to my revered parents Sri Ramesh Chandra Padhy and Smt. Narmada Padhy, who have been the perpetual source of inspiration and with whose blessings the present study could be completed.

My words of appreciation also go to the faculty friends, Dept. of Mass Communication and Journalism, Babasaheb Bhimrao Ambedkar University (A Central University) for their valuable suggestions.

Above all, I owe everything to my Lord Sri Hanumanji Maharaj and Maa Jai Santoshi.

—Author

Foreword

The need for and the acceptance of Advertising as both a business and a societal force is now a days seldom questioned. Contrasted with earlier days, this is a change of quantum magnitude.

When and why did the change in attitude occur? It was, I believe, the socially turbulent decade of the 60's that saw advertising move from the periphery to the centre of business and social action. The 60's—a time when the media posture became more aggressive towards all institutions in our society, business as well as government. The investigative reporter moved from city hall to corporate board room. Business became as frequent a subject for review and criticism as the broad way stage.

The 60's—a time when advertising came of age- a time of maturation: a time of acceptance of involvement as an effective tool for management and motivation. Now some 50 years later, we are no longer called on to explain or justify ourselves as advertising practitioners. Rather, we called on to be accountable, to show that what we do really contributes to the achievement of our target audience's goals to demonstrate through research and other measurement techniques that what we do is effective.

We are called on, to demonstrate that we, as advertising practitioners can meet out audience expectations. Coupled with these rising expectations is a near explosion in demand for advertising and public relations services. Business, governments at all levels, not for profit institutions ranging from schools to hospitals to social agencies-all are calling on advertising and public relations to contribute substantially to their missions.

The fact is that today the demand for professional advertising and public relations practice are increasingly aware of the need for people with the special skills underpinning the effective practitioner and they are intensifying their efforts- although, perhaps not enough- to educate, train and develop the public relations and advertising men and women of tomorrow.

A greater emphasis on basics and practicality is one step in the right direction. Through its history, advertising , principles, case studies and problems, now in this book has recognized the need to expose future practitioners to real life situations. It has served as a starting point for the exploration and inquiry that is the basis of effective advertising program and its implementation. Hopefully, this process will continue throughout the professional careers of those men and women who gain their first exposure to advertising from this textbook.

Professor (Dr.) Dasarathi Mishra

Chapter 1 INTRODUCTION

PART–A

INTRODUCTION TO THE STUDY

1.1 INTRODUCTION

Advertising today is a worldwide phenomenon. The modern world without advertising is something virtually inconceivable. Advertising is a measure of the growth of civilisation and an indication of the striving of the human race for betterment and perfection. Advertising has both forward and backward linkages in the process of satisfaction across the entire spectrum of needs. The explicit function of advertising is to make the potential audience aware of the existence of the product, service or idea which would help them fulfil their felt needs and spell-out the differential benefits in a competitive situation. Advertising is the best and the most convenient route to reach the consumer's mind. To make their ventures successful, advertisers spend money, time and resources at their disposal in order to dissect the intricacies of the human mind and to understand where the individual vulnerability lies.

Advertising is an inescapable part of our social lives. This is because it is rooted in the activity of persuasion, which is fundamental to the way in which we communicate with and relate to others in society. In the contemporary world, advertising has gained further significance because it provides us with a major cultural need—the need for images, icons and simulacra. We are surrounded by images in print, photographs, films, television and finally multimedia.

The important function of advertising is to introduce a wide range of goods, services to the prospective buyers, thus to support the free market economy. Advertising has become a vital marketing tool as well as a powerful communication force. It is the action of calling something to attention of the people especially by paid announcements. It is a message designed to make others known what we have to sell or what we have to buy. By using various channels of information and persuasion, it can help sell goods, services, images and ideas.

Peter Drucker has stated that the purpose of a business is to create a customer. It is the customer who is the foundation of a business and keeps it in existence. If the purpose of business is to create and keep a customer, it is imperative that he must be the focal point of all business activities. The central theme of the marketing concept is that the objective of business is to identify, anticipate and satisfy customer needs and desires. The rationale of marketing concept implies that the company management makes all decisions in terms of marketing-orientation, which begins with a customer. The concept recognises that the dictator of market success or failure, the customer, is of key concern in determining company policies and actions. All other activities of the business are integrated and balanced in terms of what is best for the company in the market place.[1]

It cannot be gainsaid that under the marketing concept the focus is on the customer—his needs and requirements—rather than on the product. The old homespun philosophy that, "If you make a better mousetrap, the world will beat a path to your door" or "we will give them any colour car they want—as long as it is black" has to be replaced by new customer logic like, "We are more interested in pleasing a customer than in making a sale", "I do not run a soap company, I run a marketing organisation". Marketing begins with the customer and ends with the customer.

'Philip Kotler' succinctly comments, "The marketing concept is a customer-orientation backed by integrated marketing aimed at generating customer satisfaction as the key to satisfy organisational goals".[2]

Advertising consists of all the activities involved in presenting to a group a non-personal, oral, or visual, openly sponsored message regarding a product, service, or ideas; this message, called an advertisement, is dissemination through one or more media and is paid for by an identified sponsor.[3]

Advertising is a highly public mode of communication. Its public nature confers a kind of legitimacy to the product and also suggests a standardized offering. Because many persons receive the same message, buyers know that their motive for purchasing the product will be publicly understood.

Advertising provides opportunities for dramatising the company and its products through the artful use of print, sound and colour. Sometimes the tools very success at expressiveness may, however, dilute or distract from the message. As a non-personal tool, advertising in spite of being public, pervasive, and expressive, cannot be as compelling as a personal salesman. The audience does not feel obligated to pay attention or respond. Advertising is only able to carry on a monologue, not a dialogue, with the audience.

Advertising plays a vital role in the society, in general, and in the business, in particular. It is a technique of modernism. *'Aaker'* and *'Myers'* believed that advertising can be considered a mirror of society.[4] Advertising not only plays a vital economic role in the scheme of national development, but it has an important educational, cultural and social part to play as well.

---

1 Ferdinand F. Mauser, *Modern Marketing Management - An Integrated Approach*, McGraw Hill, 1981, p. 8.

2 Kotler, Philip, *Marketing Management - Analysis, Planning and Control*, Prentice Hall of India Pvt. Ltd., New Delhi, p. 17.

3 William J. Santom, *Fundamentals of Marketing*, McGraw Hill, New York, 1991, p.535.

4 Aaker A. David and Myers, G. John, *Advertising Management*, Prentice Hall of India, New Delhi, 1991, p. 3.

Advertising stimulates demand of a product. It appeals to various motives of consumers so as to develop their predisposition towards the product being advertised. It supplements salesmanship and sales promotion and thus contributes to the success of the overall marketing strategy. Repeated advertising of a particular brand or service helps to develop a brand preference. It helps in increasing the sales volume, the cost per unit decreases, at least up to a certain level. It leads to increase in profits of the company. By delivering psychological utilities, advertising enhances consumer satisfaction. It boosts the image of the company and helps it in facing the keen competition prevailing in the modern business world.

Marketing is more than just distributing goods from the manufacturer to the final consumer. It comprises all the stages between creation of the product and the after-market, which follows the eventual sale. One of these stages is advertising. The stages are like links in a chain, and the chain will break if one of the links is weak. Advertising is, therefore, as important as every other stage or link and each depends on the other for success.

The product or service itself, its naming, packaging, pricing and distribution, are all reflected in advertising, which has been called the lifeblood of an organisation. Without advertising, the products or services cannot flow to the distributors or sellers and on to the consumers or users.

A successful national economy depends on advertising promoting sales, so that factory production is maintained, people are employed and have spending power, and the money goes round and round. When this process stops there is a recession. Similarly, prosperous countries are those in which advertising does its job. In Third World countries, economies are poor and advertising is minimal, especially when a large proportion of the population are young non-earners.

Most of the people seem to have quest for materialism and instant gratification. Advertising encourages the possession of material, tangible goods. The person endeavours to get more and better things, so that his ego is boosted by these acquisitions and he enjoys a higher social status partly as a result of it. This attitude is responsible for developing a sense of instant gratification that takes the human mind away from the artistic and finer things of life that are mental stimulants such as art, poetry, nature, etc.

Advertising as it is, raises a number of questions that affect the moral and aesthetic fibre of our society. Has advertising been responsible for eroding our morality? Are violence and permissiveness the outcome of advertising messages? Some advertising messages may contribute to such cultural lag and decay.

Advertising affects interpersonal attitudes, both in a positive and negative manner. Advertisements about better opportunities in life as also about better products, services and gadgets exercise an upward pull helping many people to improve their living standards. On the other hand, advertisements about air-conditioned cars, which are intended for the economically elite may breed resentment and frustration among the less affluent people. Similarly, advertisements which coast women in stereotype roles of housewives or sex objects evoke protests from women's organisations. Emphasis on youth and youthful looks may be viewed as disrespectful to the elderly and thus resented.

How does advertising affect the attitudes of our children? Does it affect our children in a negative manner, which is unacceptable to our established society? Does advertising encourage our children to behave like adults before time? Does it help put peer pressure and induce habits like smoking and taking drugs or promiscuity? Do some of the messages promote individuality so much that it results in parental disrespect? Are the young children competent enough to comprehend and process information contained in television commercials accurately? Such questions involve moral and ethical values that need research and investigation.

As the research study is based on Advertising and Lifestyle Communication: An Assessment of Media Impact on Consumer Behaviour, this can be better understood only when consumer behaviour itself is well understood.

Consumer behaviour research is a very important aspect of marketing research since consumers' together only forms the market. To effectively perform the business activities that direct the flow of goods and services from producer to the ultimate consumer or user, the needs, motives and desires of the consumer must be understood well. These are the areas, which form the bulk of the domain of consumer behaviour research. These are the factors of 'Attitude', 'Attention', 'Brand', 'Comprehension', 'Intention' and 'Action', which are so important in measuring the effectiveness of advertising, are studied in depth through various sophisticated models in consumer behaviour research. In fact, advertising or for that matter any marketing activity can be more effectively practised when there already exists an abundance of knowledge in the buyer behaviour process.

Consumer behaviour is defined as the acts of individuals directly involved in obtaining and using economic goods and services, including the decision process that precede and determine these acts.

Advertising communicates lifestyle through projection of high-class models, celebrities, such as film stars and sports stars. The concept of lifestyle is related to consumers' values and personality that represent internal states or characteristics. Lifestyles are manifestations or actual patterns of behaviour. In particular, they are represented by a consumer's Activities, Interests, and Opinions (AIOs).

Another important influence on consumer behaviour is lifestyle that is largely derived from the influence of the family. In many ways, the term is closely akin to individual differences. The term describes a distinctive mode of living. The concept goes far beyond the characterisations that result from a person's social class. This describes how people go about their daily routines. It is how people allocate their time on different activities of daily life, rather than how they spend their money, although the two problems are interrelated in many instances. What is important to individuals may be reflected by their actions. We may see that two persons belonging to the same social class and possessing the same demographic characteristics are very different in their lifestyle.

The lifestyle research can be very useful in designing and development of advertising strategy and copy. It provides data dealing with such demographic variables as sex, age and income or studies of consumer behaviour about the product and its use.

Thus, the advertising strategist attempts to learn as much as possible about the social and cultural influences on target consumers' behaviour. It will help much in designing and preparing the advertisement copy and the appeal in the right perspective effectively. By studying social and cultural influences on the behaviour of the people, the advertiser can take a decision about the medium to be used. These insights combine to permit better communication.

Advertising, one of the several incoming messages directed at the consumer, the salience of which is influenced by the emotional, physical and need state of the individual. Advertising can also be defined from a societal perspective. Advocates of advertising would argue that advertising provides a valuable service to society and its members. In general, it helps define the meaning and the role of products and institutions for the consumer. It also provides consumers with information that indicated the differences that exist between product brands and the distinguishing characteristics of companies and institutions. This information also tells the consumer what a particular brand should do when used, how to evaluate this performance, and how to compare brands and institutions.

Advocates of advertising would also claim some economic benefits. There is little doubt that advertising does create greater product turnover, which in turn produces greater profitability for the company, which in turn produces more jobs and higher wages, and so forth. Thus, our improved standard of living can be tied directly to advertising. Another economic virtue attributed to advertising is the contention that advertising assists in ridding our society of ineffectual businesses. That is, businesses that are well run and offer meaningful products tend to be helped through advertising. Businesses that are poorly managed and offer unwanted products tend to be eliminated through the impact of advertising.

Many critics of advertising feel that, advertising is a detrimental force in our society. At one extreme, some people believe that advertising represents a waste of economic resources because of its large volume. Because advertising is so pervasive, some people also believe that advertising leads consumers to purchase things that they should not or do not need, thus misallocating economic resources and creating social pressure that lead people to act in ways that they would not if it were not for advertising. These critics feel that a great deal of advertising is misleading and that it takes advantage of the inherent weaknesses found in the consumer.

Both critic and advocates agree that advertising is just a part of the total marketing effort required for success. They know that they must make a quality product that performs its function well, and that this product must be priced fairly and competitively. They know that the product must be available to the consumer in locations where they expect to find it. Finally, they know that the product must be sold through an aggressive promotional strategy that may include all the elements of promotion.

Advertising is not an unmixed blessing. It is subject to scathing criticism. Advertising is charged with creating illusions and glorifying sex. It is assailed as an instrument of monopoly, which smothers competition. It is blamed for making simple things expensive. Professor Galbraith opined that advertising tempts people to quander money on 'needless purchases'.

Advertising is very expensive and its burden ultimately goes to the consumers. It appeals to the masses and may or may not suit the individual preferences. It is many a times wasteful as its message gets diffused. It leads to creation of unnecessary wants and finally it tends to develop monopoly.

In spite of the above criticism, advertising is vital. After all, advertising is not a panacea that can restore a poor product or rejuvenate a declining market. It only helps in selling through the art and business of persuasive communication. The gains of advertising are much more than the expenses put in and this fact strongly suggests that there should be heavy advertising. McGee of Pfizer India Ltd. aptly commented that, "We hardly need reminding that for reasons of ignorance, misinformation or doctrinaire motivation, there are many who would gladly argue that the world would be a better place to live in, if advertising could be done away with".[5]

PART–B

RESEARCH METHODOLOGY

1.2 METHODOLOGY

This chapter attempts to lay down the methodology adopted in this research study for the collection and analysis of data. The scope and objectives of the study, research problem, the nature of information required for the purpose, the method of data collection, sample selection, the questionnaire used for data collection, the variables used for the analysis, and the techniques used for the analysis and interpretation of the data are outlined in this chapter. Formulation of hypotheses and limitations of the study are also included in this chapter.

Research is an endless quest for knowledge. It refers to the organised method consisting of enunciating the problem, collecting facts, critical analysis of facts and arriving at conclusions based on them. Formulation of the problem is the first ad vital step in research.[6] John Dewey says that, a problem well put in, is half solved. To find out what the problem is or which a problematic situation presents—is to be well along in inquiry. To mistake the problem involved is to cause subsequent inquiry to be irrelevant. Without a problem, there is blind groping in the dark".[7] As such, at initial stages of the study an effort was made to formulate the research problem.

Exploring design in social science research strives for discovering new facts, ideas and insights about unfamiliar phenomena. Ordinarily these studies are not terminal; rather they throw light on hitherto unknown facts and figures so that future studies can build hypotheses from the findings. When the coverage of the study becomes quite wide and much of organised data are not available, the exploratory study proves to be a highly viable method of research. The present study undoubtedly possesses wide contours both in terms of its subject and area coverage.

---

[5] Latiff, T.A.A. (ed.), *Marketing Management*, Deep and Deep Publications, New Delhi, 1993, p. 29.

[6] Parten, Mildred, *Survey, Polls and Samples: Practical Procedures*, Harper and Row, New York, 1950, p. 48.

[7] Wilkinson, T.S. and Bhandarkar, P.L., *Methodology and Techniques of Social Research*, Himalaya Publishing House, Bombay, 1992, p. 55.

No work can be comprehensive and objective, systematic and analytical, interesting and impressive, suggestive and informative, unless it is supported by or rests on adequate data. Therefore, sincere attempt has been made to collect data as much as possible to make the present work achieve the aforesaid objectives. Data being an essential ingredient for this study, a well-structured questionnaire was formed for the purpose of administration to the respondents and random sampling method was followed. Also semiotic analysis was adopted to analyse the magazine as well as television advertisements. The questionnaire pre-tested in a limited sphere was based upon the objective of the study.

The research study is the output of collation of primary data. The secondary materials from number of sources pertaining to the work are also collected for the purpose of reviewing literature. The materials collected are presented for analysis in the form of tables, and figures. The methodology used is descriptive and analytical. Standard statistical tools are used in this study. The references collected are neatly consolidated.

1.3 REVIEW OF LITERATURE

This is because of the importance of advertising in India, as in other democratic countries, the literature produced in this field is not only quite rich, informative and suggestive, but also throws much light on different aspects including the lifestyle contents and consumer behaviour, of the subject concerned. Because of its tremendous potentialities as a trendsetter and social reformer and the problems it faces, quite large number of studies have been made on it.

Chunnawala, S.A. and Sethia, K.C. (1985) says that, advertising of late has become a worldwide phenomenon and a multidimensional activity and constitutes an integral part of every society. In the modern day world, any economic activity without advertising is somewhat inconceivable. Its pervasive presence is felt in every sphere of activity. We see it on television, on the sky, on the match box, in the newspapers, on the trash containers, in the magazines, on the air mail and in the vehicles, on billboards, on radio, in the stores we visit and so on. In a way, advertising has become deeply embedded in our daily lives. It is a form of mass communication, a powerful marketing tool, a component of the economic systems, a means of financing the mass media, social institutions, an instrument of business management, a field of employment and a profession.

Sandage, C.H. (1996) says, advertising is a big business. Today we are exposed to a large number of commercial messages than at any time in the past. Newspapers and magazines are full of advertisements in various forms. Not only the number of advertisements are increasing significantly, but also the quality of advertisements have improved considerably over the past few decades. All possible means of advertising such as print, radio, television, cinema, billboard, etc. have also amply contributed to the growth of advertising in the modern day world.

Vernan, F.B. and Kim, R.Z. (1996) says that, advertisements as such are commonly associated with the mass media like newspapers, magazines, cinema, television and radio. They are also commonly found in other forms such as wall paintings, billboards, posters, brochures, danglers, direct mail, etc. Advertisements in any form are overwhelmingly used with persuasive intent *i.e.,* the advertisers are striving to alter our behaviour and/or levels of awareness, knowledge, attitudes and so on in a manner that would be beneficial to them.

Rathor, B.S. (1990) says that, advertising may be defined as the process of buying sponsor identified media space or time in order to promote a product/service or an idea. It is perhaps the most visible of all the elements in the promotion mix, and is therefore, subject to much criticism from consumer groups. It is also subject to Government regulations.

Sahu, P.K. and Rout, K.C. (1993) explains advertising an informer and persuader. Advertising usually informs the potential consumer about products and services; their benefits and utilities. As a matter of fact, it is a mass persuasion activity duly sponsored by the manufacturer/ seller for whom the advertising is done.

Sandage, C.H. (1996) describes the conceptual advertising can be thought of as a five part business where advertisers use advertising agencies and are sometimes assisted by support organisations, send their message generally through mass media to potential consumers of the product, service, or idea. Here the five basic elements are the advertisers, advertising agencies, support organisations, mass media and the consumer.

Jefkins, F. (1994) says that advertising presents the most persuasive possible selling message to the right prospects for the products or services of the lowest possible cost.

Chandan, J.S. and Singh, J. (1990) explains, as advertising in many cases, informs the target market about special features of a product/service. The existing products are also often modified for simplicity and convenience and advertisements can focus on such added/additional features. Advertising persuades potential consumers that a particular product is superior to competing products. This can be achieved simply by highlighting the superior features of the product in the advertising campaigns.

Obormeyer, D.J. (1969) says that, one of the primary objectives of advertising is to increase sales. As a matter of fact, many successful organisations of the present day world have been able to achieve their current sales volume chiefly due to the significant contributions by the most important sales promotion tool *i.e.,* advertising. Advertising campaigns are most essential when an altogether new products or a new model is introduced in the market. In fact, the arrivals of new products or new models are done through advertising.

Sontakki, G.N. (1996) says that, advertising is primarily a means by which sellers try to communicate prospective buyers the worth of their goods and services. Advertising as a matter of fact is a basic tool of marketing for stimulating demand of the product and services. Advertising as a powerful technique of sales promotion has been doing wonders in the domain of distribution because it is quite capable of influencing the course of consumption, affecting the process of production, enlarging the process of exchange and diversify the distribution system. The role of advertising in the modern business world can be examined from five distinct angles, namely, manufacturers, middlemen, sales force, consumers and the society.

Kumar, J.K. (1996) criticised advertising by saying that, advertising is too intrusive thus polluting our mental environment by repetitive loud and sometimes obnoxious messages. This criticism is primarily levied against television advertising which in the middle of an educational or an entertainment programme can be offensive.

Rathore, B.S. (1996) says that, an individual advertisement may be good or bad, truthful or misleading, decent or in bad taste. However, advertising as a process cannot be grossly blamed. It is the user who uses it for a good or bad end. Voluntary associations like Advertising Agencies Association of India (AAAI) and the Indian Society of Advertisers (ISA) are constantly striving to raise the standard of the profession of advertising by introducing a code of conduct.

Kaldor, N. (1949-50) says that, purchasing power of the masses is not static. It changes over a period of time. Advertisement therefore cannot be grossly blamed to transfer business from one concern to another. Rather it helps the expansion of business activities in a society.

Korba, A. (1992) says that, advertising billing as a percentage of the gross national product is possibly one of the most important indicators of the health of an industry. In India, it is one third of the one percent of the GNP. In USA, the figure is about 2.5 per cent and in Europe, it is about one per cent. So, there is an ample scope for Indian advertising industry to expand its business in absolute term as well as in relative terms to the Gross National Product.

Prahalad, C.K. and Harmel, G. (1998), discussed categorically about Indian advertising industry by saying that, advertising industry is preparing itself to welcome the 21st century with all its potentialities. The projected ad expenditure is likely to be as high as 1,80,000 million dollars by the year 2025. With its vast potentials on the one hand and self-regulation on the other, it is going to flourish in a big way. Advertising is no doubt a rich source of revenue for the government. Therefore, it should grant special tax concessions for its self-growth and the growth of this creative advertising industry. At the same time, the Indian advertising industry should struggle hard to keep up its image through self-regulation than government interventions.

Moslow, A.H. (1954) in his book *Motivation and Personality*, discussed in detail about the process of human motivation and personality development.

Acito, Franklin and Ford, Jeffery D. (1980) in their book *How Advertising Affects Employees,* discussed vividly regarding the nature of advertising and how it succeeded in influencing the employees in an industrial set-up.

Miller, Clyde R. (1964) in his book *Process of Persuasion*, explained in detail the persuasive techniques which are helpful in influencing a consumer's buying decision.

Ball, Michael J. (1978) written a book titled *The Role of Indian Advertising in the National Economy*, categorically discussed the nature and active role of advertising for the economic development of a developing country like India.

Rubinstein, E.A. (1978) in his book titled *Television and the Sound Viewer* speaks about the importance of television advertising and its impact on consumer behaviour.

Kijewski, Valarie (1982) in his book *Media Advertising When Your Market is in a Recession* explains about the recessionary trend in a consumer market and its revival process through the application of effective advertising.

Mohan, Manendra (1982) in his article "A Survey of Advertising Themes in 1970s" discussed in detail the advertising scenario of India.

Borden, Neil H. (1942) in his book titled *The Economic Effects of Advertising*, explains about the role of advertising and its economic viewpoint on an economy.

Lambin, Jean-Jacues (1973) in his book titled *What is the Real Impact of Advertising,* discussed regarding the usefulness of advertising and also its actual impact or influence on consumer behaviour on a larger perspective.

Simon, J.L. (1970) in his book *The Economics of Advertising* discussed the effects of advertising upon the propensity to consume of the consumer.

Steiner, Robert L. (1973) in his book *Does Advertising Lower Consumer Prices*, discussed regarding the positive aspect of advertising. As advertising sometimes enhances cost of the product but on a larger scale reduces the price of the product. Therefore, it is cost effective for the consumer.

Sen Gupta, P.B. (1989) in his book titled *Does a Developing Economy Need Advertising for Consumption*, explains the efficacy of advertising in a developing country like India for enhancing consumer demand for manufacturing products.

Dunn, Watson (1969) in his book *Advertising: Its Role in Modern Marketing*, explained the role of advertising and its techniques for the upliftment of modern marketing.

Zaveri, Bhawna (1982) in her book titled *Effect of the Use of Women in Advertising,* explained the role of women and how they are portrayed in advertisement for attracting consumer attention.

Boddewyn, J.J. (1980) in his book titled *Decency and Sexism in Advertising*, pointed out specifically the advancement of sexism, nudity in advertisement for increasing customer appeals.

Wittink, Dick R. (1977) in his book *Advertising Increases Sensitivity to Price*, discussed in detail the impact of advertising expenses on product price and the customer reaction towards it.

Stantion, William J. (1975) in his book *Fundamentals of Marketing*, says about the marketing segments, marketing mix and how advertising as an important concept of marketing succeeded in influencing consumer attention towards a product.

Colley, Russell H. (1991) in his book *Defining advertising Goals for Measured Advertising Results*, explains about the aim and objectives of advertising and its target and goal achievement.

Dhalla, Nariman K. and Winton H. Mahatoo in their book E*xpanding the Scope of Market Segmentation*, gives a comprehensive survey report on various market segmentation approaches.

Simon, Julian A. (1991) in his book *The Management of Advertising*, gives tips regarding management of effective and successful advertising campaigns.

Kelley, Richard J. (1967) in his book *The Advertising Budget*, discussed in detail the preparation of an ideal budget plan for a successful advertising campaign.

Alderson, Wroe (1960) in his book *The Productivity of Advertising*, briefs about the productive capacity of advertising for national development.

Bellur, V.V. (1987) in his book titled *Marketing Research: Theory and Practice*, explains in detail the various tools and techniques through which the nature of market condition can be identified.

Kothari, C.R. (1988) explains in detail the methodological aspects of research design in his book titled *Research Methodology: Methods and Techniques*. The literature in this book helped a lot to the researcher for systematically designing the project thesis.

Mishra, M.N. (1995) in his book *Sales Promotion and Advertising Management*, described in categorical manner the role of advertising for promoting the quality of sales and how this is to be managed in a systematic manner for better results.

Mandell, M.I. (1968) in his book *Advertising,* detailed the conceptual framework for advertising, its origin, definitions and development.

Longman, K.A. (1991) in his book *Advertising*, discussed the various aspects of advertising, its importance, need and its economic implications on a larger scale.

Miller Clyde R. (1964) expresses a brief and very analytical framework with regard to persuasion techniques in his book *The Process of Persuasion.*

Mathur, Navin (1986) says that how consumer reacts to advertising and what are the salient features that consists in advertising which appeals customers in his book titled *Press Advertising*.

Piirto (1994) in his book *Beyond Mind Games*, discussed in detail the study of fashion consumers. The study found six major groups such as older consumers, married households with college degrees, fashion foregoers, social strivers, dutifuls with high-income, and high-quality buyers. The above mentioned literature helped the researcher to shape its questionnaire and to know about the different lifestyle pattern of various groups.

Onkvisit and Shaw (1991) in their book *International Marketing*, explains the characteristics of lifestyles belonging to different countries. The study focussed on considerable lifestyle differences between Indian and American women. This literature helped a lot for the researcher to know about the tangible differences in lifestyles.

Jacob, Harnik (1981) in the journal titled *Allocation of Time to the Mass Media*, analysed the media usage pattern related to lifestyles. Magazine and newspaper reading positively related to education and occupational prestige, as well as community and political involvement. On the other hand, TV watchers tend to be unemployed, have low prestige occupations, and have a low interest in cultural matters. The researcher used the above concept categorically for this thesis.

Cyndce, Miller (1995) used lifestyles to identify consumer segments for various offerings. Modern household appliances obviously appeals much to consumers whose lifestyle demands convenience and saving time. The cross-cultural implications of lifestyle segmentation has been discussed thoroughly with this research work.

Myers and Gutman (1987) in his book *Lifestyle*, stratified the social class into various groups and discussed its significance for the marketer. The significant differences in values, attitudes, and behaviour provide a basis on which the market is segmented and obtained an enhanced understanding of the behaviour of consumers.

James Myers and Gutman (1974) in their book *Lifestyle: The Essence of Social Class*, studied about the social class structure and the income related to different lifestyle patterns. Many lifestyle items showed significant correlations with the index of social class, indicating definite but small differences between the social classes in terms of lifestyles.

Louden, D.L. and Bitta (1984) in their book *Consumer Behaviour*, studied about lifestyle and psychographic segmentation. According to him, lifestyle can be viewed as a unique pattern of living, which influences and is reflected by one's consumer behaviour. Also both of them discussed about the techniques of lifestyle segmentation.

Batra and Myers in their book *Advertising Management* studied in detail the effects of advertising on lifestyles. The key issues are which values and lifestyles are to be encouraged as healthy, which are to be avoided, and what relative impact or influence advertising has on them.

Engel, J.F. and Kollat, D.T. and Blackwell, R.D. in their book *Consumer Behaviour* studied about the mass media usage for consumer information. According to them, consumer information process consists of four stages, such as exposure, attention, comprehension and retention.

In the present work, an in-depth study has been made and the psychological aspect has been dealt with. From a review of the literature on advertising and consumer behaviour in India, it was found that there is a dearth of literature on the subject. Some of the prominent books are *Press Advertising* by Navin Mathur (Himalaya Publishing House, Bombay, 1987), *Advertising Management* by B.S. Rathore (Himalaya Publishing House, Bombay, 1984), *Advertising and Publicity in India* by S.S. Saxena (Agra University, Agra, 1952), *Essentials of Advertising* (Oxford and IBH Publishing Company Pvt. Ltd., New Delhi, 1990). Various aspects of advertising have also been covered in *Marketing Management* edited by T.A.A. Latif (Deep and Deep Publications, New Delhi, 1983), *Modern Marketing* by S.A. Sherlekar (Himalaya Publishing House, Bombay, 1981).

A number of research articles have been studied, which were published in many reputed journals such as *Advertising and Marketing, Advertising Age, Economic Times, Indian Journal of Marketing*, etc. The Indian Institute of Mass Communication at New Delhi conducted a number of research studies on advertising and consumer behaviour.

1.4 THE RESEARCH PROBLEM

The impact of advertising on the psyche of the consumers is always of crucial importance to the advertisers, media people, academicians, researchers and consumers themselves. The people involved in advertising always try to test the psychology of the consumer towards the advertisement. The formulation of the research problem in the present study involves the following questions:

(*i*) Do people watch/read advertisements and if yes, which media do they prefer the best?

(*ii*) Which is the most appealing media?

(*iii*) Are the consumers influenced by advertisements to buy or change a particular brand?

(*iv*) Do the consumers sense that advertising through lifestyle communication influences their behaviour?

1.5 SCOPE AND OBJECTIVES OF THE STUDY

Given the popularity, coverage and intensity of advertising and its wide acceptance with the consumers, the present research endeavour aims at identifying and measuring effectiveness of advertising on the consumers. The main objective is to delve into the psyche of the consumers as well as the motivational contents of advertising.

The important objectives of the research study are the following:

(*i*) To assess the impact of media advertising on change of consumer behaviour.

(*ii*) To assess the relative effectiveness of various mass media for advertising.

(*iii*) To examine the ethical aspects of various lifestyles and their presentations.

(*iv*) To make qualitative and quantitative analysis of the contents of both print and electronic advertisements and find out the trends of changing lifestyles.

1.6 HYPOTHESES

Keeping in view the broad objectives of the study, the following four hypotheses are formulated to be tested on the basis of data collected from survey and semiotic analysis.

(*i*) Advertising has significant impact on choice of brand, change of brand and buying decision of the consumer.

(*ii*) Television is the most preferred medium of advertising.

(*iii*) The lifestyle communication of ads seems to encourage the spread of unethical culture in Indian society.

(*iv*) The modern lifestyle has been greatly influenced by celebrity.

1.7 SAMPLE DESIGN

1.7.1. The Location

The sample survey was conducted in Berhampur, a city of Ganjam district in Orissa. It is considered as the commercial capital of the state. It is situated in the south-eastern part of Orissa. Berhampur city is regarded as the lifeblood of south Orissa in general and Ganjam district in particular. It lies between 190°18′ north latitudes and 840°41′ east longitudes. It is bounded in the north by

Khurda district, in the south by Srikakulam district of Andhra Pradesh, in the east by Bay of Bengal and in the west by Gajapati district. As on 1st March 2001, out of the total population of Ganjam district, total literacy was 82.25 per cent. From this, male literacy consists 93.60 per cent and female literacy 70.32 per cent. The total population of the Berhampur town was 2,89,724 on 1st March 2001. However, the population grows at a rate of three per cent per annum. Out of the total population, male population constitutes 1,50,089, while females constitute 1,39,635. Berhampur was selected as the research area because of researcher's convenience and for its suitable location. It is situated nearby Berhampur University. The city is having significant contribution to the history of Orissa journalism. A number of media institutions are located in and around its locality.

1.7.2. Determination of Universe and Sample Size

The universe comprises of the literates of Berhampur city, who have at least passed higher secondary examination. The sampling unit is an individual.

The size of the sample was 252, taken arbitrarily. It may be noted that, in conducting researches for their clients, most of the advertising agencies in India keep the sample size small, many a times between 100 and 150. In qualitative research, the sample size is generally small. Peter Sampson also supports this argument. He says, "Qualitative research is usually exploratory or diagnostic in nature. It involves small members of people who are not usually sampled on a probabilistic basis... In the qualitative research no attempt is made to draw hard and fast conclusions. It is impressionistic rather than definite".[8] The limitations of time, money, energy and research related facilities compelled the researcher to limit the size of sample to 252.

1.8 CLASSIFICATION AND TABULATION OF DATA

The data thus collected were classified according to the categories. Counting sheets and the summary tables were prepared. The resultant tables were one-dimensional, two-dimensional and in some cases, even complex.

1.9 ANALYSIS AND INTERPRETATION OF DATA

The analysis of the tabulated data involved primarily percentages and averages as statistical derivatives. The statistical conclusions thus drawn have been followed by logical and practical interpretations. The formulated conclusions have also been given at the end.

1.10 DEFINITION OF CONCEPTS

It is pertinent to define some of the concepts used in the survey.

---

[8] Quoted by Wright, John S., Winter, Willis L. and Zeigler, Sharilyn K., *Advertising,* Tata McGraw Hill Publishing Co. Ltd., New Delhi, 1982, p. 351.

1. 'Literate' refers to one who can read and understand the advertisements in English, Hindi and Oriya.
2. Age was recorded in completed years on the last birthday.
3. 'Educational qualifications' mean the last examination passed.
4. Age groups are formed as 13 to 19— teenage; 20 to 35—young age; 36 to 60—middle age and above 60 as old age.
5. 'Income' refers to income per month of the family from all sources.
6. 'Students' refer to those who are full-time or part-time students of educational institutions. Research scholars were treated as students.
7. 'Servicemen' include men as well as women in private or governmental sector. Doctors and engineers have been included in the category of professional degree holders.

1.11 EXPERIENCES OF THE INVESTIGATOR

The investigator, being unprofessionalised, faced a legion number of problems in conducting the research. The studies on advertising, lifestyle and media impact on consumer behaviour were rare. Consequently, to prepare a short and purposeful questionnaire became a baffling problem. A serious and deep thought on the subject, detailed discussions with advertising experts and psychologists helped to some extent in solving this problem. The limitations of time, energy and funds were few other problems. However, the respondents showed keen interest in filling up the questionnaire. It can safely be said that if the benefiting companies provide funds and manpower, such research studies can be conducted conveniently on a large-scale in a better-organised and synchronised manner.

1.12 THE QUESTIONNAIRE

The questionnaire has been designed with the objective of finding out the impact of advertising on consumer behaviour. The questionnaire is pre-tested in a limited sphere has been designed on the basis of the objectives of the study. The types of questions asked in this questionnaire are dichotomous, multiple choice and free response. The number of respondents has been confined to 252 from the city of Berhampur. The sample, however, have been chosen keeping in view the representativeness of the classified categories on the basis of sex, age, education, occupation and income. The sample has been divided in the following manner:

Profile of the Sample

A

Sex-wise Classification	Nos.
(*a*) Male	162
(*b*) Female	90
Total:	252

B

Age-wise Classification	Nos.
(a) 13 to 19 years (teen)	42
(b) Between 20 and 35 years (young)	135
(c) Between 36 and 60 years (middle)	70
(d) 60 years and above (old)	05
Total:	252

C

Education-wise Classification	Nos.
(a) Undergraduate	42
(b) Graduate	60
(c) Postgraduate	125
(d) Professional degree holders	25
Total:	252

D

Occupation-wise Classification	Nos.
(a) Service	60
(b) Business	60
(c) Professional	60
(d) Student	72
Total:	252

E

Income-wise Classification	Nos.
(a) Up to 5,000	40
(b) 5,001 to 10,000	52
(c) 10,001 to 15,000	55
(d) 15,001 to 20,000	51
(e) Above 20,000	54
Total:	252

1.13 STATISTICAL TECHNIQUES USED

The data collected from the administration of the questionnaire have been presented in tabulation form, analysed with the help of various statistical tools and techniques. Necessary inferences from the above have been drawn. The findings have been recorded, based upon the analysis and interpretation thereof. To arrive at the relative importance of various factors, percentages and simple weighted average methods have been made use of. The calculation of percentage method has been made as follows. First of all, the aggregate response for individual question has been analysed. Then it was divided by total number of respondents and finally multiplied by hundred to arrive at the percentage. In simple weighted average method, different weights are assigned to individual preference of an attribute in order of its merit. For example, in a set of five attributes, a weight of five (5) is given to the first preference, four (4) to the second preference, and so on. Then the weight is multiplied with the number of responses. To arrive at the weighted value of each attribute, the resultant figures were added up. Then the weighted average value for each attribute is calculated from the weighted value of each attribute by dividing them with the sum total of weights assigned to the respective attributes. The following formula is used for finding out the rank of media:

$$\Sigma WX / \Sigma W$$

Where 'W' denotes weight

'X' denotes number of items and

Σ denotes summation.

1.14 DATA COLLECTION

The sample was selected from Berhampur city, Orissa on a random basis. Since data collection was not possible from the entire state with limited resources and time constraints, the process was confined to Berhampur city only. The data collected for the above studies are primary and secondary in nature. The collection of data was done through personal contact. A total of 300 sets of questionnaire were distributed, out of which only 252 were collected. The rest 48 could not be taken due to their non-availability. The questionnaire were distributed among the respondents by the researcher personally. It is relevant to mention here that the respondents found the topic and the questionnaire very interesting and the same duly filled in were collected within a short period of time.

1.15 CHAPTER DIVISION

The research study is presented in nine chapters. Chapter I is divided into two parts. Part - A deals with an introduction to the study and Part - B contains the research methodology. Chapter II deals with a conceptual framework of advertising. Socio-economic implications of advertising are discussed in Chapter III. Chapter IV narrates the truth, ethics and social responsibility of advertising. Advertising and consumer behaviour research is explained in the Chapter V. Chapter VI discusses advertising and lifestyle communication in detail. Impact of advertising on consumer behaviour is detailed in Chapter VII. Chapter VIII is divided into two parts. Part - A deals with print presentation of lifestyle and Part - B deals with the electronic presentation of lifestyle. Chapter IX summarises the major findings with reference to objectives and hypotheses.

1.16 LIMITATIONS OF THE STUDY

There is no research study without limitations. More so, in studies on consumer behaviour, a number of limitations can be pointed out. One limitation of the present study is that, the survey has been conducted only in Berhampur city and that too among 252 respondents. Besides, the survey is based on the method of simple random sampling. It is also believed that the responses in such type of researches cannot be taken for granted, as it is a behavioural research. Again, because of constraints of time and money only two mass media such as magazine and television were taken up to represent the print and electronic media of communication.

In spite of the above limitations, it cannot be denied that the research is based on primary data and the conclusions are indicative of the behaviour of the consumers for several advertised products/ services. This indication serves as an index to the market trend. It points to the existing opportunities in the market. It can help in identifying the nature and extent of the problem and making their decisions under uncertainty. Market research is after all diagnostic like pathology and radiology and not curative. To be able to eliminate or reduce risk is not an insignificant contribution.

Chapter 2 ADVERTISING: A CONCEPTUAL FRAMEWORK

2.1 INTRODUCTION

Manufacturing of products and creation of services are of little use unless it reaches the persons for whom it is meant. However, the demand from the population for whom it is meant is not automatically generated. It has to be created because goods and services are manufactured and created in anticipation of demand. Such a creation of demand basically requires the development of considerable awareness among the prospective buyers about the availability of various products and services and the utilities and benefits thereof. Out of the various tools and techniques available for the marketer, advertising is one of the oldest, most popular and potent means of creating such awareness about products, services and ideas. As a matter of fact, advertising is the first and foremost tool of marketing products and services. It facilitates the introduction of products and services in the market through persuasion of the potential consumers in favour of such products/ services. Advertising also increases the familiarity of the consumers with the products and services as a result of which, the consumers feel more about the same while making their purchases. Advertising aims to create and maintain an idea or an attitude in the mind of people. Almost all products or services possess certain special selling often referred as Unique Sales Propositions (USP).

Advertising of late has become a worldwide phenomenon and a multidimensional activity and constitutes an integral part of every society. In the modern day world, any economic activity without advertising is somewhat inconceivable. Its pervasive presence is felt in every sphere of activity. We see it on television, on the sky, on the match box, in the newspapers, on the trash containers, in the magazines, on airmail and in the vehicles, on billboards, on radio, in the stores we visit and so on. In a way, advertising has become deeply embedded in our daily lives. It is a form of mass communication, a powerful marketing tool, a component of the economic systems, a means of financing the mass media, social institutions, as instrument of business management, a field of employment and a profession.

Moreover, advertising is a big business today; we are exposed to a large number of commercial messages than at any time in the past. Newspapers and magazines are full of advertisements in various forms. Not only the number of advertisements are increasing significantly but also the quality of advertisements have improved considerably over the past few decades. All possible means of advertising such as print, radio, television, cinema, billboards, etc., have also amply contributed to the growth of advertising in the modern day world.

Advertising is a potent tool of marketing and a component of overall promotion activities. The marketing operation of any business operation is guided by its market plan; which has the best possible mix of four variables, namely, the nature of the product, the price of the product, the channels of distribution which take the product to the consumer from the producer, and the promotional activities. In every book on marketing, these four variables are referred to as product, price, place and promotion. A combination of these four elements, which are common to the movement of goals, affects the ultimate sales success. This combination is known as the marketing mix. The variables are commonly called 4Ps. Advertising is a sub-component of the overall promotion component - one of the 4Ps. Another important aspect to be borne in mind is that these four variables are inter-dependent and are influenced by each other. Therefore, every advertising decision is influenced by the various components in the mix. The logical step, therefore, in studying the fundamentals of advertising is to understand the marketing concepts.

To many outside the field of marketing, it seems as if marketing has the magic power of converting a sick business into a profit-making one, into making breakthroughs to growth from stagnancy, and converting the single-product, single-market status into a multi-products, multi-market status of a company. But marketing is not magic; it is in fact, a logic, a style of managing a business. Peter Drucker, the famous management thinker and writer, in his recent work, *Management: Task, Responsibilities, Practices*, has rightly observed:

Marketing is so basic that it cannot be considered a separate function (*i.e.,* a separate skill or work) within the business, on a par with others, such as manufacturing or personnel. Marketing requires separate work and a distinct group of activities. But it is, first, a central dimension of the entire business. It is the whole business seen from the point of view of its final result, that is, from the customer's point of view. Concern and responsibility for marketing must, therefore, permeate all areas of the enterprise.[1]

The underlying principle behind Drucker's philosophy is customer-orientation of the marketing operations of any business. Successful marketing means the satisfaction of the consumer's wants and needs. "The consumer is king" is the theme, which guides every marketing decision and activity.

2.2 NATURE AND SCOPE OF ADVERTISING

Advertising and other forms of promotional activities should be viewed as a means of implementing a communication strategy. Unlike personal selling and some sales promotion and public relations techniques, advertising is an impersonal means of communication. It is an impersonal communication to groups that is paid for by an identified sponsor. It focuses upon groups of persons, rather than upon individuals. Marketers cannot tailor advertising messages to the peculiarities of individual consumers, but aim at the group. In addition, the advertisement feedback mechanism is not as precise as it is in personal selling. Advertising is impersonal and is addressed to groups. An

[1] Drucker, Peter, Management: Task, Responsibilities, Practices, p. 32.

identified sponsor pays for advertising. Each advertising message indicates who the sponsor is. Further, this means of promotion is paid for. Unlike publicity, it is not free. Advertising is a means of reaching groups. It is a form of mass communication. This method of promotion enables the marketer to address large number of target consumers at a low cost per consumer contacted.

Advertising is any one element of the promotion mix, but it often takes special prominence in the overall marketing mix design. Because of the high visibility and pervasiveness, it is an important social and economic topic in Indian society.

Promotion may be defined as "the coordination of all seller-initiated efforts to set up channels of information and persuasion to facilitate the scale of a good or service". The bulk of promotion is directed toward facilitating and enhancing specific products and brands. Thus, promotion is most often, intended to be a supporting component in a marketing mix. This does not mean that it is any the less important than the product or other marketing decision areas. Rather promotion decisions must be integrated and coordinated with the rest of the marketing mix, particularly product/brand decisions, so that it may effectively support an entire marketing mix strategy. The promotion mix consists of four basic elements:

(*i*) Advertising, which is the dissemination of information by non-personal means through paid media where the source is clearly identified as the sponsoring organisation;

(*ii*) Personal selling, which is the dissemination of information by non-personal, usually face-to-face, contacts between audience members and one or more employees of the sponsoring organisation. The source of information is identified as the sponsoring organisation;

(*iii*) Sales promotion, which is the dissemination of information in a very broad sense through a wide variety of activities, including free samples, gifts, coupons, point-of-purchase signs and displays, stamp programmes, reduction sales, contests, shows, and exhibitions, demonstrations, and various non-recurrent efforts not made in the ordinary course. In other words, sales promotion includes those marketing activities other than personal selling, advertising and publicity which stimulate consumer purchasing and dealer effectiveness;

(*iv*) Publicity, which is the dissemination of information by personal or non-personal means and is not directly paid by the organisation and for which the organisation is not clearly identified as the source.

2.3 DEFINITIONS

On definition of 'advertising', David M. Potter, Professor of American History at Yale University said:

Advertising as an institution has suffered almost total neglect. One might read fairly widely in literature, which treats of public opinion, popular culture, and the mass media in the US. Without even learning that advertising now compares with such long-standing institutions as the school and the church in the magnitudes of its social influence. It dominates the media, it has vast power in the shaping of popular standards, and it is really one of the very limited groups of institutions, which exercise social control. Yet analysis of society has largely ignored it. Historians seldom do more than glance at it in their studies of social history, and when they do, they usually focus attention upon some picturesque or titillating aspect, such as the way in which advertising has reflected or encouraged a new frankness about such previously tabooed subject as ladies' underwear. Histories of American periodicals and even of the mass media deal with advertising as if it were a side issue. Students of radio and of the mass circulation magazines frequently condemn advertising for its conspicuous role, as if it were a mere interloper in a separate, pre-existing, self-contained aesthetic world of actors, musicians, authors, and script writers; they hardly recognise that advertising created modern American radio and television, transformed the modern newspaper, evoked the modern sleek periodicals and remains the vital essence of each of them at the present time. Marconi may have invented the wireless and Henry Luce may have invented the news magazine, but it is advertising that has made both wireless and news magazines what are in America today... [2]

Advertising Age defines advertising as:

The dissemination of information concerning an idea, service or product to compel action in accordance with the interest of the advertiser.[3]

Blake points out that:

Advertising is the presentation and promotion of a product, service or idea where such presentation and promotion is identified with and paid for by a sponsor... Advertising seeks not only to inform but to promote... to persuade people to buy a product or service.[4]

Borden states that:

... Advertising messages are identified with the advertiser either by signature or by oral statement... Advertising is a commercial transaction involving payments to publisher or broadcasters and others whose media are employed.[5]

From the above definitions on advertising, this can be concluded that, "Advertising is dynamic". Its definition also changes along with the changing markets, lifestyles, methods of distribution and the changing techniques of communications. During the past few years, there are significant developments of advertising and as a result, the definitions are changed. Advertising is an institution, which performs both social and economic functions and should be recognised in the context of total marketing strategy. Advertising becomes more sophisticated in use of research to better understand consumer behaviour and motivation. The new definitions include a more concerted effort to build favourable 'brand' and corporate identities. It becomes greater in use of information, bearing on

---

2 Potter, David M., *Advertising Age*, October 4, 1954.

3 Jha and Singh, *Marketing Management in Indian Perspective*, Himalaya Publishing House, Bombay, p. 549.

4 Blake, Reed H. and Maroldson, Edwin O., *A Taxonomy of Concepts in Communication*, Hastings House Publishers, New York, p. 47.

5 Borden, Neil H. and Marshall, Martin V., *Advertising Management - Text and Cases*, p. 3.

media audiences, and a burgeoning concern about consumer welfare. Therefore, "advertising is the communication link between the seller and the buyer or the consumer and provide information about products and services and an active attempt to influence and persuade people to action or belief by an overt appeal to reason or emotion".

The Definitions Committee of the American Marketing Association defined advertising as:

...any paid form of non-personal presentation of ideas, goods or services by any identified sponsor. It involves the use of such media as the following: magazines and newspaper space, motion pictures, outdoor (posters, signs, skywriting, etc.), direct mail, store signs, novelties (calendars, blotters, etc.), radio cards (car, bus, etc.), catalogues, directories and references, programmes and menus and circulars. This list is intended to be illustrative, not inclusive.[6]

The definition on advertising as is explained by the American Marketing Association (1948) remained almost identical even in 1963 except the inclusion of 'promotion of ideas'. The American Marketing Association recommends this definition in 1963 in the following words:

Advertising is any paid form of non-personal presentation and promotion of ideas, goods and services by an identified sponsor.[7]

This definition falls short of incorporating the effects of advertising. Not only, advertising 'presents' ideas, goods and services, but must also persuade people to respond positively to the advertised message. The definition can be refined to state:

Advertising is any controlled form of non-personal presentation and promotion of ideas, goods and services by an identified sponsor that is used to inform and persuade the selected market.[8]

Today, the management of advertising is sophisticated, analytical and state of the art while at the same time being relevant and practical in planning, decision-making and control. But the focus is on decision-making, specifically the decisions connected with setting advertising objectives, launching advertising campaigns, developing media strategies and measuring advertising results.

The advertising management is made up of a system of interacting organisations and institutions, all of which play a role in the advertising process. At the core of this system are the advertisers, the organisations that provide the financial resources that support advertising. Advertisers are private or public sector organisations that use mass media to accomplish organisational objectives. It is the decision to invest resources in purchasing time or space in such mass media as television, radio, newspaper or magazines that basically distinguishes advertisers from non-advertisers. Advertisers make use of mass media. Non-advertisers do not.[9]

Advertising developed in the United States during the first half of this century into marketing revolution, taking over from where the industrial revolution had left. Economic progress and recent

---

[6] Report of the Definitions Committee, *Journal of Marketing*, 12(2), 1948.

[7] Alexander, Ralph S. (ed.), *Marketing Definitions, American Marketing Association*, Chicago, 1964, p. 9.

[8] Bolen, William H., *Advertising*, John Wiley and Sons, 1984, p. 4.

[9] Aaker, David A., and Myers, John G., *Advertising Management*, Prentice Hall of India Pvt. Ltd., New Delhi, 1986, p. 3.

scientific discoveries are the main causes of the rise of 'advertising' as a new marketing tool. The competition in the market makes it necessary to learn the art of selling more of a particular product. To entice probable customers to a new product, a relatively low cost is resorted to, but only advertising can make the advantage known to them. In a free enterprise system, consumer is the king and his wants are translated into actual purchases. And during growth of the market, it is the woman who is more interested in advertising. In this context, Senator Clinton P. Anderson, Chairman of the Joint Committee on Atomic Energy, while addressing the Newspaper Advertising Executive Association, defined advertising thus:

The main idea of advertising is to provide the millions of lines of interesting copy which will be needed to tell my wife and millions of other housewives in America what new products they should buy.[10]

2.4 HISTORICAL PERSPECTIVE

As the markets grew larger and the number of customers increased, the importance of attracting them grew. The task of personally attracting customers became enormous and more expensive. Increasing reliance was placed on advertising methods of informing many consumers about the availability of the merchant's products. These advertising methods were more economical in reaching large numbers of customers and informing them of the products' availability. While these advertising methods were more economical in reaching large numbers of consumer and informing them of the products' availability. While for informing and reminding, they could not do the whole promotional job. They were used only because it was physically and economically impossible to reach each consumer personally. The merchant still used personal persuasion once the customers were attracted to his store.

It has been wrongly assumed that the advertising function is of recent origin. There is evidence to suggest that the Romans practised advertising; but the earliest indication of its use in this country dates back to the middle ages, when the use of surname indicated a man's occupation. The next stage in the evolution of advertising was the use of signs as a visual expression of the tradesman's function as well as a means of locating the source of goods. This method is still in common use.

The potentialities of advertising multiplied when the hand press was invented at the end of the 15th century. By Shakespeare's times, posters had made their appearance, and there is evidence to prove that advertising had assumed the function of fostering demand for existing products. Another important development at this time was the emergence of the pamphlet as an advertising medium. The early examples of these pamphlets disclose their sponsorship by companies intent on generating goodwill for their activities. The slight cost of posters and handbills encouraged a number of experiment with other methods.

[10] Anderson, Clinton P., *The New York Times*, July 13, 1955.

2.5 EFFECT OF URBAN GROWTH ON ADVERTISING

The need for advertising developed with the expansion of population and the growth of towns with their shops and large stores; mass production in factories; roads and railways to convey goods; and popular newspapers in which to advertise. The large quantities of goods being produced were made known by means of advertising to unknown customers who lived far from the place of manufacture. This process developed some two hundred years ago in industrialised countries.

Advertising grew with the development of media, such as the coffeehouse newspapers of the seventeenth century, and the arrival of advertising agencies such as White's in 1800 to handle British government lottery advertising. Charles Barker and George Street flourished in the early nineteenth century.

2.6 ADVERTISING: ITS ROLE AND IMPORTANCE IN THE MODERN BUSINESS WORLD

Generally speaking, advertising is a relatively low-cost way of conveying selling messages to numerous prospects, and is important in most marketing programmes. It is used not only to stimulate demand but for many other purposes. It can secure leads for salesman and middleman by convincing readers to request more information and by identifying outlets handling the product. It can force middlemen to stock the product by building consumer interest. It can help train dealers, salesman in product uses and applications. And it can build dealer and consumer confidence in the company and its products by building familiarity.

The marketing management's most frequent assignment in advertising is to stimulate market demand. By using advertising to 'pre-sell' customers, that is, to arouse and intensify their buying interest in advance - the management hopes to facilitate the salesmen's selling task. While sometimes advertising alone may succeed in achieving buyer acceptance, performance, or even demand for the product, it is seldom that, it can be solely relied upon. Usually, advertising is most efficiently used with at least one other sales method, such as personal selling or point-of-purchase display, which is generally more effective in directly moving customers to buying action. Effective advertising by a manufacturer often arouses a consumer's interest, but it will rarely send him to retail stores actively seeking the product. However, when in a store, an alert salesman or an attractive display calls his attention to the manufacturer's product, the impact of previous advertising often helps in persuading him to buy.

2.6.1. Importance

Advertising has become increasingly important to business enterprises - both large and small. Outlays on advertising certainly attest to the management's faith in the ability of advertising efforts to produce additional sales. It would be difficult to conceive of a firm that does not attempt to promote its product in some manner or another. Most modern institutions simply cannot survive without advertising.

Non-business enterprises have also recognised the importance of advertising. The attempt by army recruitment is based on a substantial advertising campaign, stressing the advantages of a military career. The health department popularises family planning through advertising. Even labour organisations have used advertising to make their viewpoints known to the public at large. In fact, it is reasonable to say that promotion now plays a greater role in business than it ever did in the past.

Advertising strategies that increase the number of units sold stimulate economies in the production process. Lower consumer prices then allow these products to become available to more people. Similarly, the price of newspapers, professional sports, radio and TV programmes, and the like might be prohibitive without advertising to share the expense. In short, advertising pays for many of the enjoyable entertainment and educational aspects of contemporary life, as well as lower product costs.

The criticism that "most advertising messages are tasteless" and that "advertising contributes nothing to society's well being" sometimes ignore the fact that there is no commonly accepted set of standards or priorities within our social framework. We live in a varied economy characterised by consumer segments with differing needs, wants and aspirations. What is tasteless to one group may be quite informative to another. An advertising strategy generally suffers from the averaging problem that escapes many of its critics. The one generally accepted standard in our society is freedom of choice for the consumer; customer-buying decisions will eventually determine what is an acceptable practice in the market place.

Advertising has become an important factor in the campaigns to achieve such societal-oriented objectives as the discontinuance of smoking, family planning, physical fitness, and the elimination of drug abuse. Advertising performs an informative and educative task that makes it extremely important in the functioning of the modern Indian society.

2.7 DEFINING ADVERTISING GOALS FOR MEASURED ADVERTISING RESULTS (DAGMAR)

Before an advertising budget and programme are developed, advertising objective must be set. These objectives must flow from prior decisions on the target market, market positioning and marketing mix; the marketing mix strategy defines the job that advertising has in the total marketing plan. At the same time, there are many specific communication and sales objectives that may be assigned to advertising.

Russel H. Colley has distinguished fifty-two possible advertising objectives.[11] He has outlined a method called DAGMAR for turning advertising objectives into specific measurable goals.

An advertising goal is a specific communication task to be accomplished among the defined audience in a given period of time. DAGMAR outlines a specific approach to measuring whether advertising goals have been achieved.

[11] Colley, Russel H., *Defining Advertising Goals for Measured Advertising Results.*

The development of operational objectives usually starts with a consideration of the ultimate behaviour that advertising is to influence. Operational objectives provide criteria for decision-making and standards against which to evaluate performance, and serve as a communication tool. Short-run sales usually do not provide a basis for operational objectives for two reasons:

(*i*) Advertising is usually only one of many factors influencing sales; and

(*ii*) The impact of advertising often occurs primarily over the long run.

Whatever the ultimate behaviour, it should be possible to conceptualise and perhaps estimate its value to the firm-hopefully in terms of the profit stream over time. There may be behavioural measure—for example, the number of new customers attracted-that may provide the basis for advertising objectives. However, it is usually be helpful to consider the communication and decision process that will lead to the desired behaviour and to identify key intervening variables in that process. These intervening variables, such as brand awareness, image or attitude, will, then, either by themselves or in conjunction with behavioural measures, provide the basis of advertising objectives. Further, to provide information for the development of objectives, it is useful to study the market dynamics and to determine the various brand images and consumer attitudes that prevail.

One possible target for advertising is made up of potential new customers. The number of people enticed into trying the brand may then form the basis of advertising objectives. Often, however, a process of learning and attitude development precedes the decision to try the brand, and advertising concentrates more profitably on this process. It may also attempt to increase or maintain the loyalty of existing customers. Here, it may be useful to concentrate on improving an image or on maintaining awareness levels, for it is believed that such results will affect loyalty over time. Advertising may also increase the product usage of existing customers. This approach to setting objectives is a refinement and extension of DAGMAR's approach.

DAGMAR defines an advertising goal as a specific communication task to be accomplished among a defined audience in a given time period. Thus, a communication task is based on a hierarchy model of the communication process involving awareness, comprehension, conviction and action. The goal is specific, with a definite measure, a starting point, a defined audience, and a fixed time period. In defining the audience, a particularly useful segmentation scheme is based on the steps in the hierarchy model. Thus, it may be useful to direct a campaign to an audience that is not aware of the brand. For implementing the approach, DAGMAR suggests that, the decision-maker analyse the situation in terms of merchandise, markets, motives, messages, media and measurements.

By introducing the behavioural science theory into advertising management, DAGMAR provides the framework for the development of more operational objectives. However, this has been challenged through the years on several fronts. Some critics are of the opinion that the only appropriate measure of advertising is sale. Another objection is that it is difficult to select a hierarchy level on which to base objectives, and to know how to move people up the hierarchy. Others believe that the approach is limited by measurement problems and noise in the system. By providing guidance to operating people, DAGMAR is said to inhibit the development of the great idea. The most fundamental attack is that the hierarchy model of the communication process is not appropriate. There is, for example, empirical evidence that changes in behaviour may precede and cause changes in attitudes in some situations.

Refinements of DAGMAR made an attempt to draw on research to improve the communication model on which DAGMAR was based. In refinement, the emphasis has been to determine which of the many models of the communication process will be appropriate in a given application. Of late, more analytical models have been developed that make the link between intervening variables and behaviour.

An important question in many advertising campaigns is to determine which intervening variable should be the focus of the campaign. One approach is to determine those hierarchy levels that have not yet been reached by a large number of potential customers. An extension would not only consider the size of the segment but the difficulty and, therefore, the cost of moving them (variables) up the hierarchy, as well as the likelihood of their eventually making the desired decision once they have moved up.

To implement the DAGMAR approach, people often need to be influenced about a particular intervening variable. For a durable product, one method is to compare it with the brand image of other brands. Another method was given by Claycamp and Liddy in their model, which made an attempt to specify the primary variables, which determine the achievement of adequate levels of awareness and trial purchasing. A model test showed that advertising expenditures were an important contribution to awareness if the advertising quality was high and that the awareness level, in turn, contributed to trial purchasing.

2.8 ADVERTISING IN MARKETING MIX

2.8.1. The Marketing Concept

Marketing was defined by the American Marketing Association as "the performance of business activities that direct the flow of goods and services from producer to consumer or user".[12] However, marketing is much more than the mere physical movement of goods from the points of production to consumer outlets. The key marketing functions include distribution, promotion, selling and standardisation, financing of marketing inputs, risk bearing and also gathering of market information. These activities blended together constitute marketing environment.

A more recent definition of the term probably better reflects the broad-ranging scope of marketing:

Marketing is a total system of interacting business activities designed to plan, price, promote, and distribute want-satisfying products and services to present and potential customers.[13] The

[12] Alexander, Ralph S., *Committee on Definitions*, American Marketing Association, Chicago, 1963.

[13] Stantion, William J., *Fundamentals of Marketing*, McGraw Hill Book Company, New York, 1975, Ch. 1, p. 5.

modern concept of marketing has helped emphasise certain principles that are basic in understanding both marketing and advertising. Some of the principles are stated below:

2.8.2. Marketing Focuses on the Consumer

Planning in the modern marketing concept starts with the consumer. Therefore, understanding the consumer has become the first step. The entire marketing organisation has to work together to determine what the consumer wants, how best to produce and sell the products, which can satisfy these wants, and also, how to motivate the purchase of a product. The same approach will apply to promoting the acceptance of worthwhile ideas in the area of non-commercial marketing.

2.8.3. Marketing is a Flow Process

Marketing is a dynamic process, which reflects changes in economic and social activities. The economic and social environment in which the firm operates undergoes frequent changes. The tastes and preferences of customers are in a process of flux. Marketing must respond to environmental changes.

2.8.4. Interaction with other Activities

Marketing includes many interacting activities, and marketing managers consider many of these factors, such as economic environment and government policy, while appraising the firm's marketing mix. This is of special relevance to business in India. The Government of India has strict regulations regarding licensing and other measures, such as the Monopolies and Restrictive Trade Practices Act and Foreign Exchange Regulations Act. The marketing mix is inevitably influenced by regulating policies.

2.8.5. The Marketing Mix

The concept of marketing is associated with the deployment of the total resources of a business firm towards the determination and satisfaction of wants and needs of consumers and customers in such a way that it enhances the achievement of a firm's overall objectives. The application of the marketing concept helps to lessen the imbalance between the supply and demand for a product or a service, especially when broken down by specific market segments.

2.8.6. Role of Advertising in the Marketing Mix

Advertising effort must essentially be integrated with the rest of the marketing plan. It is a part of the total marketing mix and has a supportive relationship with its various components. The need to coordinate advertising activities with other parts of the programme may be seen in the following features of the interaction of advertising with other components of the marketing mix.

2.8.7. Personal Selling

A salesman can point out to customers how his company's products fit their needs. It is also necessary to undertake selling to channels of distribution by pointing out that dealing in the company's products can contribute to their net profits. The salesman treats each customer as an individual and tunes the message to increase its receptiveness to an existing or potential customer.

Personal selling and advertising have to work together. Advertisements in magazines and newspapers may provide leads and equities which salesman can follow. Similarly, a salesman may bring to the attention of his company's dealers the help they receive in their marketing efforts from advertising. Advertising is designed to appeal to large audiences and its advantage over personal selling lies in the cost. An advertising exposure costs much less than personal selling.

2.8.8. Product Planning

Product planning has an important place in the marketing mix. Recent strategies in the product-planning area have been directed towards manufacturing better products and bringing about improvements in existing ones. Consistent efforts are being made to improve the quality of products, increasing their variety and also for devising new uses for them. Rapid changes in technology and myriads of innovations have made product planning a complicated task. Advertising highlights the superiority of a firm's brands or products over other brands or products and also seeks to enhance awareness and knowledge of new uses.

2.8.9. Brand Policy

The brand provides to the customer a certain guarantee and assurance that the quality of the product is satisfactory as the brand name connotes accountability. To the manufacturer it represents a means of gaining customer loyalty by building a consumer franchise around his particular brand. Advertising decisions are affected by a company's brand policy. For example, a company or a group of affiliated companies may produce several products, all under a family or company name. The Modi group of companies manufacture a number of products including tyres, textiles, paints and carpets and 'Modi' is the common brand name used for all products.

2.8.10. Price

One of the major considerations in determining price should be its role in achieving the targeted sales of the product. Sometimes price may not make much difference to sales as in the case of essential commodities where the demand is inelastic in relation to price. In the case of some products, it may even be possible to achieve higher sales at a higher price. For example, in the case of premium varieties of cosmetics, quality-conscious consumers may not be convinced of the quality of a brand or product if it is priced low. When a firm develops a prestige product at a high price, advertising emphasises its high quality, image and prestige.

2.8.11. Packaging

Packaging is also an important part of the marketing mix, although its importance varies with the type of product. For many products, packaging is one of the most powerful aids to selling, as there is constant competition for the customer's attention. In the case of products such as toiletries, cosmetics, and confectionary, it is of prime importance that packaging should be attractive. It is one of the factors, which can influence sales considerably. In such cases, packaging serves as an advertisement for the product by emphasising not only the contents but the containers as well. A typical Nescafe jar with its yellow top is prominently featured in the Nescafe advertisement.

2.8.12. Distribution

The role of advertising includes provision of support to distribution channels in a large measure. It is through advertising that the 'pull' effect may be created amongst potential buyers. This in turn, will motivate the channels to stock the product in anticipation of a smooth and speedy off take.

2.8.13. Promotion and Displays

Sales promotions can be used to increase sales to wholesalers, retailers, and through salesman, to consumers by offering premiums, concessions, coupons and prizes and by window displays and special deals. Premiums and 'point of sale' displays are also widely used in consumer-oriented promotions. In cases where coupons, premiums and the like are used, announcements of these schemes made to customers through the mass media generate a great deal of interest and have a high attention-getting value.

2.8.14. Advertising Decisions

The important point is that advertising decisions are influenced by their interactions with marketing objectives. Advertising does not exist in isolation, but must dovetail with and reinforce the rest of the marketing programme. In fact, all components of the marketing mix should strike a balance with each other. They should be in consonance with each other and should contribute to the organisation's marketing objective in their totality. For instance, advertising objectives should be derived from the marketing objective as a whole and there should be no conflict between them.

2.8.15. Factors Influencing the Marketing Mix

Factors that tend to influence the marketing mix are:

(*a*) The marketing objectives.

(*b*) The attitudes and behaviour patterns of potential consumers.

(*c*) Attitudes and motivation of the trade.

(*d*) Characteristics of the products or the services to be sold.

(*e*) Competitors' strategies.

All decisions taken at the planning stage will affect the communication strategy and the advertising programmes should reflect the type of results advertising should produce out of several alternatives such as the following:

(*a*) Increased brand awareness

(*b*) Improved brand opinion

(*c*) Change in the market share

(*d*) An attitudinal change

(*e*) Motivation of actual purchase

(*f*) Short-term gains in profits and for sales

(*g*) Medium-long-term gains in contribution, profits and sales.

2.9 MARKET SEGMENTATION

An important factor, which determines the role of advertising in the marketing mix, is the concept of market segmentation. As consumer behaviour is the most significant factor in advertising decision making and developing marketing programmes, the strategy has to be planned with specified types of consumers in mind. The importance of this factor in developing a marketing programme has led to the development of the concept of marketing segmentation.[14]

Market segmentation isolates those groups of consumers who may have similar attitudes about the purchase and usage of a particular brand or product class. Once these groups have been identified, they are studied in depth in order to understand the cognitive domain and parameters of value judgements of consumers. The concept behind market segmentation is based on the observation that all potential customers are not identical. Therefore, a company should develop different marketing programmes for different subgroups of the target audience, wherever necessary. For each segment to be identified, the following need consideration:

(*a*) What these particular consumer needs and desire are, especially as they relate to the brand and the product class under study.

(*b*) How consumers' perception of the brand and product class relate to the benefits they desire.

2.9.1. Advantages of Segmentation

There are various advantages of market segmentation:

(*a*) It is possible to direct advertising and marketing strategy to prime segments and decide how to frame the message appropriate to the brand and the product, considering the attitudinal disposition of consumers in this segment.

---

[14] A comprehensive survey of various market segmentation approaches as given in Dhalla, Nariman K. and Winton H. Mahato, *Journal of Marketing*, 40, April 1, 1976, pp. 34-41.

(*b*) It helps in selecting the proper media and knowing what types of media and programmes should be compatible with personalities and lifestyles of the prime segment.

(*c*) It also helps to uncover areas of product development and to find out if large groups of unfulfilled needs exist. In that case, entirely different kinds of products could be acceptable. A product may have certain unique benefits that are not being advertised.

2.9.2. Reaching the Target Segment

There are two ways by which the target audience can be reached:

(*a*) Controlled advertising

(*b*) Customer self-selection.

In a controlled-coverage situation an advertising-decision maker tries to reach a desired target segment and also to avoid reaching those who are not in the target segments through releasing advertisements in the media most accessible to the identified segment.

Customer self-selection is an alternative approach. Here the advertising programme is directed to a mass audience of which the target segment may be only a small part. People in the target segment may be only a small part. People in the target segment are attracted by the marketing effort since it is designed for them. Those who are not in the target group will probably avoid exposure either consciously or unconsciously. This applies to industrial advertisements in English dailies in India. There may be considerable waste of advertising as the cost of exposure for the target audience becomes rather high because a very small fraction of the audience may, in fact, be composed of potential buyers of industrial products.

2.10 ADVERTISING PROCESS

2.10.1. Advertising and Psychology

Advertising is a specific form of communication where the aspects of cost and corresponding benefit assume a special significance. In order to understand the way advertising can work, it is necessary to give some attention to the basic processes of communication. Invariably, one is tempted to go into the domain of psychology. It will neither be possible, nor necessary to discuss details of human psychology. It may suffice to realise that decision-making in the area of business, or for that matter in the domain of non-commercial activity, will be influenced quite considerably by patterns of behaviour of concerned persons, individually and in groups. Human beings belong to different types of backgrounds, which have an effect on their behaviour. Furthermore, regardless of education, training and group or organisational framework constraints, rationality may be expected only up to a limit.

Man is simply not a totally rational being; psychology has nonetheless endeavoured to introduce some order to the selectivity and bias with which he processes communication.[15]

2.10.2. Triangle of Communication

The process of advertising communication may be succinctly expressed in the form of a diagram, the eternal triangle of communication. The advertiser's objective is to communicate with the audience in order to obtain the desired results arising from the responses of the audience.

2.10.2.1. Advertiser

The advertiser is commonly interpreted as a commercial organisation, which has the paramount objective of making profits out of its business activities. Profits are usually generated through marketing or trading activity, apart from the financial investments. Even in the last case, marketing has a role to play, as the yield for investments in other companies and assets will, in turn, depend on the marketing activity of the latter. The communication logic, will, however, also apply to the types of advertisers, which may have a societal or political objective. Advertising for family planning, road safety and the like, and election campaigns are no different in this respect.

2.10.2.2. Audience

The term 'audience' has to be interpreted with care. Readers of a newspaper or magazine, listeners to the radio, or viewers of cinema or television would not necessarily constitute the audience for an advertiser. The audience for specific advertising has to be defined and identified by the advertiser. The need for market segmentation, which would help in defining and identifying the audience has been emphasised. It may be added that identification of the target audience is no less important for non-commercial advertising. The concept of target audience will, therefore, be applicable in all situations whether an advertising campaign or a detailed advertising programme for a product or service is under consideration.

2.10.2.3. Media

The third element of the triangle of communication is the media and that is where advertising tends to differ from other forms of communication. Advertisers, as a rule, will not control the media. Hence they will have to depend on the availability of media, and its appropriateness to reach their target audiences. The concept of REACH is a vital aspect of the advertising process.

2.10.2.4. Dynamic Concept

Thus, the triangle of communication consists of advertisers who are trying to convey advertising messages to their target audience through media, which are independent of advertisers. The basic concept, however, is not constrained to a static situation. First, the triangle may be interpreted both at the micro and macro levels, *i.e.,* for an advertiser or for one campaign and collectively for several advertisers in a community or a country. More importantly, all three elements of the triangle are subject to continuous change. Audience alter their patterns of behaviour under the influence of factors such as education, occupation, mobility, and so forth. Definitions of target audience invariably

---

15 McLeod, Jack M., "The Contribution of Psychology to Human Communication Theory", Frank E.X. Dance (Ed.), *Human Communication Theory*, Holt Rinehart and Winston, New York, 1967, p. 202.

need revisions. Advertisers produce and market products and services, which may cater to the needs and tastes of their clientele. The media, serving as the link, is influenced primarily by audiences to whom they have to relate. The cost economics of media, at the same time, involves advertising revenues. Both advertisers and media are ultimately dependent on the mass of buyers from amongst whom both select their respective target audience.

2.10.2.5. Choice and Competition

The creative aspect of advertising comes into play when an advertiser formulates an appropriate message to be beamed across to its target audience for a specific campaign. Even if we assume that segmentation has been efficiently done, it will be necessary to formulate the message and present it in such a way that it should appeal to the audience. This is essential when there is choice, and correspondingly, competition. The importance of appeal will obviously be less when there is little or limited choice, unless the advertiser has the objective of market development.

2.10.2.6. Matching Message with the Media

The media has two major roles. First, it is the question of matching audience to media, the type of persons who constitute the relationship, listenership, and viewership of the media vehicles. The second dimension is that of the frequency with which a specific media vehicle can put across the message to the target audience and the choices available to the advertiser. Both these dimensions are combined with the concept of exposure, which is translated into opportunity To See, commonly known as OTS. A further dimension of the suitability of certain types of messages to a specific media, whether print, audio, or audio-visual, should be kept in mind.

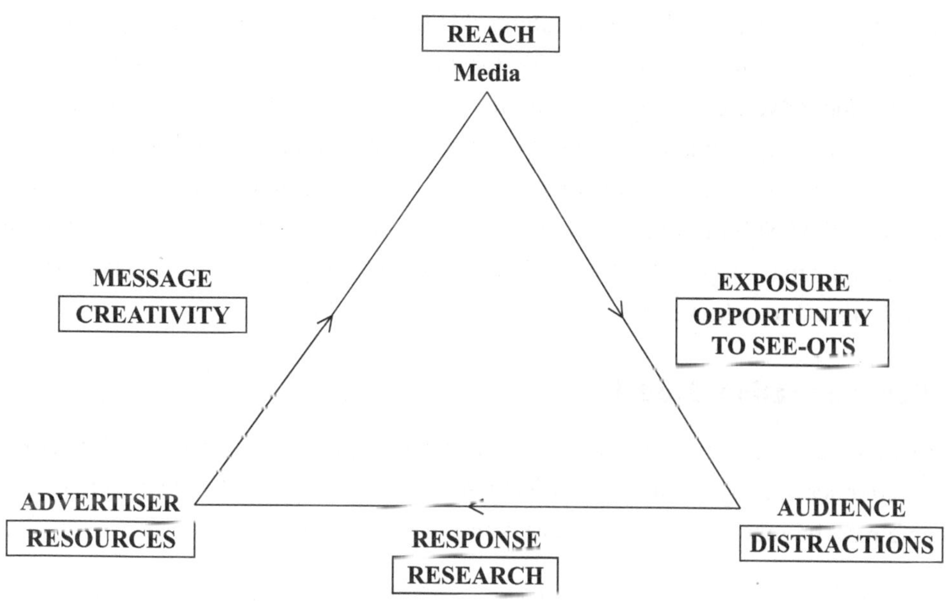

Fig. 2.1. Triangle of Communication

Source: Mohan, Manendra, *Advertising Management: Concepts and Cases*, p. 66.

2.10.3. Distractions for the Audience

The following two factors aggravate the disturbances and distractions operating on the audience:

(*a*) Competition between Media: A number of media vehicles would normally compete for the attention of the audience.

(*b*) Situational Setting: Reception of the advertising message may also be affected by the time and occasion of reading, listening or viewing of the audience.

2.10.4. Resource Constraints

Completing the cycle of communication, it is obvious that advertisers have their own resource constraints, both of funds as well as time. They can only afford to spend a certain amount of money on advertising in accordance with their marketing and advertising appropriation-the preparation of advertisements need time. Finally, the feedback from the audience is an important input for the advertisers.

2.11 EFFECTIVENESS OF ADVERTISING

The ultimate test of effectiveness of advertising obviously consists in the degree of achievement of the objectives set by an advertiser in consultation with the advertising agency working on the account. In the case of typical marketing situations this may take the form of an increase in the sales or market share or penetration into a new market segment. There has been a continuing debate on the subject of whether advertising works or does not work as measured in terms of specific marketing parameters. A recent study sponsored by the Institute of Practitioners in Advertising has sought to give a definite lead in this direction. This took the form of inviting entries for awards on the theme, "Advertising Works".[16] Submissions by advertisers and their advertising agencies, of case histories of specific campaigns made it possible to establish a casual relationship between advertising and the results it was designed to achieve.

2.11.1. Communication Models

There are various models of the advertising communication process, which aim at explaining the possible sequence through which advertising may eventually affect buyer/user behaviour. A simple scheme may be represented by a linear diagram as follows:

---

[16] Broadbent, Simon (ed.), *Advertising Works*, London, 1981.

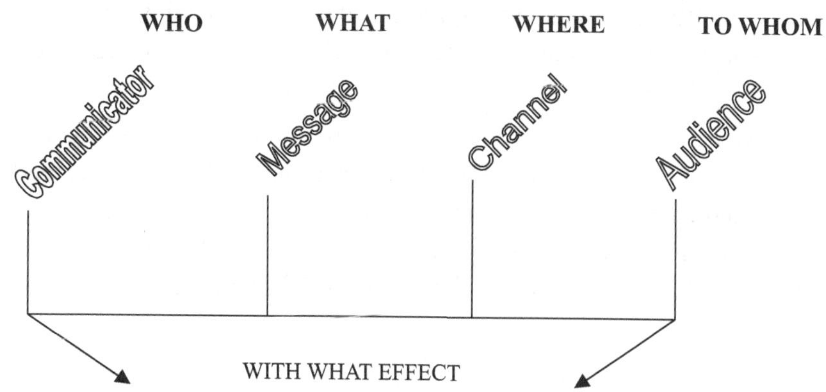

Fig. 2.2. Linear Communication Model

The feedback can be built in by a reverse arrow from the audience to the communicator under the caption, "To What Effect".

2.11.2. The AIDA Model

The effect is the action into which a prospect may be induced as a result of advertising. The following sequence may operate.[17]

Attention ⟶ Interest ⟶ Desire ⟶ Action

This was one of the earliest of such models developed in the 1920s in the USA and has come to be known as the AIDA model of hierarchy of effects. It highlights the importance of catching the eye/ear of the prospects and creating interest through the advertising message and its presentation. The desire to obtain advertised goods/services may be generated, albeit to varying degrees, amongst different prospects as a result of advertising. The final stage of action will depend not only on the determination of the prospect but also on other factors, such as availability, which is a function of the distributive system and its efficiency.

2.11.3. Lavidge and Steiner Model

Models of hierarchy of effects developed later gave more importance to cognitive stages. It was apparently felt that with an increase in competition and an enhancement of discerning abilities of potential buyers and users, information would play a greater role. The persuasive power of advertising could itself be a function of the information content. One such model is depicted below.[18]

Awareness ⟶ Knowledge ⟶ Liking

Purchase ⟵ Conviction ⟵ Preference

[17] Strong, F.K., The *Psychology of Selling*, McGraw Hill Book Co., New York, 1925, p. 9.

[18] Lavidge, Robert J. and Gary A. Steiner, "A Model for Predictive Measurements of Advertising Effectiveness", *Journal of Marketing*, 25 October 1961, p. 61.

This model is slightly more elaborate than that devised by Colley for the Association of National Advertisers under the auspices of the ANA Committee on 'Corporate Management Approach to Advertising Development'.[19]

The Lavidge and Steiner model takes cognisance of the competitive situation. Such competition may arise between brands of a product or even between substitute products as perceived by prospects constituting the target audience. The stage of linking following those of Awareness and Knowledge may refer to the advertising thus emphasising the creative aspects. Preference for the product or the brand may be the combined effect of product characteristics and their relevance to the target audience, and of advertising.

2.11.4. Innovation Adoption Model

A variation of the hierarchy of effects model, which builds in the experience of usage, was provided by Rogers in his 'Innovation Adoption Model' depicted below.[20]

Awareness

↓

Interest

↓

Evaluation

↓

Trial

↓

Adoption

Roger's model is of special relevance to new product introductions and particularly useful for adoption of non-commercial services or practices in developing countries. The stages of evaluation and trial before adoption (or purchase) are very typical in uninitiated communities were benchmarks for comparison might not exist. In this context, the importance of word-of-mouth communication may also be pointed out. Word-of-mouth is also a possible effect of advertising. It can serve as an important input for buying decisions as well as for moving prospects from the stage of interest to that of evaluation. The decision in favour of making an evaluation is likely to be influenced by information available from various sources including advertising. Evaluation obviously is a major step towards the adoption of the product /service.

2.11.5. Operational Model

O'Brien has tried to develop an operational model which could integrate various stages of decision making by buyers as follows:

---

[19] *Ibid.*, p. 48.

[20] Rogers, Everett M., *Diffusion of Innovations*, Free Press, New York, 1962, pp. 79-86.

Cognitive activity (non-evaluative thinking)

↓

Affective activity (evaluative-mental-activity)

↓

Conative activity (plans for actions and actions)

2.12 MEDIA SELECTION FOR ADVERTISING

2.12.1. Role of Media

Media has a vital role in the process of advertising communication. Effective advertising is possible only if suitable media are available. The appropriateness of media used, vis-à-vis the target audience and their reach, are of critical importance. Both these are, in turn, dependent on the editorial content in the case of print media and the nature of programmes for radio and television. For cinema advertising, the types of films screened as well as the locations of theatres will be relevant. In addition to the market potential, business policies of newspapers and periodicals are also likely to have an effect on their circulation. The government policies bearing on the nature of programmes influence listnership and viewership of radio and television.

A substantial proportion of the advertising budget allocation to the mass media is spent on buying space and time. Therefore, media decisions assume considerable importance when financial implications come to the force.

Four important terms that refer to this activity of determining the most effective media for informing the public about products are:

(*i*) Media selection,

(*ii*) Media planning,

(*iii*) Media strategy, and

(*iv*) Media research.

(*i*) Media Selection

'Media Selection' refers to the selection of a specific vehicle or a combination of vehicles, or more broadly the selection of a specific medium or a combination of media. Thus, the *Times of India* group of newspapers may be selected for the launch of a new filter cigarette for upper-middle class women, or a new detergent may be introduced into the market by ad films in the cinema and the television, with the press and outdoor media being selected as 'reminder' media.

(*ii*) Media Planning

'Media Planning' however is a more general term, taking within its compass all decisions regarding the time and place of advertising, in addition to the selection of the media. A 'media plan' thus outlines how advertising time and space in various media will be used to achieve the marketing objectives of the company through advertising. Media planning thus involves not only 'Media Selection' but also the drawing of advertising 'schedule'. Single insertion in a single medium is rare for consumer products.

(*iii*) Media Strategy

'Media Strategy' is a part of the marketing strategy; hence the 'media plan' is part of the overall market plan, and media selection is the final stage in the process of the promotion of a product through advertising. As it is often remarked, advertising is only one element in the 'marketing mix'; the primary objective is marketing the product, and advertising is just the means of creating a need for the product.

(*iv*) Media Research

'Media Research' involves the collection of data about the various advertising media, surveying consumers on their media preferences and habits, and carrying out primary and secondary research on effectiveness of each medium for selling particular types of products. Few advertising agencies or advertising departments in India have 'media research departments', where these exist; it is the department's responsibility to draw up media plans and strategies. Most ad agencies, however, have a media plan and strategies. Most ad agencies, however, have a 'media department' or 'media division', which carries out the task of media planning. The majority of agencies depend upon outside marketing agencies to conduct readership or audience surveys for them.[21]

2.13 NEED AND IMPORTANCE OF MEDIA PLANNING

Media planning has taken an importance during the last decade or so because of the phenomenal growth of the media, and inflation of media costs, and the need for 'scientific' decisions on the selection of media. The media scenario has changed now with individual vehicles vying aggressively to woo advertisers through incentives, extra services, and clubbed rates for sister publications. Daily newspapers have in recent years launched special supplements on business, advertising, marketing, management, education, travel and tourism, the hotel industry and other subjects with the sole purpose of providing the facility of 'segmentation' of consumers to advertisers. 'Segmentation' allows advertisers to target their ads of specific groups with special interests and belonging to a particular class or socio-economic status.

The rise in the number of rival brands and products too has made it all the more necessary to advertise competitively in carefully selected media and vehicles. The old practice of selecting women's magazines for women oriented products, for instance, will not work any longer, because there are so many women's magazines in different languages. This is equally true of business magazines and investment magazines. With over 20 special interest magazines flooding the market, the choice of the advertiser is not easy to make.

[21] Churchwalla, Kumar, Sethia, Subramanian, Suchak, *Advertising: Theory and Practice*, 2002, pp. 205-206.

But perhaps the primary reason for the importance of media planning is that advertisers are asking for returns from advertising expenditures; they expect ad agencies to justify their media decisions and plans.

Media planners, therefore, have to address the following key questions:

(*i*) What are the media available that will serve advertisers' interests in the most effective manner?

(*ii*) Which individual medium in each general category of media selected will be the best vehicle for a client's total advertising?

(*iii*) What would make the best 'media mix' for the client's total advertising?

(*iv*) What would be the most effective media schedule for the release of client's ads in each of those media?

2.13.1. First Step in the media Plan: Target Market Study

The first step in the media planning is the gathering of useful data about the target market or audience to be reached by advertising. All possible data regarding the interests, attitudes, socio-economic status, age groups, male-female composition, professions, religious beliefs, language, cultural background, will need to be collected. Much of this data can be had from the consumer research organisations like the Indian Council of Applied Economic Research. The kind of data needed about the target audience could be classified into the following:

(*i*) Demographic data, that is population data regarding age, sex, income, religion, language, etc.

(*ii*) Psychographic data, that is, 'psychological' data about the *lifestyles* of various segments of the population, their varied cultures and beliefs and tastes.

(*iii*) Consumer profiles, that is, the tastes, and preferences of the target audience with reference to different products, and in particular to the specific product or brand that is to be advertised.

(*iv*) Media profile, that is the media habits and preferences of the target audience.

2.13.2. Second Step: Deciding the Ad Message

The second step is to decide upon the nature of the message to be advertised. The message will be determined by the consumer profile and media profile of the target group. The message will have to be in terms of cultural and social background of the target group. If, for instance, the target group of a soft drink advertisement is the young college students of Berhampur, the message must make sense to him or her; it must speak his or her language, and must appeal to his or her cultural values through familiar copy and illustration. What are the buying motives of the target group? What are the selling points of the product? Which of the selling point or points (the USP of unique selling proposition) is to be focussed on in the ad?

2.13.3. Third Step: Matching Media and Target Group

The third step is to search for the ideal match between the target group's various profiles and the appropriate media. The young college student of the earlier example does not spend much time with television except on weekends. So, would there be any point in showing the soft drink ads targeted at college youth on weekly evenings? Perhaps he heads the film and video magazines, which are not as prestigious to advertise in. It is clear that, the media planner has other considerations in mind: the cost, the product prestige, the client's reputation, the rival brands' advertising media.

2.13.4. Fourth Step: Media Selection

The fourth and final step in media planning is deciding the media vehicle, the reach, the frequency and size of the advertising campaign. The 'media vehicle' is the individual newspaper or magazine or radio programme or TV serial or video film to be used for exposing the advertisement.

2.14 MEDIA SELECTION

As an electrical current flows from one end to the other through a conductor, so the advertising message is transmitted through the advertising media from the advertiser to the target audience. Advertising media are the vehicles, which carry the advertising messages. Various kinds of media are available to an advertiser. But the significant point is to select the appropriate medium for a particular advertising.

Effective advertising refers to informing the public about the right product at the right time through the right medium. Conveying a right message through a wrong medium at the wrong time would be a definite waste of resources. Therefore, the right media selection is the crux of the success of the entire advertising campaign. However, the right message, the right timing, and the right place of advertising are equally important. Media selection decisions refers only to the selection of a specific medium of advertising, such as the newspaper, a magazine, the radio, or television, the mail service or outdoor advertising, whereas media planning is a general term encompassing decisions involving the time and place of advertising in addition to the selection of the medium. A media plan outlines how advertising time and space in various media will be used to achieve the marketing objectives of the company through advertising.

In selecting media, advertisers will need to consider the following elements:

1. The objectives of the advertising campaign;
2. The 'coverage' and 'reach' of the media;
3. Media costs; and
4. The nature of the message.

An advertising plan is based on an overall promotional strategy; and media planning follows the advertising plan. Media strategy is thus a part of the marketing strategy. In other words, the media plan is part of the overall market plan, and media selection is the last stage in the process of promotion through advertising. Media decisions are mainly concerned with the following:

- What are those available media, which will serve our advertising needs best? Examples: newspaper, magazine, radio, television, direct mailing, outdoor etc. Which individual medium in each general category of media selected above will be the best vehicle for the advertising? Examples: TOI, India Today, Frontline, Radio, and Delhi TV Commercials.
- What could be the best combination of mix of media for our total advertising?
- What would be the best specific schedule for the release of our ads in each of these media?

Media Planning and Media Selection assume significance in the light of frequent reports that advertising is wasteful. The effectiveness of a well-designed advertising message depends upon 'when' and 'where' it is released. These are 'time' and 'place' decisions. In short, we may say that the success of advertising depends upon the right selection of media, the timely release of the advertisement message, its frequency and continuity, and the place of its release. All this signifies media planning.

For the right media planning and selection, the advertiser must know the consumer profile accurately and the market to be reached, *i.e.,* the target market. If you direct advertising to people who have neither the inclination nor the money to buy the product, it is a waste in effort which otherwise may be good advertisement effort in itself. In this case, the advertisement is effective, while advertising is ineffective. Therefore, in order to get the most out of the rupees spent on advertising, it should be directed to the right audience. For each target, there is an effective message; and it is this effective message reaching the right audience, which makes advertising most successful.

2.14.1. Types of Media

The media are classified into two categories:

(*i*) ***Above-the-line Media*:** Press, TV, outdoor, posters, cinema and radio. The recognised agencies get 'commission' from these media.

(*ii*) ***Below-the-line Media*:** Those who do not give commission to the ad agency. The agency adds a percentage as a handling or profit charge or charge of service fee. The examples are: Direct mail, merchandising, exhibitions, and sales literature.

The following are the various categories of media available to a media buyer or an advertiser:

I. Print Media

(*i*) Newspapers:

(*a*) Daily

(*b*) Weekly

(*c*) Sunday

(*d*) Weekend supplement.

(*ii*) Magazines:

(*a*) Consumer Magazines: General interest, special interest magazines like Auto World, Interior India.

(*b*) Business publications: Industrial publications, trade publications, institutional publications, etc.

(*iii*) Direct Advertising: Direct Mail.

II. Broadcast Media

(*i*) Radio: Vividh Bharati, FM.

(*ii*) Television: Terrestrial channels like DD and Satellite Channels like Star, Zee TV.

(*iii*) Narrow-cost-Media: Video and cable TV, Cinema, Ad films.

III. Outdoor Media

IV. Transit Advertising Media

V. Other Media

(*a*) Speciality Media: T-Shorts, buttons, caps, stickers, badges, etc.

(*b*) Direct advertising or Direct Marketing (DM)

2.14.2. Media Planning Process

This process answers the questions:

— When (the timing of the release)
— Which (the media selection)
— How (the coordination in media planning)
— How much (the budgetary allocation)

In short, this process designs a course of action that shows how advertising time and space will be used so as to contribute to the achievement of marketing objectives. Media plan is the end product of media planning process.

The media objectives are set keeping in mind the background of the market, the firm's market strategy, and its creative strategy. Media objectives thus contribute to the overall attainment of marketing objectives.

Media objectives lead us to a definite media strategy to translate media goals into general guidelines involving planner's selection and use of media. The best alternatives are selected.

The details of the media plan are then filled up such as selecting the broad classes, selection of media within these classes, and the actual media use decisions for each medium selected.

The degree of synergy between message content and media provides the missing piece of the jigsaw that media selection often is. For substantive messages, TV may be a right medium.

2.15 MEDIA RESEARCH

Media research is concerned with collection of data on the reach and exposure of each media in general, and of vehicles within each media in particular. Such data provide quantitative and qualitative information on the basis of which objective decisions regarding media and vehicle selection can be made.

Some of the areas that media research studies include:

(*i*) Investigation of a single medium or a single vehicle for advertising effectiveness.

(*ii*) Comparison of several media, or of several vehicles of a single medium.

(*iii*) Studies in 'Media Mix' and 'Vehicle Mix'.

(*iv*) Basic research and methodological studies.

(*v*) 'Image' studies of media and vehicles.

(*vi*) Reviews and decisions of advertising strategy and research methods.

2.15.1. Functions of Media Research

(*i*) The primary function of media research is to find out the most efficient media by measuring and comparing different media and different vehicles in terms of 'vehicle distribution', 'vehicle exposure' and 'advertising exposure'.

(*ii*) 'Vehicle distribution' refers to the number of copies of a newspaper or magazine circulated within a region or the entire country. In the case of broadcast and non-broadcast media, it refers to the number of programmes distributed on each channel.

(*iii*) 'Vehicle exposure' refers to the number and kind of people reading an advertising issue of a newspaper or magazine; it also includes the number of times each person reads an average issue. In the broadcast and non-broadcast media, however, 'vehicle exposure' refers to the number and kind of people in the audience.

(*iv*) Finally, 'advertising exposure' refers to the number of people exposed to the advertising message and also to the number of times each person exposes himself or herself to the advertising message. Again, in the broadcast and non-broadcast media, 'advertising exposure' relates to the number and kind of people exposed to the advertising message.[22]

All these four factors are taken into account in the determination of the most appropriate vehicles and media for a client's advertising. This exercise of determining the most appropriate vehicles and the most appropriate media for an advertising campaign is termed 'media planning' or 'media schedule'.

2.16 PRINT MEDIA AND ADVERTISING

Advertising in the print media is the oldest and the largest in terms of advertising billing. The print media carry their messages entirely through the visual mode. These media consist of newspapers, magazines and direct mail.

2.16.1. Newspapers

A sizable share of the total advertising budget is spent on advertising in newspapers. Newspapers in our country virtually reach most of the homes in the cities and many members of the

[22] Chaunawalla, Kumar, Sethia, Subramanian, Suchak, *Advertising: Theory and Practice*, 2002, pp. 163-164.

family read them. Their message can be longer than those of the radio and TV; and the message may therefore be more complex and lengthy. Since newspapers are local, marketers can easily use them to reach particular markets. This selectivity is easily available. The closing times for ads in newspapers are not rigorous. Some are in the twelve-hour range. From the viewpoint of the advertiser, newspapers offer several advantages; they are local in content and appeal, and provide opportunities for direct communication between a product and its local dealers or distributors. Because newspapers supply news, they offer an atmosphere of factual information and of currency that may be favourable for some advertising situations. Advertisers can reach a very broad audience through newspapers, which offer great flexibility. The advertiser may choose the specific areas to be covered, and the advertisement, can be placed in newspapers at very short notice as compared with other media. Much of the advertising carried by newspapers is local promotion by retail stores, cinemas, and other local organizations.

A disadvantage of using newspapers is that the cost of reaching a national or large regional market may turn out to be high. In addition, the printed copy does not reproduce the ad as finely as a magazine does. Further, consumers do not keep the issue for long periods of time; nor do they pass it on to others, as they often do with a magazine. Finally, in the eyes of consumers, newspapers do not have the prestige of TV and some magazines.

2.16.2. Magazines

Magazines are a means of reaching different markets, both regional and national, and of general and specific interest. An organisation may approach national market through such publications as the *Business Week, Femina, Sports Week and Filmfare*. Regional magazines are available for those markets who do not want a national coverage. Some marketers divide their markets on the basis of such variables as age, educational level and interests. They are likely to be concerned with special interest magazines. Magazines are divided into those that serve business, industrial consumers, ladies, sports, etc. The diversity of magazines is tremendous. Some offer news or other 'general interest' content to huge audiences. Others are highly specialised, technical, or even exotic. In general, magazines offer advertisers the opportunity to reach highly selective audience.

The primary advantages of magazine advertising are: selectivity of market targets; quality reproduction; long life; the prestige associated with some magazines; and the extra services offered by many publications. The quality of magazines reproduction is usually high. Consumers sometimes keep individual copies for long periods of time, reread them, or pass them on to others. Some magazines have prestige value. Magazines offer high-quality printing for advertisements. The paper used and the presses employed in magazine printing make possible the reproduction of the right colour, sharp details, etc. Advertisements may be read more carefully and with greater depth of interest in a magazine than elsewhere, both because magazines tend to be kept longer and sometimes read repeatedly, and because of the specialised character of their contents.

The primary disadvantage is that, magazines lack the flexibility of newspapers, radio and TV. Another disadvantage is the high cost. Because of the high cost factor, many small advertisers do not employ this medium. Another problem is waste circulation, that is, individuals who are not targeted consumers are exposed to the advertising. Finally, magazines have long closing periods, sometimes as long as a month.

2.16.3. Outdoor Media

Outdoor advertising involves the use of signs and billboards, posters or display and electric spectaculars. The marketers may purchase billboards on the basis of showings. A showing indicates the percentage of the total population of a particular geographic area that will be exposed to it during a one-month period. Here, the number of billboards is as would attract approximately 90 per cent of the local population about 20 times during a month. Signs are usually smaller than billboards and are erected and maintained by the marketer rather than by the advertising media.

This form of advertising has the advantages of communicating quick and simple ideas, of repetition, and of the ability to promote products that are available for sales. Outdoor advertising is particularly effective in metropolitan cities. Another advantage of outdoor advertising is that the advertiser can use this medium to bring the product to the attention of consumers; or to remind them of the product, while they are on shopping trips or are disposed towards shopping. Consumers see the billboards or signs many times as they drive to and from work, shop, and run errands. Advertisers may utilise this medium to economically reach a large mass of people or small-local markets.

2.16.4. Direct Mail

It is one of the most important classes of advertising media. The concerns that employ direct mail brochures, sales letters, post cards, leaflets, folders, booklets, catalogues, and house organs, etc. In a sense, the advertiser act as their own media.

The direct mail offers the advertisers a maximum of selectivity and flexibility. They do not generally use advertising media, such as TV or magazines. Direct mail advertising is generally much more expensive than advertising in other media, because of the high costs of delivery messages individually. It also suffers from a lack of prestige-unhappiness with junk mail is widespread. Marketers often experience difficulty and incur high costs in obtaining a list of good prospects and in updating the list as new prospects appear and old prospects disappear. Further, the cost per contact can be high in relation to other media.

The advantages of direct mail include selectivity, intensive coverage, spread, format flexibility, complete information and the personalisation of each mailing piece. Direct mail purchases also tend to be consistent buyers by mail. The effectiveness consideration makes direct mail an ideal medium.

A disadvantage of direct mail is its high cost per reader. Direct mail advertising is, moreover, dependent on the quality of the mailing list.

2.17 BROADCAST MEDIA AND ADVERTISING

Advertisers use two types of media to reach target consumers over the airwaves: radio and TV.

2.17.1. Radio

Advertisers using the medium of radio may also be classified as national or local advertisers. The radio is a prominent vehicle of advertising in our country, and accounts for a large sum of the total advertising budget. Radio serves principally local rather than national or large regional markets. Many small advertisers use the radio so do some large organisations.

The advantages of radio advertising are immediacy, low cost, flexibility, practicality, low-cost audience selection, and mobility. The radio is an extremely mobile broadcast medium. It reaches virtually every one, either in their homes, cars, or elsewhere, providing a means of reaching a mass market. The radio is an inexpensive medium for every one. Marketers may purchase commercial time. It is, moreover, a flexible medium; and it has the latest deadlines for the submission of commercial materials. Others such as magazines often require that advertisers submit their messages months before they are to be presented to the public.

The disadvantages of the radio include fragmentation, the unavailability of the advertising message for future reference, and less research information. The medium cannot take advantage of the visual means of communication as TV and the print media do.

2.17.2. Television

Of late in India, a growing class of advertising media has been the TV. In our country, commercial advertising on TV is severely limited because broadcast timings are only in the evenings. The TV is a unique combination of sight and sound, and achieves a deeper impact than the other media do. This is particularly advantageous for advertisers whose products require demonstration. TV advertising offers advantages of impact, mass coverage, repetition, flexibility and prestige.

TV appeals to both the senses of sound and of sight. As a result, it combines the two to produce high-impact commercials. Finally, the fact that a product or service is promoted on TV may build a prestigious image of the product, and its sponsors. The lifestyles communicated through various models on television derive pleasure from watching TV.

The disadvantages include relinquishing control of the advertising message to the telecaster, high cost, some evidence of public distrust and lack of selectivity. Only a limited message is possible because of the limitations of time. It is not as selective as some of the other media. TV time is expensive and it is not easy to get prime time. Quite apart from TV time, it is bit expensive to produce a commercial.

2.18 CREATIVITY IN ADVERTISING

Creativity in advertising means the process of selecting and presenting the message in an effective manner so that it may attract the attention, create the interest in product and stimulate action. It is an art of advertising. Various artists, writers, poets, novelists, play-writers, etc. combine the product attributes with the ideas, words and phrases. The effectiveness of advertising depends upon the copy design. Copy design or layout arranges various elements of advertisement, copy-headlines, sub-headlines, slogans, illustrations, etc. in an attractive manner. In designing the copy various principles are followed.

In designing, themes and appeals and various other information about the product and market conditions must be thoroughly considered. Themes and appeals create the image of the product and of the company. Theme must be sound, effective, true and convincing.

The creativity or designing must also consider the use of colours in advertisement. They attract attention and endow an advertisement with a feeling of quality and prestige. But, it is rarely possible in newspapers due to their poor quality of paper. However, magazines print colour advertisement but they charge higher rates for printing.

The creative part of advertising involves the process of selecting and presenting the messages. We see daily thousands of advertisements and commercials in print and on air. This is most often known as the 'art' of advertising. The business of conceiving, writing, designing and producing these messages is called 'advertising creativity'.

Creativity is an art. An artist, writer, poet, novelist, play-write takes well-known ideas, words, and phrases and relates them in a fresh, often brilliant manner while preparing an advertising copy. They combine the product attributes and the ideas, words and phrases in such a manner that persuades the consumers to buy the product. This combination really represents an art and creativity.

The effectiveness of the advertising depends very much on proper message design. A successful basic message design may be used over and over again, creativity in advertising most assuredly draws on 'pure' writing talent but as it is obvious, the nature of business demands a certain kind of discipline, not found in creative writing circles. Writers must be very rich in the language concerned (spellings, grammar, punctuations and idiomatic expressions) and they must have an overall knowledge of marketing environments and awareness of consumer learning abilities and selective processes. Creativity in advertising, therefore, must be disciplined creativity.

2.19 CREATIVITY IN COMMUNICATION[23]

Communication is an advertisement emerges from a powerful idea—an idea that is unique and does not get lost in the world. Creativity remains an enigma to most people—people think, 'we are born creative or we are not'. Creativity is a complex process whose outcome depends upon the forces within the individual and outside.

Creativity is thus a range of abilities. Yes of course, in IQ there is a strong genetic factor. However, the genetic factor is much weaker for the abilities that constitute creativity, except for adaptive flexibility can be built into people. Creativity is both convergent and divergent thinking. Creative thinking is largely a function of divergent thinking—the discovery of identification of many alternatives. Creative ad people have to overcome the constraints of deadlines and time pressure by

[23] Sharma, Sandeep, Kumar, Deepak, *Advertising: Planning, Implementation and Control*, Mangal Deep Publications, 2001, p. 91.

developing relaxed atmosphere of working. Creative people exhibit an ability to go off the beaten track, a capacity to respond to reality and keep their feet on the ground.

A checklist for exploring the creative element:

- Restate the problem in as many ways as possible.
- Question the assumptions underlying the problem.
- Combine the ideas in unusual ways, related with unrelated.
- Question the problem itself.
- Have a concern to discover problems.
- For being creative, learn to relax.

To quote David Ogilvy, The Goliath of Advertising to emphasise that the ad that sells of more importance to marketers than anything else. He says, "When I write an advertisement, I don't want you to tell me that you find it creative. I want you to find it so interesting that you buy the product".

2.20 ADVERTISING APPEALS

A huge amount of time, energy, and money go into developing advertising appeals to influence the buying behaviour of consumers. The purchase decisions of prospective customers are attempted to be influenced by advertisers rationally or emotionally by the use of appeals of various kinds; which are generated out of the different kinds of product attributes or features. The advertisement appeals aim at influencing consumer perception of the advertised product or brand; and change their attitude towards the product. Ad appeals can be either product-oriented or consumer-oriented. Consumer-oriented appeals have their ground rooted in the hierarchy theory of needs put forth by A.H. Maslow. As per this theory, there are five levels of human needs arranged in a hierarchy. They are:

(*i*) Safety needs of personal and family security, and protection;

(*ii*) Psychological needs of hunger, thirst, sex, etc.;

(*iii*) Love needs or the needs of affection and belongingness;

(*iv*) Esteem needs or the needs of self-respect, prestige, social approval, achievement, etc.; and

(*v*) Self-actualisation needs or needs of self-fulfilment and self-expression, etc.

These needs occur one after the other is fulfilled. The first two levels of needs *i.e.,* the psychological needs and safety needs are the basic or primary needs for any human being. Then come the three levels of needs one after the other; which are more psychological in nature and are termed as secondary needs. Satisfied needs lead a person to a stage of unsatisfied needs; which motivate the behaviour of a person. Much of human behaviour is motivated by subconscious and unconscious needs, which a person may fail to admit consciously. Generally, many needs act together to give rise to a given behaviour response; but only some needs are more important in behaviour than others. These are the key needs, which need to be identified and appealed to, directly or indirectly, in the advertising messages.

Appeals can be broadly classified as rational, emotional and moral. Rational appeals are those appeals, which are directed at the thinking of the audience. It involves some sort of deliberate reasoning process on the part of the receiver of the advertising message, which he or she believes would be acceptable to other members of his or her social group. In such cases, the product is expected to yield the functional benefit that is wanted of it. However, many a time it becomes difficult to clearly demarcate between rational and emotional motives; but certain buying motives like high quality, low price, long life, performance, resale value and economy in the operating expenses are normally considered as rational under ordinary circumstances. Industrial users are normally guided by more rational motives than anything else. Emotional appeals as a contrast to rational appeals are appeals, which are not preceded by careful analysis of the pros and cons of making a buying decision. They are normally below the level of consciousness, and may not be recognised by a person. Sometimes even if the person is aware of the motive operating, he or she refuses to admit it because he or she feels that it would be unacceptable as a good reason for buying among his associates and colleagues. Emotional appeals are designed to agitate some positive or negative emotions in the minds of the people, which are expected to motivate product interest or purchase. Emotional appeals can be both positive and negative. But researchers show that negative emotional appeals have greater impact than the positive ones. Fear appeals or the threat approach is probably the most common and effective of the negative appeals. The bad-breath advertisements of Colgate and many other toothpaste companies, and the advertisements of most insurance companies use this method of appeal to extract quick response from the prospects. Fear appeal is very well used in the public messages to wear helmet or stop smoking.

Positive appeals use the strategy of reducing a person's anxiety about buying and using a product whereas negative appeals use the strategy of increasing a person's anxiety about using a product or service. A positive appeal emphasises the positive gains to a person from complying with the persuasive message, while the negative appeal emphasises on his loss if fails to comply. The basic differentiating factor is that when products are of little interest to consumers if rational appeals are used, fear appeals are used; and when products fulfil a generally recognised need, positive appeals are used. However, fear appeals are always more effective because they always talk about the dangerous state one has to go through if the product is not used. Fear appeal can also be better used if the market is segmented. Because consumers of different age, sex, education, or social status have fear of different things, positive emotional appeals highlight product benefits and attributes capable of influencing consumer behaviour. Love, pride, prestige, humour, and joy are some of the positive appeals. "The love and care soap" slogan of Dettol is one good example of it. Many advertising in fact, combine both emotional and rational motives in their appeals because it is widely felt that the basis of purchase is actually a blend of both kinds of buying motives.

Moral appeals are those appeals, which touches to the sense of right or wrong of the audience. Appeals to donate generously for the earthquake victims in Gujarat, is an example of it. Messages intending to arouse favourable response to social causes like prohibition, adult literacy, rural development, equal rights for women, etc., use moral appeals.

Advertising appeals can further be classified into direct and indirect appeals. Direct appeals clearly communicate with the consumer about a given need; and follow it up with a message extolling the advertised brand as a product satisfying that need. Indirect appeals do not stress on a human need, but refer to a need indirectly. Advertisers have some ambiguity in the message so that the consumers may be free to interpret it and the need to which the advertiser is appealing. Since the interpretation is not difficult, there is no risk involved in keeping the ambiguity in the message.

Indirect appeals can be either product-oriented or consumer-oriented or both combined. Product-oriented Indirect Appeals can be of three types:

(*i*) Feature-oriented Appeals: Here the basic message is about product features, attributes and characteristics.

(*ii*) User-oriented Appeals: The message here emphasises on specific in-operation and/or post-operation advantages of the brand advertised.

(*iii*) Product-comparison Appeals: The basic message stressed on the differences between the advertised brand and the competing brands.

Consumer-oriented Indirect Appeals are classified in the following ways:

(*i*) Attitude-oriented Appeals: The basic message is structured in a manner to be in line with the consumer's attitude, belief and value system.

(*ii*) Significant Group-oriented Appeals: The message stresses on the group, which uses or approves of the advertised brand. The group may be a reference group, a social group, or a peer group significant for the consumer target.

(*iii*) Lifestyles-oriented Appeals: The basic message emphasises an identifiable lifestyle relevant to a defined target market. Wills brand cigarette ad uses the appeals of its strange taste, which runs as "For some hard smokers, a strong cigarette can only give relaxation, particularly after a day's hard work, one needs a Wills Flake".

(*iv*) Subconscious-oriented Appeals: The cream of the message is distinguished and directed of the consumers' subconscious or unconscious need. These messages are aimed at the buyer's dream world; but are shrouded in some manner by messages appealing to the buyer's conscious mind.

(*v*) Image-oriented Appeals: Brand image is created by all kinds of advertising appeals; but here the advertiser purposefully tries to create a brand image of specific type, which suits to the self-image or self-ideal image of the target market.

Although various kinds of appeals can be used in advertising to motivate the audience, the purpose can be unfulfilled if the advertising messages are not structured properly.

2.21 CREATING AND PRODUCING AN ADVERTISEMENT

David Ogilvy has laid down commandments for creating advertising campaign.[24] They are:

(1) What you say is more important than how you say it;

(2) Unless your campaign is built around a great idea, it will flop;

(3) Give the facts;

(4) You cannot bore people into buying;

(5) Be well-mannered, but don't clown;

(6) Make your advertising contemporary;

(7) Committees can criticise advertisements, but they cannot write them;

(8) If you are lucky enough to write a good advertisement, repeat it until it stops pulling;

(9) Never write an advertisement which you wouldn't want your own family to read;

(10) The image and the brand;

(11) Don't be a copycat. Nobody has ever built a brand by imitating somebody else's advertising.

William Bernbach of Doyle, Bernbach, and Dane believes in the following for successful creation of advertisements.[25]

(1) Don't talk down to an audience. The copy should be honest; puffery, clichés, and heavy repetition should be avoided.

(2) The approach has to be clean and direct. It should be simple, swift, and as penetrating as possible.

(3) The advertisement must standout from others by having a character of its own.

Besides David Ogilvy and Bill Bernbach, there are many others from the world of advertising who have given their own views about advertising creativity and also proved them successfully. Now is the time to turn to the process of the creation and production of advertisements. The model of the creation and production process[26] given in the figure below lays out the details of it.

---

[24] Ogilvy, D., *Confessions of an Advertising Man*, Atheneum, New York, 1964, pp. 93-103.

[25] Aaker, D.A., and Myers, J.G., *Advertising Management*, Second Edition, Prentice Hall of India Pvt. Ltd., New Delhi, pp. 349-350.

[26] *Ibid.*, p. 361.

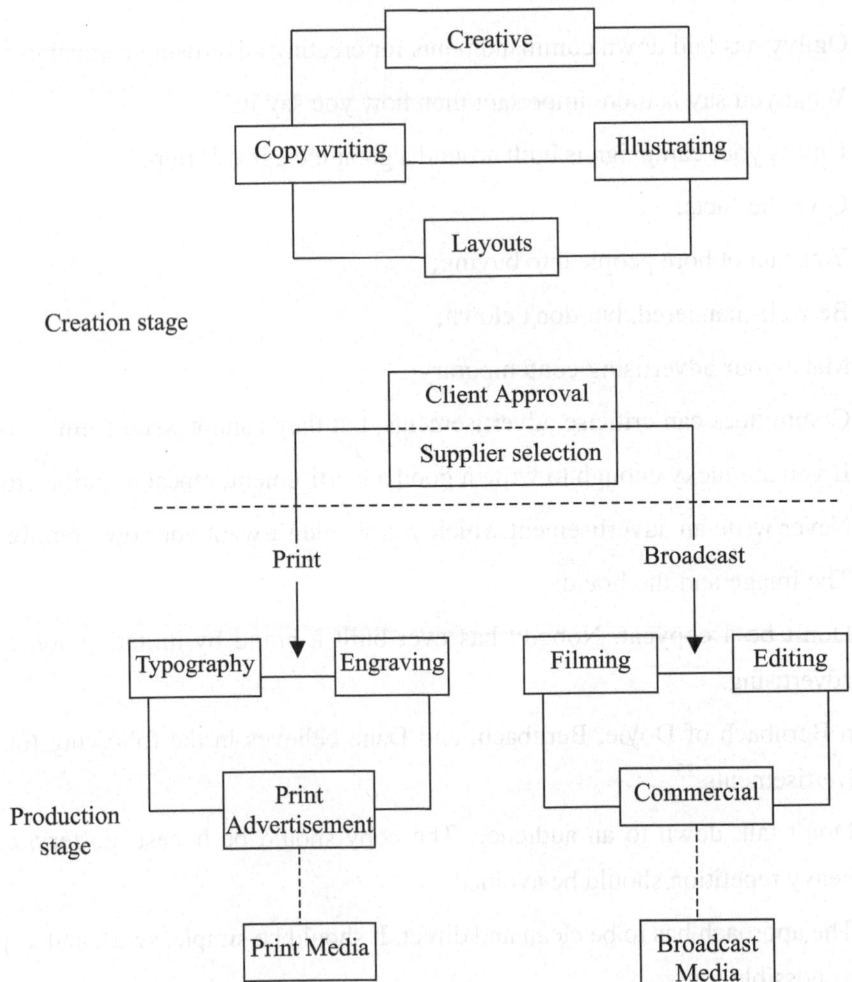

Fig. 2.3. Model of the Creation and Production Process

2.21.1. Creation Stage

Much of the local advertising is normally taken up at the client or media level for the creativity; but in almost all cases of national advertising, an advertising agency is involved. The agency's creative department holds the responsibility for generating alternative advertising ideas and for picking up one or a few that will be sent forward for production. The creative department comprises copywriters and artists. The following is a description of the steps that comprise the creation stage.

2.21.1.1. Creative Process

Alex Osborne lays down the following as the starting point of the creative process.[27]

[27] Osborne, A.F., *Applied Imagination*, 3rd Revised Edition, Scribner's, New York, 1963, p. 11.

(A) Fact-finding:

(*i*) Problem-definition: Picking out and pointing up the problem.

(*ii*) Preparation: Gathering and analysing the pertinent data.

(B) Idea-finding:

(*i*) Idea-production: Thinking up tentative ideas as possible leads.

(*ii*) Idea development: Selecting from the resultant ideas, adding others, and reprocessing by means of modification, combination, etc.

Fact-finding should include factual information about the company, the product, competition, the target audience along with their language, needs, motivations, and desires. Fact-finding also includes a careful discussion of the advertising objectives. The constraint implied by the objectives should be challenged by the creative team; and in doing so, new alternatives can be generated and new objectives can be formulated. Solutions to tough problems spring up when the focus of the problems is broadened. Fact-finding also should have a digestion and incubation time. Facts need time to be absorbed and assimilated. The best ideas emerge only after a period of incubation.

After fact-finding comes the idea finding or idea generation, which is the soul of the creative process. It is always wise to generate large number of ideas. Evaluation of the ideas and choosing an alternative come next, which are not as difficult a job as generating alternative ideas. In fact, many sophisticated methods have been evolved to choose among alternatives; but idea generation still remains a very difficult job. The creative process leads to the specific activities of writing copy, illustrating, and layout.

2.21.1.2. Copywriting

All the written or spoken words in an advertisement including the headline, slogan, and even the address of the sponsor constitute the copy. Copywriting in print is the activity of actually putting words to paper, those contained in the main body of the text *i.e.,* the main argument and appeals used. In broadcast media, the copywriter is in effect a scriptwriter who develops a script or scenario to be used in radio or TV. Different advertisements are designed differently to meet different problems *i.e.,* attaining different specific objectives. To handle the different kinds of problems, different kinds of copies are written. Burton and Kreer describe them in the following manner.[28]

(*a*) Straight-line Copy: In such copies, the body text begins immediately to develop the headline and illustration ideas in direct selling of the product, using its sales points in order of their importance.

(*b*) Narrative Copy: A story or specific situation is established in such copies, which leads into a discussion of a product's selling points. In institutional advertising, a copy is also a narrative one, which sells an idea, organisation, service, or product, instead of presenting the selling features.

---

[28] Burton, P.W. and Kreer, G.B., *Advertising Copywriting*, 2nd Edition, Englewood Cliffs, N.J., Prentice-Hall, Inc., 1962, pp. 115-116.

(*c*) Dialogue and Monologue Copy: Characters used in the advertisements do the selling in their own words in such copies.

(*d*) Picture and Caption Copy: In such kinds of copies, the story is told by a series of illustrations and captions rather than by use of a copy block alone.

(*e*) Gimmick Copy: The selling power in such forms of copies depends upon humour, poetry, foreign words, great exaggeration, gags, and other trick devices.

2.21.1.3. Copy Alternatives and Creative Styles

Copy alternatives are created in advertising media context situation. Copies of infinite variety of forms can be created; but the constraints are imposed from production technology and media forms available. All kinds of copies essentially end up in one of the three media forms, viz., visual only (print), audio only (radio), audiovisual (television). Copywriter's creativity is restricted by the limitations of the medium involved.

In prints, copies can use words and for numbers. Many kinds and sizes of typefaces can be used to draw the attention of the readers. There can be long copies using many words and short copies using a few words to have a right impact. A long copy explains the product features and fills the advertising space whereas a short copy is used to gain reader's attention and highlight the product's existence. Another ingredient of print copy is the various kinds of pictures, cartoons, tables, charts, logos, trademarks, brand or company symbols that can be used. Use of colour, blank space, and the size of the advertisement can also render effectiveness to the copy in print media.

In audio (radio), copy is associated only with sound. Voices, music, and special effects can be used in numerous ways to create various audio copy alternatives.

In television, a copywriter can utilise the full spectrum of both sight and sound possibilities. The added advantage here is that of the moving pictures. Within the legal restrictions, the copywriter virtually has a limitless vista for creation before him.

2.21.2. Image and Positioning Strategy

Advertising can be used to mould and reinforce an image.[29] Advertising campaigns frequently use the development of an image as one of their most crucial objectives. Images can be stable over the years or extremely unstable and dynamic.

The term 'position' or 'positioning' are often used these days to mean 'image' with the specific quality of comparison with the competition. Image is associated with the company, its products, and its brands. All these can be positioned with respect to competitive alternatives.

2.21.2.1. Positioning Strategies

A positioning strategy provides the focus in the development of an advertising campaign. There can be several approaches to positioning strategy.

(*a*) **Using product characteristics or customer benefits:** A commonly used positioning strategy is to associate an object with a product characteristics or customer benefit. For example, an automobile manufacturer may emphasise an economy and reliability of its products or its durability or engineering efficiency to position it against the

[29] Aaker, D.A., and Myers, J.G., *op. cit.*, pp. 133-157.

competition. Sometimes a product can be positioned with respect to a product characteristic that competitors have ignored. Physical characteristics are objective and cannot be measured on some physical scale such as colour, temperature, intensity, sweetness, distance, thickness, weight, fragrance, etc. There are also pseudo-physical characteristics, like spiciness, smoky taste, greasiness, creaminess, etc., which cannot be measured. These characteristics can be used for positioning strategy.

(*b*) **Positioning by Price-Quality:** It is an important area, which is frequently used in positioning strategy. In many product categories brands are deliberately offered with more features in terms of service or preference. Such brands normally cost more to cover the cost of production. At the same time the higher price also intends to communicate that the product is of higher quality. In advertising, products are thus positioned either in terms of their low price or higher quality against competing brands.

(*c*) **Positioning by use:** An image of the product can be communicated by associating the product with a use or application. Milkmaid in its advertising positions itself as a sweet dish product against the other competing food products. Products can have multiple positioning strategies too; but the more the numbers, the more the difficulties and risks in terms of effective communication.

(*d*) **Positioning by Product use:** This positioning strategy uses the approach of associating a product with a user or a class of users. This is one of the very important reason why advertisers use models or celebrities to position their products. Lux toilet soap is positioned by using glamorous movie stars. Lifebuoy soap is positioned by using macho men.

(*e*) **Positioning by Competitor:** Positioning strategy is based on the concept of competitors. But it is sometimes useful to use the competitors well-crystallised image developed over many years to one's own advantage by using it as a bridge to help communicate another image referenced to it. Comparative advertising are examples of such positioning strategy.

(*f*) **Positioning by Product class:** Some products make critical positioning decisions that involve product-class associations. Maggi Noodles have felt it necessary to position their product with respect to other kinds of food items. Maaza has positioned its mango drink with respect to ripe mango fruits.

2.21.2.2. Determining the Positioning Strategy

How to determine as to what should be the positioning strategy. It can be difficult and complex process. However, it can become more manageable by adopting a six-step approach aided by thorough market research. The steps are to:

(*a*) identify the competitors;

(*b*) determine how the competitors are perceived and evaluated;

(*c*) determine the competitors positions;

(*d*) analyse the customers;

(*e*) select the position; and

(*f*) monitor the position.

SUMMARY

Advertising is any paid form of non-personal mass presentation or promotion of ideas, goods, or services by an identified sponsor. It includes all the activities involved in presenting to a group, a non-personal, oral or visual, openly sponsored message regarding a product, service or idea. Thus, advertising is a process, and advertisement is the message communicated by the sponsor through the various media available to the intended receivers, made possible through the process of advertising. Advertising should not be confused with public relations, propaganda, and publicity; which have their own special meanings. Sales promotion is another term often confused with advertising. It supplements advertising, but has its own identify. The activities other than personal selling, advertising, and publicity that stimulate consumer purchasing and dealer effectiveness come under sales promotion. The examples of such activities are: window displays, shows and exhibitions, demonstrations, premiums, games, contests, and sweepstakes, etc.

The main objective of advertising is to increase sales. But the specific objectives can be to increase the number of units purchased, to introduce new products, to counteract competition, to increase the number of product uses, to increase sales in off-season, to maintain brand loyalty, to build a positive business image, to obtain dealer support, to secure leads for salesman and many more.

Consumer-oriented advertising can be national, local, or cooperative. Advertising aimed at business buyers can be trade advertising, industrial advertising, farm advertising, professional advertising, etc. Advertising management as an important area of marketing management is a system of interacting organisations and institutions; all of which play very important roles in the advertising process.

Media is another important area of advertising because they are vehicles that carry the advertising message from the sponsor to the target market. Above-the-line media includes print, TV, radio, outdoor, etc. Below-the-line media are the ones like direct mail, point-of-sale, merchandising, exhibitions, etc., used usually in sales promotion. In advertising, we are mainly concerned with the above-the-line media. Selection of media involves a whole of planning, which is the lookout of the media department in the ad agency. Media planning and scheduling are very important aspects of advertising and include many smaller details about the media.

An advertising goal is a specific communication task to be accomplished among a defined audience in a given period of time. DAGMAR lays down a specific approach to measure if advertising goals have been achieved.

Advertising appeals are of prime importance in advertising. Therefore, a huge amount of time, energy and money go into developing advertising appeals to influence the buying behaviour of consumers. Purchase decisions of prospective consumers are attempted to be influenced by advertisers rationally or emotionally by the use of appeals of various kinds, which are generated out of the different kinds of product attributes or features. Appeals can be rational or emotional. They can also be direct or indirect.

Chapter 3

SOCIO-ECONOMIC IMPLICATIONS OF ADVERTISING

3.1 INTRODUCTION

In the previous chapter, advertising in general has been discussed. The present chapter is devoted to a description of economic and social implications of advertising. It includes descriptions on business environment and advertising, explicit role of advertising, effects of advertising on product quality, and increase in economic activity and employment.

The role of advertising in society has often been a subject of much debate. Advertising may be useful for consumers, considering that dissemination of information is necessary when buyers have to make a choice from the various products and services or from the different brands of a product. The opposite view is based on the contention that consumers are duped by misleading advertising and hence advertising should either be eliminated or strictly regulated. It will be fallacious to draw any conclusion without considering the various aspects of interface of advertising with individual and institutional buyers and society. It may be useful to look separately into the economic and social effects of advertising. Economic implications of advertising may arise from its role vis-à-vis the overall business environment and also with respect to various macro and micro situations. The social relevance of advertising lies in its qualitative content and creative exposition.

The cumulative effect of advertising is particularly relevant to the discussion of both economic and social implications. There is a strong temptation to evaluate advertising in isolation from its context. It must be realised that advertising is created in tune with the prevailing social norms and behaviour patterns. It is, however, possible that the inherent futuristic orientation of the advertising profession may be instrumental in projecting some ideas or images which may be ahead of the times. Moreover, the carryover effect of advertising on its audiences dictates the need for bringing in changes in order to maintain the magnetism of the inherent appeal. A systematic approach as well as susceptibility to change are essential ingredients of purposeful advertising.

3.2 ECONOMIC EFFECTS OF ADVERTISING

Questions have often been raised about the effects of advertising on consumer welfare and the functioning of the economic system. Of late, this subject has assumed great importance due to a growing consumerism movement. A lobby of public opinion considers expenditure on advertising wasteful and an increase in advertising expenditure undesirable.

Advertising is closely linked with economic development in the long-run term, considering that it can be a vital marketing input for new product introductions. It can thus be a valuable aid in the process of market development. Economic growth is the outcome of expansion in demand on the one hand and augmenting of resources on the other. Advertising can also perform a useful function in the dissemination of technology and creating favourable conditions for the acceptance of innovative approaches. Economic systems are basically constituted of a series of transactions between individuals, organisations and sectors. The relevance of advertising may be seen at all stages of interface between a supplier and a buyer at a micro level and also in the macro-economic content.

3.2.1. Business Environment and Advertising[1]

A study conducted by the Strategic Planning Institute indicates the utility of advertising in periods of economic recession. Recession, according to this study, refers to periods of sluggish economic and industrial activity when the rate of growth of the market served is substantially lower than the long-run trend. Deviations of short-term trends from the long-run market trend indicate periods of expansion and recession.

The analysis of the Strategic Planning Institute (1990) showed that during recessionary periods, average businesses recorded gains in their market shares, apparently at the expense of smaller competitors and those who were less willing to defend themselves. During expansion periods, however, some businesses have difficulty in meeting growing demand, thus allowing competitions on easier entry into the market.

In either case, business can help improve their market shares by increasing the expenditures on media advertising. About a quarter of these made a major increase in their expenditure on media advertising during recessionary periods and they gained an average of 1.5 points of the market share. During market expansion periods, over 50 per cent of the businesses increased advertising expenditures and no spectacular gains in market shares were achieved. Those businesses, which reduced media advertising expenditures during the expansion phase, on the other hand, suffered losses in their market shares.

---

1 Mohan, Manendra, *Advertising Management: Concepts and Cases*, Tata McGraw Hill, 2001, pp. 17-18.

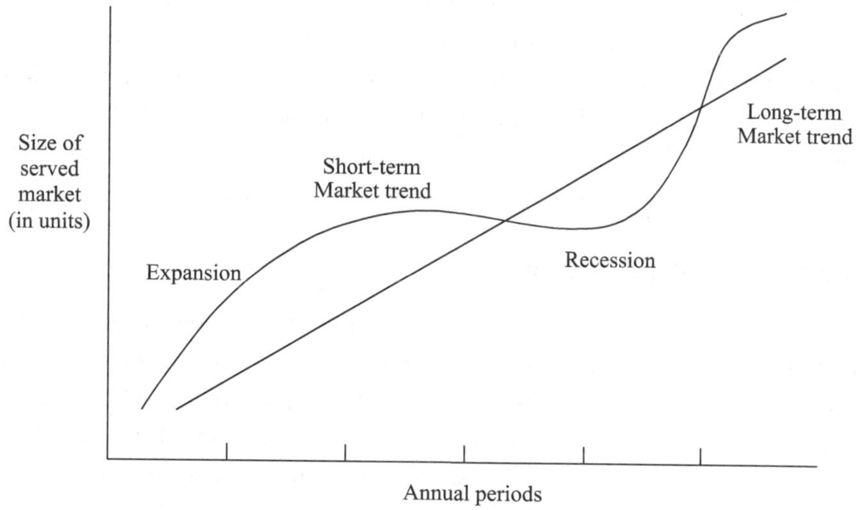

Fig. 3.1. Long-term vs. Short-term Business Trends

Source: Mohan, Manendra, *Advertising Management*, p. 18.

3.3 EXPLICIT ROLE OF ADVERTISING

An assessment of the role of advertising in the economic system should include its role as a guide to prospective buyers, its effect on primary and selective demand, product differentiation, propensity to consume and on innovation and on the financial support that it provides to the media. Indirect effects of advertising may be seen in its influence on the efficiency of production and distribution, lowering of prices, economic well-being, improvements in product quality and finally in its contribution to national income.

3.3.1. Guide to Prospective Buyers

Advertising is an instrument of persuasion and information. The informative role of advertisements consists in provision of information about products and their specifications, features, functions, and prices to prospective buyers.

Tull, Boring and Gonsior (1994) comment on the utility of such information:

Conventional demand theory endows the consumer with a vast amount of information. The consumer is held knowledgeable of the configuration of attributes that comprise a product or a service. Further he is assumed to be aware of the product price alternatives available to him and has well defined tastes and preferences and can determine his marginal role of substitution for each product for the other possible alternative products involved in a particular purchase decision.[2]

[2] Mohan, Manendra, *op. cit.*, p. 19.

In real life, however, consumers would not be so well informed. They have to rely on whether information they can gather from various sources including advertisements. There can be little doubt about the genuine need for a certain amount of information for the process of making decisions about the purchase of products and judicious exercise of choice between products and their substitutes and amongst several brands. Kaldor (1972) observes that if advertisements were not provided free, consumers would be quite willing to pay for the supply of information.[3]

3.3.2. Primary and Selective Demand

The demand for a class of product as a whole may be termed primary demand and the demand for an individual company's products the selective demand. Borden points out that advertising may shift the demand for a class of product when the demand for that product is expansible, *i.e.*, subject to increase through appeals to consumer's buying motives.[4] In influencing the shape of the demand curve for any type or class of products, advertising may make the demand either more or less elastic. If a company is able to shift its demand curve with the help of advertising, it will attain a longer share of the industry's total sales unless the primary demand expands in equal ratio. If the product does not present a good advertising opportunity, it does not bring a change in a company's demand schedule.

Advertising has not only increased the demand for some products but has also changed the shape of the demand curve by the introduction of new products. In the early stages, there may be a relatively small and inelastic demand. Later, with aggressive advertising, public acceptance is built up and other firms start initiating the product. Thus the shape of the demand curve is altered. Advertising tends, in some instances, to make the demand for specific brands of some products relatively price inelastic for varying lengths of time. If the brands have won the loyalty of consumers, they maybe expected to regularly use them even when their price relationships with existing brands are disturbed.

3.3.3. Product Differentiation

Another factor affecting the firm's capacity to influence demand is product differentiation. In product differentiation rests the opportunity to influence consumers to develop brand preferences. Products in which differentiation is not possible will not be affected by advertising. Advertising plays a part in expanding the range of merchandise through the stimulation of product differentiation among brands has been much more direct than their influence in widening the range through new inventions of a major character.[5] The desire on the part of producers to offer a variety of products under their brand names has led them to continue experimenting with different combinations of desirable product qualities. Technology has contributed towards developing new products, which might gain consumer acceptance.

---

3 Kaldor, N., "The Economic Aspects of Advertising", *Review of Economic Studies*, 18(1), 1972, p. 5.

4 Borden, Neil H., *The Economic Effects of Advertising*, Richard D. Irwin Inc., Homewood, USA, 1942.

5 *Ibid.*, p. 613.

3.3.4. Encouraging Innovation

Advertising encourages product development by providing an economical way of informing potential buyers about the launch of new products or of improvements in some products. In many situations, new product introductions require extensive research and development expenditures and substantial investment in production facilities. Advertising can help in recovering these research expenses.[6]

3.3.5. Propensity to Consume

There can be two hypotheses, according to Simon,[7] about the effects of advertising on the propensity to consume:

(*a*) Advertising does affect aggregate spending.

(*b*) Advertising does no more than affect the allocation of the budgeted amount by people.

The considerable stability in the average propensity to consume over many decades is consistent with an allocation hypothesis. Simon makes a reference to the Milwaukee Journal experiment of systematically blacking out selected advertisements. A newspaper strike provides a real life situation for the same purpose. The evidence collected from data on department stores sales suggests that consumer spending declines when normal advertising flow is cut off.

Advertising affects the long-run propensity to consume by influencing tastes, though it is doubtful that the effect could occur so rapidly as to affect spending over a business cycle. On the other hand, advertising might affect the short-run propensity to consume by informing consumers of bargains. The study of Lambin[8] shows that a 1 per cent increase in advertising expenditures result in an average short-term increase of 0.1 per cent either in sales or market share. In the long-term it was observed that a 1 per cent increase in advertising was correlated with an average of 0.25 per cent increase in the sales or market share. While advertising apparently created a preference for the advertised goods; the sales response to advertising did not rise in proportion to the increase in advertising expenditures.

3.3.6. Financial Support to Media

The major functions of the mass media are to provide education, entertainment and information to the audience. The revenue from subscriptions alone is quite inadequate to support the publication of newspaper and magazines. Radio and television networks have to depend on the support of the state exchequer through license fees. Alternatively, they must have access to advertising revenue. Selling of space or time by the media to advertisers is essential for the financial viability of the

---

6 Aaker, David and Myers, John G., *Advertising Management*, Prentice Hall Co. Ltd., New Delhi, 1977, Ch. 16 "The Social and Economic Effects of Advertising", p. 553.

7 Simon, J.L., *Issues in the Economics of Advertising*, University of Illinois Press, Urbana, Chicago, 1970, Ch. 8 "The Effect of Advertising Upon the Propensity to Consumer", pp. 193-217.

8 Lambin, *op. cit.*

media. Availability of advertising revenue is a pre-requisite for the growth of media through introduction of new media vehicles and continuance of existing ones.

3.4 INDIRECT ROLE OF ADVERTISING

Advertising may also have many indirect effects on products and their prices, market situation and economic and business activity. These effects are generally apparent after a certain time lag. The major effects are described below:

3.4.1. Lowering of Prices

Advertising can help in lowering prices by reducing the costs of production and distribution and expanding the market. Advertising encourages mass consumption and, consequently, may lead to substantial increases in production. This enables manufacturers to reap the benefits of the economies of scale. Since the cost of production per unit is brought down, prices will be lowered and consumers will thus be benefited. This has been the long-term experience of a number of industrial nations.

An obvious objective of advertising is to influence prospects favourably towards the products and services advertised. This is commonly termed the 'pull' effect and can help in reducing the costs of distribution. A study by Steiner shows how advertising affected prices and trade margins in the toy industry in the USA.[9]

This study indicated that there was a substantial decline in the retailer's margin as well as consumer prices of toys between 1955 and 1970. Advertising on TV and in the print media led to a major upsurge in demand. Strong competition emerged and this resulted in a rapid turnover and massive discount offers.

Advertising, which has brought wide acceptance of a product, frequently has had the effect not only of shifting the demand curve to the right, but also of changing its shape. Koldor suggested that advertising may lead to a lowering of prices by making a product wantable. Some sellers may be highly effective in bringing a large number of purchasers into the market, particularly consumers in low-income groups, to whom low price has an effective appeal.[10]

3.4.2. Advertising and Competition

Lambin's study indicated that a company's advertisement had a negative impact on rivals' sales and market shares. However, the study did not uncover any explosive pattern leading to advertising wars. Rival advertising efforts tend to cancel each other out.[11] Advertising encourages

---

9 Steiner, Robert L., "Does Advertising Lower Consumer Prices", *Journal of Marketing*, 37(4), October 1973, pp. 19-26.

10

11 Labin, *op. cit.*

competition and consequently firms will vie with each other to provide the best products and services to buyers so as to create and sustain brand loyalty. This encourages firms to undertake consumer research and come out with products more suited to consumer needs.

3.4.3. Effects of Advertising on Product Quality

Advertising not only tends to improve product quality through competition and product differentiation but also influences product quality in another way, namely, by inducing producers to maintain quality as claimed under their brand names. The system of branding has the effect of giving protection of product quality to consumers, because the self-interest of the sellers leads them to ensure a high quality of the merchandise sold under their brand names. A seller does not wish to maintain the quality of his brand only because he is an advertiser. It is in his long-term interest to enjoy the benefits of patronage of satisfied customers, whether he advertise extensively or not.[12]

3.4.4. Increase in Economic Activity and Employment

Advertising and selling may have played a part in expanding the economic system by stimulating consumers into buying more. Advertising and aggressive selling have led people to want more things and to get them too. They have been induced to work harder than they would otherwise. This has had the effect of raising the aggregate level of the production of goods and services in the economy.

In the long run, aggressive selling and advertising have probably played a major part in making people favourably disposed towards high levels of consumption and in creating the acceptance of new products and new ideas. Advertising is particularly important in inducing the initial sale to pioneering adopters of a product in the introductory stage of its lifecycle.[13]

3.4.5. Effect on Business Cycles

Advertising could be a tool for alleviating the extremes of business cycles. When an economy is in a recessionary phase, some firms increase their advertising. This may have the effect of preparing purchase decisions, especially for industrial products, machinery and plants and thus diminishing the amplitude of business cycles.

3.5 CRITICAL ANALYSIS OF ADVERTISING

Advertising invites a lot of criticism from various quarters. Some of the major targets of such criticism are described below:

3.5.1. Product Proliferation

Critics of advertising point out that advertising encourages unnecessary product proliferation. It leads to the multiplication of products that are almost identical, resulting in wastage of resources, which could otherwise have been used to produce other products.

[12] Borden, *op. cit.*

[13] *Ibid.*, pp. 681-713.

3.5.2. Inefficient Manufacturers Stay in Business

One of the short-term effects of advertising is that it can enable inefficient manufacturers to sell their substandard products by extensive advertising and thus stay in business. This is detrimental to consumers if they can be lured by advertising into buying low-quality products.

3.5.3. Barriers to Entry

There is a general belief that advertisements promote industrial concentration to a greater or lesser degree. The extent of such concentration may vary with the character of the individual trade, the advertisability of the product and the technical conditions of its production.[14] However, studies on this subject are not conclusive. The evidence of positive association between advertising and concentration is weaker than can be expected, as indicated in a study by Telser.[15]

3.5.4. Advertising and Propensity to Consume

It is generally believed that advertising raises the propensity to consume. While this may be desirable for industrial nations, can a developing economy afford a high propensity to consume? Arguments cited in favour of higher propensity are the following:[16]

(*a*) Consumption stimulates productivity because people are motivated to work harder and earn more in order to satisfy their needs. This extra effort on their part also increases productivity and helps develop the economy.

(*b*) Advertising for mass consumption goods can help in gradually reducing disparities and breaking down barriers, as those between the urban elite and others, by making more products available in rural areas.

Raising the propensity to consume can be undesirable as it can lead to conspicuous consumption. Thus, money can be frittered away on inessentials. It is also argued that the higher the propensity to consume the lesser will be the savings. This leads to problems of capital formation and so investment may be hindered. Supporters of this view ignore the fact that advertising has been used as a very potent tool for promoting banking services and saving habits and for raising funds from the public for investment in equity and debenture capital and fixed deposits. Over subscription of a larger number of capital issues in India in recent years is a testimony to effective and purposeful use of advertising.

3.6 SOCIAL ISSUES IN ADVERTISING

A discussion of the social issues in advertising covers the means of advertising as well as its effects. Means of advertising include creative and media strategies. Advertising is criticised on the

[14] Koldor, *op. cit.*

[15] Aakers and Myers, *op. cit.*, p. 559.

[16] Sen Gupta, P.B., "Does a Developing Economy Need Advertising for Consumption?"

grounds of deception, manipulation, and bad taste. The points raised below include questions of manipulation of consumers against their will. Matters of taste in advertising and possible preoccupation with exploiting sex appeal will also be discussed.

The second objection relates to the social effects of advertising such as its influence on social values and *lifestyles*. It is believed that the pervasiveness of advertising has an impact on the value systems of society.

3.6.1. Deception

Deception occurs when an advertisement is introduced into the perceptual process of the audience and the output of that perceptual process either differs from the reality of the situation or affects buying behaviour to the detriment of the consumer.[17] Thus, deception refers not only to the information content in advertising but may also arise from misplaced emphasis in presentation. Greyser has formulated five simple questions, which may be applied to the information provided in advertisements.[18]

(*a*) Is the claim testable?

(*b*) Is a competitive claim of superiority defensive in terms of either normal or extraordinary but reasonable use?

(*c*) Does the claim apply to all models and types in the product range, or just to some?

(*d*) Can the message be misinterpreted by a reasonable person?

(*e*) Finally, the test for relevance is also important. Does the advertisement address itself to what consumers want to know?

The Federal Trade Commission of the USA reviews advertising referred to it in accordance with the following criteria laid down by the Supreme Court.

Advertising as a whole must not create a misleading impression although every statement, separately considered, may be literally truthful.

Advertising must not observe or conceal material facts. Advertising must not be artfully continued to distract and direct readers' attention from the true nature of the terms and conditions of an offer.

Advertising must be free of fraudulent traps and strategy which would induce action which would not result from a forthright disclosure of the true nature of the offer.[19]

---

17 Aaker and Myers, *op. cit.*, p. 569.

18 Greyser, Stephen G., "Advertising Attacks and Counters", *Harvard Business Review*, 50(2), March-April 1972, pp. 28 and 145.

19 Dunn, Watson, *Advertising: Its Role in Modern Marketing*, 2nd Edition, Holt, London, 1969, Ch. 6, p. 92.

3.6.2. Manipulation

Critics of advertising feel that the freedom of choice of consumers is restricted by the power of advertising since it can manipulate buyers into making a decision against their will or interest.[20] Such manipulation can be brought about by playing on the subconscious motives of people using emotional or subliminal appeals. Even the genuine persuasive power of scientific advertising can have such effects. It must be pointed out that the manipulating power of advertising through a careful application of techniques of motivation research has been overstated. People probably make choices most of the time for reasons best known to them. Although marketing professionals have accepted the reduced scope of motivation research, the layman is still haunted by the spectre of the 'hidden persuaders'.

The communication of factual information about a product is usually accepted as being of value to the consumer. However, when advertising utilises appeals or associations that go beyond such a basic communication task, the charge of manipulation via emotional appeals is raised. The implication is that consumers will be led to make less than optimal decisions by such emotional appeals.

There is also a view that advertisers have the power to manipulate their audiences. Many large companies have the capacity to get a large number of exposures for their advertisements. Furthermore, these companies can utilise advanced and very scientific advertising techniques and thus make an impression on consumers. It must be realised that even the most sophisticated approaches have their own limitations. Secondly, buyers' choices are determined by many basic behavioural characteristics and so advertising usually exerts only a marginal influence.

3.6.3. Taste

Some critics feel that advertising has adverse effects, as creative exposition may not always be in good taste. The most common criticisms are:[21]

(*a*) Moral concern about the advertising related to the product itself, *e.g.* cigarettes, alcohol, etc.

(*b*) Objections to the occasion of exposure to advertisement. This will be specially relevant to television advertising when children may be among the audience.

(*c*) Objections to appeals employed, *e.g.,* overemphasis on sex appeal.

(*d*) Objections to the techniques of advertising strategy like excessive repetition of the claim or advertisement, or clearly unaesthetic presentation.

3.7 CONTROVERSIAL EFFECTS OF ADVERTISING

The persuasive role of advertising is presumed to have an impact on society's values and *lifestyles.* In determining the ill-effects of advertising there still remains the issue of whether

[20] Aaker and Myers, *op. cit.,* pp. 537-542.

[21] Greyser, *op. cit.,* p. 28.

advertising creates such negative effects or whether it merely reflects the values and attitudes that are created by more significant sociological forces. The casual relationships are far too complicated to yield conclusive pointers. Advertising is probably effective in creating an image rather than in changing society's values.

3.7.1. Materialism

Advertising is accused of promoting materialism by inducing people to attach too much importance to the material aspects of life. It creates the notion that acquisition of things will gratify basic and inner needs and aspirations. As Mary Gardiner Jones of the Federal Trade Commission has put it:

It is the message of the commercial that all of the major problems confronting the individual can be instantly eliminated by the application of some external force - the use of a product. Externally derived solutions are thus made the prescriptions for life's difficulties. In the world of the TV commercials, all of our individual hopes and fears can be instantly yield to a material solution and one, which can work instantly without any effort, skill, or trouble on our part.[22]

3.7.2. Advertising and Sensitivity to Price

There is a belief that advertising affords differentiation among closely resembling brands and thus dulls the consumers' sensitivity to the price. However, a study of Wittink showed that the relative price elasticity increases with an increase in advertising, implying that advertising increases sensitivity to price.[23]

3.7.3. Advertising Creates Insecurity

Advertising can make people worry about tooth decay, body odour, lack of self-confidence and many other ills while claiming that the advertised products will reduce these worries.[24] There is no evidence that advertising can create a fear where no fear actually exists. However, it can magnify latent fears. An advertisement for Naturelle Herb Cream, for instance, has the following headline:

The time to worry about wrinkles is when you are still young and pretty.

3.8 CONCLUDING COMMENTS

Advertising has come to stay as a part of modern systems and present day society. Communicating to consumers, the vast variety of goods and services available is obviously impossible

[22] Aaker and Myers, *op. cit.*, pp. 547-548.

[23] Wittink, Dick R., "Advertising Increases Sensitivity to Price", *Journal of Advertising Research*, 17(2), April 1977, pp. 39-42.

[24] Dunn, Watson, *op. cit.*, p. 101.

without advertising. Emerging *lifestyles* and patterns of buyer behaviour call for such communication in the interest of prospective buyers. It may be added that advertising is not merely a vehicle for promoting purchases and stimulating consumption. Considerable criticism of advertising veers around advertisements of consumer goods. That should, indeed be taken note of. Advertising is also an essential input in the marketing of industrial products and investment goods. The contribution of advertising to the promotion of savings and investment has been referred to above. Advertising approaches and techniques are also being effectively used for the promotion of a number of important social causes such as family planning, healthcare and prevention of accidents.

It is in the interest of both consumers and advertisers to ensure that advertising follows certain norms of quality and maintains standards, which may be laid down by competent authorities. There are provisions for the regulation of advertising in a number of countries and codes for guidance have been drawn up. The British Code of Advertising practice, for instance, specifies that advertisements should be "legal, decent, honest and truthful". The Advertising Standards Authority, an independent body although financed by the advertising industry, has the responsibility of administering the code. The code is kept under review and consumer research is conducted by the Advertising Standards Authority to record the changing attitudes and keep this code updated. Only very few advertisements are found to violate the code. Advertisers as well as advertising agencies have a basic concern for consumer taste and acceptance and are willing to abide by the discipline of self-regulation.

Chapter 4 ADVERTISING: TRUTH, ETHICS AND SOCIAL RESPONSIBILITY

4.1 INTRODUCTION

In the previous chapter, the economic and social implications of advertising have been discussed candidly. The present chapter focuses on truth and ethics of advertising and its social responsibilities in detail. It includes discussions on ethics and morality, need for creative imagination, obligations of advertising, responsibilities of advertising men, sex and advertising and its various legal aspects.

"The objectives of advertising are mainly long-range to assure the firm eternal life and a place in the sun... The purpose of advertising is to increase demand for the company's product above what it would otherwise be."[1]

4.2 ETHICS AND MORALITY

Ethics means a set of moral principles and values. Morality means set of principles of right and wrong behaviour. Morality is broader in meaning than ethics, and is concerned with the right type of conduct. Ethics refers to a system of certain values that govern the conduct of individuals or groups in a community. Morality is a dynamic system.

Advertising, in order to be effective and successful has to guide the customers to buy certain products. Advertising is a business practice as well as a social service. Advertising has to be good because it cannot afford to be bad. Advertising has to be right. The objective should be accomplished only by ethical advertising. Unethical advertising on the other hand, may cut the very throat of the competitor who resorts to it and lead to a chain of adverse effects.

Some attention has been paid to the economic effects of advertising; but little has been done to analyse, ascertain and measure the adverse effects of unethical advertising. This is so because a measurement of the adverse effects of unethical advertising is as difficult as, it not more difficult than, measuring the economic effects of advertising, for unethical advertising has effects or reaction, which are quite indirect and are in uncertain directions. Moreover, it is not easy to differentiate between ethical and unethical advertising because it is difficult to draw the line between the two. It is mostly a matter of values, opinions and judgements. However, this differentiation is necessary.

[1] Rathor, B.S., *Advertising Management*, Himalaya Publishing House, 1996, p. 57.

Ethical advertising can shift the demand curve of a firm to the right; unethical advertising can shift the demand curve of a firm to be left. The use of such adjectives like better, more, best, largest, tastiest, or only can make all the difference. Words like these may transform an ethical advertisement into an unethical one.

Unethical advertising may result in the following adverse effects:[2]

(*i*) *Affects competition and encourages growth of monopoly*: The combined advantage of an increasingly larger market share for one firm naturally reduces competition and ultimately develops into monopoly power, leading to disadvantages to the consumer and to society in the political sense.

(*ii*) *Reduces efficiency*: Weakness or absence of competition reduces efficiency.

(*iii*) *Discourages innovation*: The firm that has gained monopoly power may have the required financial strength and the advantage of size to invest in research and development for innovation. However, the tendency would be not to do so because of the absence of competition.

(*iv*) Psychological reaction by rivals leading to loss of market share for the companies to give only such slogans as reflect the inferiority of other competing products and the superiority of one's own product. If consumer behaviour is any guide, this action and tendency to reaction may lead to loss of market share in the case of one and a gain in favour of the other. Who wins the unhealthy race is uncertain.

4.3 ADVERTISING AND SOCIAL RESPONSIBILITY

In the present era of "*garibi hatao*", it is vital that advertising people pay serious attention to their obligations to the society in which they live, and develop a sense of responsibility in their daily working life.

The basic obligation of an advertising man is to his profession. This obligation does not end with selling goods or promoting services; it involves that he work efficiently, developing advertising skills commensurate with the requirements of the time and place, and that, at the same time, he should bear in mind the fact of the inherent competitive nature of advertising.

As more and more goods are produced in the country, it will become increasingly necessary for advertising to use all its skills efficiently and effectively to ensure the smooth functioning of the distribution pipeline.

In the course of the past few years, the amount spent on advertising has been increasingly at a fairly healthy rate. Today, the advertising message is conveyed to people in all walks of life, and through all the mass media. The vast media-mix poses a big problem in the context of the literacy and living habits of our people. This is a problem that may be solved only by using specialised skills, both in media planning and creative approach.

---

[2] *Ibid.*, p. 59.

4.3.1. Need for Creative Imagination

It obviously presents a tremendous challenge to all those engaged in advertising. It requires a greater depth of understanding of the people as well as of the market. However, creativity by itself is not enough. The people in advertising should understand the needs of the business community and, at the same time, pay adequate attention to what is required for the common good of the people. It is only in this way that the activities and projects of advertising agencies would lead to better living standards for our people.

This creative imagination must not only take into consideration the facts and figures of the market, but should do so in the context of our cultural traditions, economic aspirations as well as the social objectives of our society. Sly headlines, over-dramatization, overplay of sex, exaggeration and half-truths are sometimes considered to be clever, gimmicks, and necessary for success. Such vulgarities and unethical distortions, however, give a bad name to advertising. A common perception can be earmarked as, "Bad Advertising is Bad Business".

4.3.2. Obligation of Advertising and the People in it

Whether it is the manufacturer who meets the needs of the community with the help of advertising, or it is advertising that helps manufacturers to create needs for their products, is not a relevant point. What is important is that mass production cannot be economical without mass distribution; and mass distribution cannot be achieved without the use of mass media, in a manner that only advertising skills can supply. Advertising is thus the cornerstone of mass distribution, the result of which—mass consumption—is the fruit that may be enjoyed, but only with the aid of advertising.

4.3.3. Responsibilities of Advertising Men

Advertising is neither good nor bad. It depends for its effects on the people responsible for it. These days, too much emphasis has been laid on specialisation, be it by the industry, by the government, or by the people at large. This emphasis on specialisation at the cost of a well-balanced human being is, to some extent, responsible for many of the ills in the world today. In this craze for specialisation, people forget that man is basically a human being, an important member of the human society.

To be a good advertising man, therefore, each man in the profession should understand the full social implications of advertising and his responsibilities to the profession. This understanding, though is not easy, is very necessary. Advertising people can bring about a change even in the thinking of businessman. To do this, they should have a high social consciousness, and feel, not only for the people, but also for society as a whole.

Today, advertising needs more and more men and women with broad education and greater social consciousness, who have the requisite advertising skills, and, at the same time, a thorough understanding of the market.

4.3.4. Sex and Advertising

"I wouldn't be shy of sex in advertising if people want to spend their money on the display of nude girls," says a top advertising executive. But he warns against overemphasis on nudity. If the nude figure is really attractive, the reader may remember the girl and not the product.[3]

Another member of the trade says that advertising has to keep pace with the country's cultural development; and sex is a dominating factor in today's culture. It can't, therefore, be altogether eliminated from ads.

The Press Council of India receives every year crores of complaints against newspaper for indecent display of nude figures of women in advertisements, which offend public ethics. Rejecting most of them as frivolous, it observes in its latest report: "If these pictures cause sex excitement, it must be a case of the abnormal and pathological condition of the reader and not of anything intrinsic in the pictures themselves".

Advertising is an important phenomenon of modern society; and there is a coterie of people working to consummate the sale of each product advertised. It is the most effective mass communication medium designed both to inform and influence its audience. In a short time, it has come to hold a respectable status, and is now regarded as a service to society. The profession itself is one of the most paying in developed countries.

The broader aspect of the relevance and need for advertising, especially taking into account the vale systems and consumer satisfaction, should also be given its due importance. The impact of advertising on children is a subject, which has aroused a lot of interest in recent years, and a lot of research is being undertaken in several countries.

4.4 OBLIGATION TO VALUE SYSTEM AND LIFESTYLE

A frequently made change against advertising is that life tends more and more to be influenced by advertising, and that as a result, the values of our world are not only dominated but also even debased by advertising. The researcher does not support the change. One thing that advertising is able to do is widely disseminate news about the majority's value systems to a huge audience, some of whom perhaps are not aware of them. In a sense, then, advertising informs some parts of our culture what the predominant value system is as reflected through advertising copy and layout.

It is believed that advertising promotes products that satisfy the materialistic requirements of consumers, and hence it is accused of promoting materialism in our population. It is also true, however that, advertising is used to promote 'back to nature' items such as natural food, camping equipment, etc., all representing a rejection of the materialism of the establishment. The criticism also includes the idea that advertising brought about the 'revolution of rising expectations' among our people with the concomitant demand for instant gratifications of material desires. But, for all this advertising cannot be blamed. The responsibility of advertising in this regard should, to be effective,

[3] *Ibid.*, pp. 69-69.

reflect the attitude of its intended audience. It is true that advertising is the chief means of communicating to people the range of reasons for which they might want to acquire material objects. If our culture recognises the reasons, *e.g.*, if an item is a symbol of status the advertising is not performing any unsociable act. If we regard these materialistic values undesirable for our society, we should look beyond advertising for change.

4.5 LEGAL ASPECTS OF ADVERTISING

Advertising is an integral part of modern life and its persuasive ability has a wide impact on society. It has a large responsibility within our economic system and is a highly visible and important institution affecting many people. But it injures the buyer and the economy if the advertisement is deceptive. Deceptive advertisement means when the information provided in the advertisement is misleading, deceptive, manipulative or undesirable. It represents an unethical behaviour of the businessmen that has unfortunate effects on consumers ranging from misspent money on an item that did not live up to the expectations developed in the advertising to hazardous accidents resulting from the misrepresentation of faulty goods.

Three major institutions in the society that protect consumers against misleading or fraudulent advertising are:

(*i*) Government agencies enforcing laws against offenders;

(*ii*) Advertising industry association and media groups that impose self-regulation upon their member firms and advertisers;

(*iii*) Advertisers themselves acting through enlightened self-interest and a sense of social responsibility.

Advertising is self-publicising. The content of advertising message is a matter of public record. Competitors and consumers both are in a good position to expose the dishonest or misleading advertising. It is, therefore, good if the business imposes the self-regulation upon themselves and not to publish any advertisement that contains a false statement whatsoever. Advertisers should realise that truthful advertising leads to consumer satisfaction, is the only successful long-range strategy to follow. Developing loyal consumers through misleading ads is difficult, if not impossible. Therefore, enlightened companies establish their own guidelines designed to ensure that their advertising does not violate the general rules of honesty and fair play.

The advertising industry associations and individual firms should impose self-regulation upon their members and themselves. They should be honest in their trade and should not accept the advertisements containing misleading or deceptive statements because they also have certain social responsibility towards customers and society.

4.5.1. What is False and Deceptive Advertising?

False claims about products, when made in advertisements destroy public faith in advertising. Advertisements containing false statements amount to deception. Conceptually, deception exists when an advertisement is introduced into the perceptual process of some audience and the output of that perceptual process: (*i*) differs from the reality of the situation, and (*ii*) affects buying behaviour to the detriment of the consumer. The input itself may be determined to contain falsehoods. The more difficult and perhaps more common cause, however, is when the input, the advertisement, is not obviously false, but the perceptual process generates an impression that is deceptive.

4.5.2. Legal Restrictions on Advertising in India

Advertisements and sales promotion have become well-established modes of modern business techniques. However, it should be noted that these techniques are often used to deceive the customers. At present we do not have any legislation preventing deceptive advertisements or sales promotion methods. The MRTP Act also is silent on these matters perhaps on the assumption that if dealers, manufacturers or producers are prevented from distorting competition, the consumers will get a fair deal. This indirect restriction is neither enough nor will it prevent the sellers from publishing misleading advertisements or adopting unfair methods or sales promotion.

Today, in India, a growing concern is being felt against these kinds of deceptive advertisements. The Sachar Committee, which was appointed to revise the Companies Act and MRTP Act pointed out: "The objection taken is not to the advertisement to the product, which it may be necessary to do in order to acquaint the public with the articles. What is however insisted on is that there is an obligation on the part of the seller that if he advertises he must speak the truth".

4.5.3. Recommendations of Sachar Committee

The Sachar Committee has recommended the following acts of sellers as unfair trade practices:

(1) Misleading advertisements and false representation. A seller should not falsely represent that:

  (*a*) The goods are of a particular standard, quality, grade, composition, style or model, if they do not possess that qualification;

  (*b*) The rebuilt, second hand goods are new goods.

(2) Offering of gifts or prizes with the intention of not providing them and conducting professional contests.

The Committee is of the opinion that all the aforesaid unfair trade practices should be punishable as an offence or any person or undertaking indulging in any of these activities should be liable to be prosecuted before the committee.

4.5.4. Legal Protection provided to Trademarks

The protections provided to trademarks are:

(*i*) The registration party can claim ownership. After registration date, no other party can use the mark or can start using the mark, even if done in good faith or without knowledge of registrant's claim;

(*ii*) A mark may become incontestable after five years and give exclusive right to its use even though another party may have used the mark prior to its registration by the registrant.

SUMMARY

Conceptually, deception exists when an advertisement is input to the perceptual process of some audience and the output of that perceptual process (1) differs from the reality of the situation and (2) affects buying behaviour to the detriment of the consumer. A misrepresentation or mission can occur in at least nine situations:

(1) Suggesting that a small difference is important.

(2) Artificial product demonstrations.

(3) Using an ambiguous or easily confused phrase.

(4) Implying a benefit that does not fully or partially exist.

(5) Implying that a product benefit is unique to a brand.

(6) Implying that a benefit is needed or that a product will fulfil a benefit.

(7) Incorrectly implying that an endorser uses or advocates the brand.

(8) Omitting a needed qualification.

(9) Making a claim without substantiation.

Puffing, the subjective statement of opinion concerning a product's quality, using terms such as "best", is permissible. However, the distinction of puffery and deception has been narrowed over time. Deception in advertising can also be controlled by competition lawsuits and by self-regulation. The Lanham Trademark Act has been used as a vehicle to combat damage when a competitor is disparaged unfairly in a comparative ad. The advertising industry has developed an ambitious programme of self-regulation, which rests largely on the support of industry itself.

Chapter 5 ADVERTISING AND CONSUMER BEHAVIOUR RESEARCH

5.1 INTRODUCTION

Media impact on consumer behaviour can be better understood only when consumer behaviour itself is well understood. In the earlier chapter, truth and ethics in advertising has been discussed in detail. In the present chapter, we talk about consumer behaviour because the actual purchase is the result of that; and the behaviour of the consumer is very much influenced by advertisement. It is said that to understand the act of purchasing, it is necessary to probe the events that precede and follow the purchase. This maxim entails an in-depth study of consumer behaviour and how advertisement affects a purchase as an event preceding the purchase and an event following the purchase to condition subsequent purchases of purchasing behaviour.

Consumer Behaviour research is a very important aspect of marketing research since consumers together only form the market. To effectively perform the business activities that direct the flow of goods and services from producer to the ultimate consumer or user, the needs, motives and desires of the consumer must be understood well. These are the areas, which form the bulk of the domain of consumer behaviour research. These are the factors of 'Attention', 'Brand Comprehension', 'Attitude', 'Intention' and 'Action', which are so important in measuring the effectiveness of advertising, are studied in depth through various sophisticated models in consumer behaviour research. In fact, advertising or for that matter any marketing activity can be more effectively practised when there already exists an abundance of knowledge in the buyer behaviour process; but also deals with the family decision-making process involved in buying situations. The faculties of 'information and experience', 'evaluative criteria', 'attitude' and 'personality' embedded in the brains of the consumer together form a filter, which allows or disallows messages to come in. This filter has to be understood well by the advertisers, which can be done only through the understanding of consumer behaviour. Therefore, the present chapter deals with consumer behaviour research at length.

5.2 CONSUMER BEHAVIOUR

Consumer behaviour is defined as the acts of individuals directly involved in obtaining and using economic goods and services, including the decision processes that precede and determine these acts. Social scientists sometimes used the word 'behaviour' to include only overt or observable actions, but it is increasingly recognised that the overt act is only one portion of the decision process. A realistic analysis of consumer behaviour must necessarily include less observable processes that accompany consumption. Consumer behaviour involves the study not only of what people consume but where, how often, and under what conditions goods and services are consumed.[1] The study of consumer behaviour in most part is the study of consumer buying rather than the actual consumption.[2] "It is the motivation of the purchasing agent which is most directly relevant to marketing. The prospective consumer of a given purchase and the person making the purchase are often two different people. In many cases, the purchase is made for a household, and the purchasing agent is only one of those who will share in its use".[3] Although the buyer is the normal focus point of all consumer research activities, yet a careful analysis must include the influences of the total family or other group on the behaviour of the actual buyer or the purchasing agent.

In this chapter, the researcher talk about consumer behaviour because the actual purchase is the result of that; and the behaviour of the consumer is very much influenced by advertisements. It is said that to understand the act of purchasing, it is necessary to probe the events that precede and follow the purchase. This maxim entails an in-depth study of consumer behaviour and how advertisement affects a purchase as an event preceding the purchase and an event following the purchase to condition subsequent purchases or purchasing behaviour.

The decision process approach used[4] to analyse consumer behaviour uses the above-mentioned concept, *i.e.,* to understand a purchase; which is only one stage in the decision process, it is pre-emptory to analyse the events that precede and follow the purchase. The combination of external inputs, mainly from the social environment, and internal influences like the psychological processes typical to the person, evolves into a decision by a consumer to make a purchase. However, there may not be any purchase even though the decision has been made. Such a situation arises "when the marketing system does not provide adequate resources to stimulate execution of the transaction". [5]

Consumer behaviour is an applied discipline. It borrows and applies findings from many disciplines in an attempt to solve practical problems. The disciplines relied upon are social psychology, individual psychology, sociology, cultural or social anthropology, economic geography, linguistics, political science, philosophy and economics. The applied disciplines of consumer behaviour are useful in developing ways for the more efficient utilisation of resources of marketing. It also helps in solving marketing management problems in more effective manner. By the study of consumer behaviour both macro and micro marketing problems can be better understood. Therefore, to understand the marketing process and all its components in a valid manner, one has to understand

---

1 Engel, J.F., Kollat, D.T., and Blackwell, R.D., Consumer Behaviour, 2nd Edition, Holt, New York, pp. 5 6.

2 Alderson, W., Dynamic Marketing Behaviour, Homewood III, Irwin, 1995, p. 144.

3 Alderson, W., Marketing Behaviour and Executive Action, Homewood, III, Irwin, 1977, pp. 165-166.

4 Ibid.

5 Ibid.

consumer behaviour thoroughly, *i.e.*, what the consumer needs are, how they are formed, and how they are influenced by various marketing activities. In the layman's language, consumer behaviour is to be studied to improve predictions about the products, the consumers will buy and under what conditions they will buy them. Thus, the study of consumer behaviour helps in the satisfactory and efficient performance of all the marketing functions; and advertising is no exception. So, advertising can be more efficient and advertisement can be more effective if the buying behaviours of the consumers are better understood.

Study of consumer behaviour leads to the evaluation of consumer goods with unsatisfied needs or desires. That helps the firms to organise their resources to meet the unmet needs; and helps them in practising the "marketing concept". The analytic framework of discussion process can be laid down mathematically as:

$$Y = f(x_1, x_2 \ldots\ldots x_n)$$

Where y = an aspect of consumer behaviour (output)

x_1 = the various processes or stimuli (inputs)

f = the function, or the rule that pairs each possible value of 'x' with at most one value of 'y'.

Given the function rule and the values of x_1, 'y' can be predicted.

Consumer analysis reveals the underlying conditions that are true about consumer; and thus opens avenues for increasing the efficiency of existing strategies and tactics of marketing. Many questions about marketing strategies and tactics can be answered through the analysis of consumer behaviour. Some such questions relating to advertising are:[6]

1. Do the consumers pass through a hierarchy of response stages in evaluating products?
2. How models of consumer behaviour are useful in the development of marketing strategy?
3. How is sensation translated into meaning about brands or products?
4. What types of advertising appeals are the more effective in different product categories?
5. How can the 'boredom barrier' of advertising be broken?
6. Is 'subliminal' advertising effective?
7. How do buyers learn about new brands and products?
8. How do new residents learn about stores and brands?
9. How perusable are prospective buyers?
10. Does advertising really bring about much attitude change?
11. Does the development of favourable attitudes towards a brand lead automatically to more sales?
12. What is persuasive communication?
13. How many times should an ad run?

[6] Engel, Kollat and Blackwell, op. cit., pp. 16-17.

14. How important is a particular segment in the development of a marketing strategy?
15. Does one segment respond to marketing strategies differently than others?
16. Can marketing efforts effectively increase informal conversation about a particular product enough to result in additional sales?
17. To what member of the family should promotion be directed?
18. Can buyers be stimulated to buy products for which they do not recognise a need?
19. How and when do buyers seek information about a product?
20. What are the most influential information sources about a product?
21. How does the importance of information source vary among market segments?
22. Under what circumstances does a marketing program have follow-up or 'sleeper' effects?
23. Are some customers more 'loyal' to a brand than others? How does this influence marketing strategy?
24. Are some persons consistently buy new products before other segments of the population?

Consumer analysis, on the whole, is essential in evaluating and understanding the new market opportunities, choosing market segments, increasing efficiency of marketing strategy and tactics, and improving retailing performance. To study consumer behaviour empirically, three basic approaches normally used are:[7]

(*a*) The distributive approach focusing on behavioural outcomes;

(*b*) The morphological approach dealing with the way a decision is made; and

(*c*) The analytical approach, which is similar to the morphological approach, but also assesses the impact of various influences like that of advertisements or displays on purchases.

The morphological and analytical approaches are highly similar; and are frequently referred to jointly as the decision-process approach.

(*a*) **Distributive Approach**

In this approach, relations are attempted to be established among the independent variables like economic, demographic, and social-psychological with the outcomes of consumer decision-making. Here behaviour is understood and studied as an act rather than as a process. With the distributive strategy, consumer analysis becomes relatively simpler. This approach is quite effective when there is very high correlation among the independent variables and the brand purchased. In such cases, marketing potential can be quite effectively predicted and the selection of advertising media and vehicles also can be done with greater accuracy. But this strategy treats consumer behaviour at a very superficial level by treating behaviour as an act rather than a process. A correlation is established; but why it is so, is not explained.

[7] Ibid., pp. 45-49.

(*b*) **Decision-Process Approach**

This strategy has five processes in tandem. They are: (*a*) problem recognition, (*b*) alternative evaluation (internal search), (*c*) alternative evaluation (external search), (*d*) purchase, and (*e*) the outcomes. These processes are connected in a sequence. In this approach, the assumptions are: (*i*) the consumer need not be aware that he passes through these phases or processes for decision-making about the purchase of a product; (*ii*) like any other process, this one also has some time dimensions; which means a person may go through this process in seconds or for months or years depending on the purchase situation; and (*iii*) all the phases of the process do not always occur as some may be skipped. Unlike Distributive Approach, the Decision-Process Approach has the clear advantage of treating consumer behaviour as a process rather than an act. While the former is only concerned with the decision, the latter probes to find out the way the decision is arrived at, the stages of decision-making that precede and follow the decision along with the decision itself. Thus, the Decision-Process Approach provides more information for marketing decision-making. "Knowledge about such things as the process resulting in problem recognition, the relative importance of various information sources, the criteria used to evaluate alternative brands, and so on, is useful in designing product, pricing, channels, and particularly, advertising and sales strategies.[8]

5.3 CONSUMER RESEARCH

Consumer research provides the basis for the development of new product and service concepts to meet targeted consumer needs. It also enables the marketer to build consumer 'meaning' into the product or service by discovering which attributes are most important to the target market and integrating them into the product or service design.[9]

The field of consumer research developed as an extension of the field of marketing research, focusing almost exclusively on consumer behaviour rather than on other aspects of the marketing process. Just as the findings of marketing research were used to improve managerial decision-making, so too were the findings of consumer research. The initial reason for studying consumer behaviour was to enable marketers to predict how consumers would react to promotional messages, and to understand why they made the purchase decisions they did. Marketers assumed that if they knew everything there was to know about the consumer decision-process, they could design marketing strategies and promotional messages that would influence the consumer in the desired way. In the belief that marketing was simply applied economics, the economic man theory prevailed the assumption that consumers are rational decision-makers who objectively evaluate the goods and services available to them and select only those that gives them the highest utility at the lower cost.

---

[8] Ibid., p. 47.

[9] Schiffman, L.G. and Kanuk, L.L., Consumer Behaviour, 6th Edition, pp. 24-26.

5.3.1. The Consumer Research Process

The major steps in the consumer research process include:

(1) defining the objectives of the research,

(2) collecting and evaluating secondary data,

(3) designing a primary research study,

(4) collecting primary data,

(5) analysing the data, and

(6) preparing a report on the findings.

The following model depicts the consumer research process.

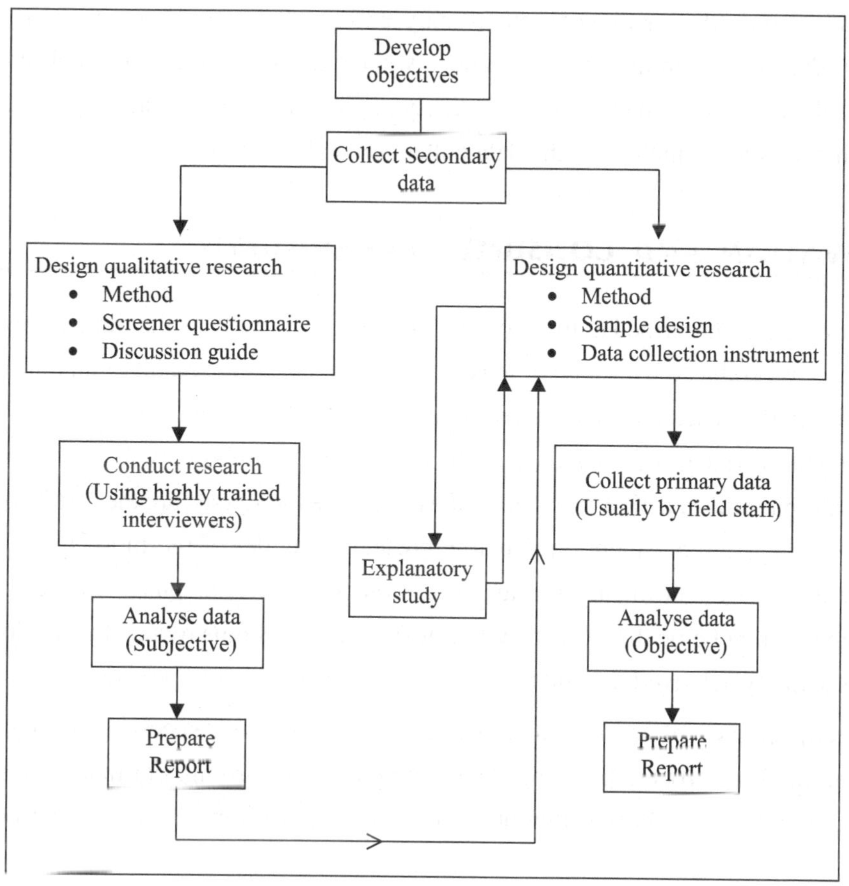

Fig. 5.1. Consumer Research Process

5.3.2. Developing Research Objectives

The first step in the consumer research process is to define carefully the objectives of the study. Is it to segment the market for wide-screen television? To find out consumer attitudes about cellular phones? To determine what percentage of men use cologne? It is important for the marketing manager and researcher to agree at the outset on the purposes and objectives of the study to ensure that the research design is appropriate. A carefully thought out statement of objectives helps to define the type and level of information needed.

For example, if the purpose of the study is to come up with new ideas for products or promotional campaigns, then a qualitative study is usually undertaken, in which respondents spend a significant amount of time face-to-face with a highly trained professional moderator who also does the analysis. Because of the high costs of each interview, a fairly small sample of respondents is studied; thus, the findings are not projectable to the market place. If the purpose of the study is to find out how many people in the population use certain products and how frequently they use them, then a quantitative study that can be computer-analysed is undertaken. Sometimes, in designing a quantitative study, the researcher may not know what questions to ask. In such cases, before undertaking a full-scale study, the researcher is likely to conduct a small-scale explanatory study to identify the critical issues to include in the data collection instrument.

5.4 MOTIVATION AND CONSUMER BEHAVIOUR[10]

Motivation can be described as the driving force within individuals that impels them to action. This driving force is produced by a state of tension, which exists as the result of an unfulfilled need. Individuals strive both consciously and subconsciously to reduce this tension through behaviour that they anticipate will fulfil their needs and thus relieve them of the stress they feel. The specific goals they select and the patterns of action they undertake to achieve their goals are the results of individual thinking and learning. Fig. 5.2 mentioned below presents a model of the motivational process. It portrays motivation as a state of need induced tension that exerts a 'push' on the individual to engage in behaviour that he or she expects will gratify a need and thus reduce the tension. Whether gratification is actually achieved depends on the course of action being pursued.

The specific courses of action that consumers pursue and their special goals are selected on the basis of their thinking process (*i.e.*, cognition) and previous learning. For that reason, marketers who understand motivational theory attempt to influence the consumer's cognitive processes.

[10] Ibid., p. 83.

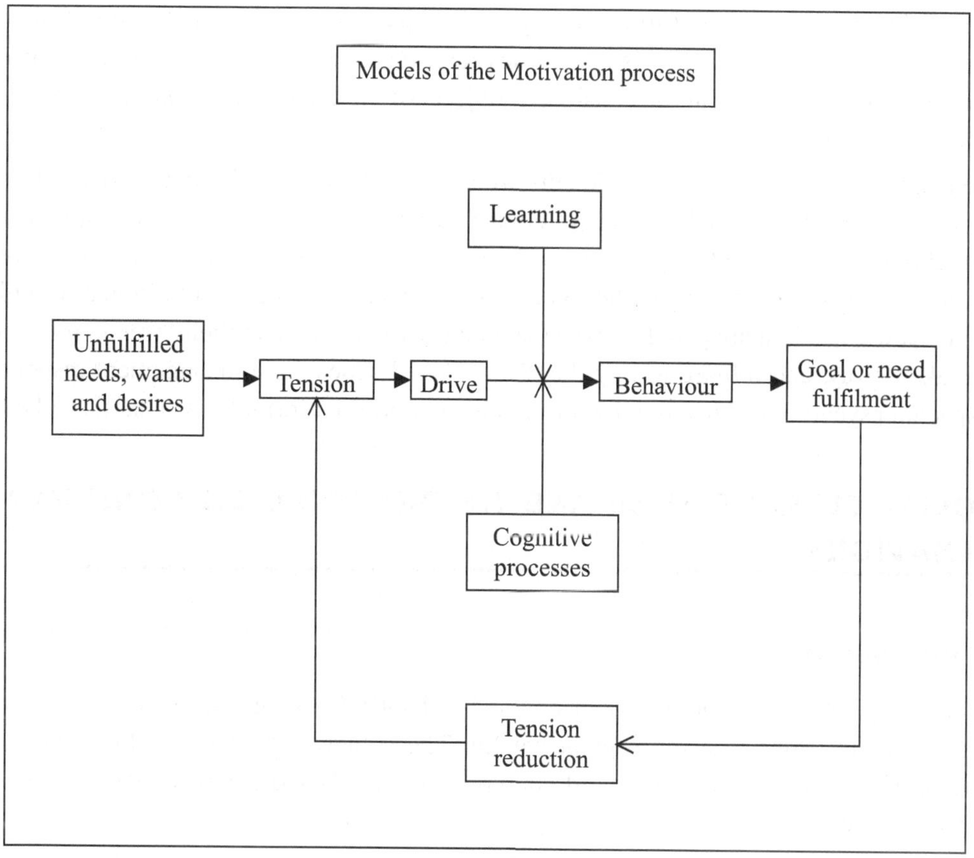

Fig. 5.2. Model of the Motivation Process

5.4.1. Positive and Negative Motivation[11]

Motivation can be positive or negative in direction. We may feel a driving force toward some object or condition, or a driving force away from some object or condition. For example, a person may be impelled toward a restaurant to fulfil a hunger need and away from motorcycle transportation to fulfil a safety need.

Some psychologists refer to positive drives as needs, wants, or desires, and to negative drives as fears or aversions. However, although positive and negative motivational forces seem to differ dramatically in terms of physical activity, they are basically similar in that both serve to initiate and sustain human behaviour. For this reason, researchers often refer to both kinds of drives or motives as needs, wants, and desires. Some theorists distinguish wants from needs by defining 'wants' as product-specific needs. Thus, to use an earlier example, a person may experience thirst; she/he may want Lipton's Iced Tea as a means of alleviating her/his thirst.

[11] Ibid., p. 86.

Goals, too, can be positive or negative. A positive goal is one toward which behaviour is directed and thus is often referred to as an approach object. A negative goal is one from which behaviour is directed away and thus is sometimes referred to as an avoidance object. Since both approach and avoidance goals can be considered objects of motivated behaviour, most researchers refer to both simply as goals.

Sometimes people become motivationally aroused by a threat to or elimination of a behavioural freedom (*e.g.,* the freedom to make a product choice without undue influence from a retailer). This motivational state is called psychological reactance and is usually manifested by a negative consumer response. For example, in 1985, when the Coca-Cola Company changed its traditional formula and introduced "New Coke", many people reacted negatively to the fact that their "freedom to choose" had been taken away, and refused to buy the "New Coke". Coca-Cola management responded to this unexpected psychological reaction by introducing the original formula as "Classic Coke".

5.5. SOCIAL CLASS LIFESTYLE AND ITS INFLUENCE ON CONSUMER BEHAVIOUR

5.5.1. Introduction

In the early 1990s an economic boom, coupled with more liberal government policies, enabled some individuals in China to acquire great wealth. These 'new rich' became big spenders and flaunted their wealth by enrolling their children in private schools and buying expensive items such as cars, TVs and VCRs.

Initially, many of the new rich were admired because they had 'bucked the system'. But when it became known that their newfound prosperity had come at the expense of many others whose standard of living had greatly decreased, making them the 'new poor', their status changed. The new rich are now looked upon with resentments and are often accused of acquiring their wealth illegally. The new rich have reacted by becoming very careful not to be conspicuous and draw attention to themselves. As a result, over 20 per cent of China's night clubs have closed as expense accounts have dried up and the rich have become more philanthropic. Lavish spending still occurs, but it is now more private. As evidence, China is the largest market in the world for expensive cognac, at $ 186 million a year.

This example illustrates how social class can influence acquisition, consumption and disposition. The concept of social class implies that some have more power, wealth and opportunity than others. Some consumer show off their wealth or possessions by engaging in conspicuous consumption, and certain products/services such as car and cognac can serve as status symbols. Finally, this example illustrates how some can raise their social standing, whereas, others may fall to lower levels.

Social class is another factor that can influence consumer behaviour. This portion examines what determines one's social class (*e.g.,* occupation, education, income). Finally, it discusses how social class lifestyle affects' specific outcomes, such as conspicuous consumption, status symbols, compensatory consumption and the meaning of money.

5.5.2. Social Class[12]

Most scientists can be divided into a social hierarchy, whereby some individuals have higher status than others. These social classes are identifiable groups of individuals whose behaviours and lifestyles differ from those of other classes. Members of a particular social class tend to share similar values and behaviour patterns. It is important to stress that social classes are of formal groups with a strong identity but rather loose collections of individuals with similar life experiences.

Many societies view social class distinctions as important to their existence because they recognise that everyone has a necessary role to play if society is to function smoothly. However, some of these roles (*e.g.*, medical doctor, executive) are more prestigious and valued than others. This does not mean that the concept of social class is inherently negative. Even though inequalities are present, social class distinctions can help individuals determine their role in society or what they would like it to be (their aspirations). Furthermore, all levels of the social class hierarchy make an important contribution to society.

5.5.3. How does Social Class Affect Consumer Behaviour?

Social class is often viewed as a cause of or motivation for acquisition, consumption, and disposition. This portion examines four major topics:

(*a*) Conspicuous consumption

(*b*) Acquisition of status symbols

(*c*) Compensatory consumption

(*d*) Meaning of money.

5.5.3.1. Conspicuous Consumption

Formally defined, conspicuous consumption is the acquisition and visible display of luxury goods and services to demonstrate one's ability to afford them. Thus, conspicuously consumed items are important to their owner because of what they tell others. The visibility of these goods and services is critical because the message will not be communicated if others see them.

Initially, the concept of conspicuous consumption was used to describe the behaviour of the upper classes who would buy and display very expensive items to communicate their wealth and power. Today, however, conspicuous consumption can be observed in most social classes. In other words, individuals at all levels acquiring and displaying the trappings that are characteristic of respected

[12] Hoyer, Mac Innis, Consumer Behaviour, 1999, p. 325.

member of their class. For example, a middle-class family might buy a personal computer, showing their neighbours that they can afford it and that they want their children to get ahead.

In the Arab World, the newly rich upper classes engage in the conspicuous consumption of items such as cars, planes, and other technologically advanced products. Even in former communist countries, consumers now show consumption competitiveness. The idea is that one might be the "Shame of the Village" if one cannot keep up with others. In addition, consumers can engage in conspicuous waste. For example, wealthy individuals may buy houses they never use, pianos that no one plays, and cars that no one drives.

5.5.3.2. Status Symbols and Judging Others[13]

Highly related to conspicuous consumption is the notion that people often judge others on the basis of what they own or possess. In other words, people often use products, or services that become status symbols to indicate who they are in the social hierarchy. Someone who owns a Rolex watch or a Mercedes will likely be viewed as upper class. In the inner city, drinking premium liquor or wearing gold jewellery is often considered a status symbol. Owning a cellular phone or taking on expensive cruise indicates status in India, and the same is true of a rock garden or a golf club membership in Japan.

Thus, some acquisition and consumption behaviours can be explained by consumer's quest to acquire items that reflect not only their current social class but also their class aspirations. Middle class consumers, for example, characteristically display a strong desire to own a nice house in a respectable neighbourhood so that others will judge them in a positive manner.

Interestingly, status symbols can sometimes move in a reverse direction, which is called a parody display. In addition, if certain status symbols become widely possessed, they can lose their status connotations and become fraudulent symbols. As an example, designer jeans were an important status symbol in the 1980s, but lost popularity after too many people owned them.

5.5.3.3. Compensatory Consumption

The concept of compensatory consumption is also related to social class. This is an attempt to offset for deficiencies or a lack of esteem by devoting attention to consumption. In other words, a consumer who is experiencing frustration or difficulties in life, particularly in terms of career advancement or status level, can attempt to compensate for this lack of success by purchasing desired status symbols, such as car, hose or nice clothes. These acquisitions help restore lost self-esteem.

5.5.3.4. The Meaning of Money

An important concept related to social class is that of money. At the most basic level, economists define money as a medium of exchange or standard of payment. Under this view, money fulfils a very functional or utilitarian purpose and facilitates the acquisition of items needed for everyday living.

---

[13] Ibid., p. 337.

Thus, money and what it stands for are very important in developing an understanding of consumption patterns. In the present context, money enables the acquisition of status objects that are indicators of social class standing. Money is also viewed as a way of rising to a higher level of enabling us to acquire more.

To conclude, the consumption patterns of for specific social classes were examined. The upper class is hardworking, healthy, socially conscious and especially concerned with conspicuous consumption. The middle class wants to buy the 'right things' and live in a nice neighbourhood, and has strong aspirations to raise its social standing. The working class is characterised by strong family ties and a local orientation. The homeless are engaged in a struggle for survival by recycling, and collecting. These class distinctions pose important marketing implications in areas of product and service development, advertising and personal selling messages, media exposures, and outlet selection.

5.6 DECISION PROCESS[14]

Consumer behaviour, by definition, is a decision process and physical activity of making a purchase. An ultimate purchase activity is preceded by interplay of several variables, and some of the variables also affect after the purchase has taken place. All these variables are a part of the decision process. The mental activity resulting into the final purchase may be complex and may happen over a period of time, or it may be quick and simple.

5.6.1. Role of People in the Context of Consumer Behaviour

The consumer as a first step recognises his unfulfilled need or want. It is called problem recognition. It actually leads to information search and evaluation. The information search can be deliberate or prolonged or can happen without the consumer being even aware of it. He can rely on past experiences or can seek information from external environment, *e.g.*, friends, shopkeepers and advertisements. The consumer evaluates the collected information to arrive at a purchase decision. Then having decided to buy, he makes the actual purchase, making a choice regarding the outlet to buy from. He consumes the product, which either satisfies him, confirming correctness of his decision or dissatisfies him, leading to a search for alternative choices, and evaluation afresh.

5.6.2. Individual Determinants

Two individuals from one family may show entirely different purchase preferences. One may like Neem Soap, Oriya feature film, while the other may like Debonair, English dramas and Le Sancy Soap. Why do they show variations, though the family environment is the same? The answer may be their individual motivation and involvement, attitude, self-concept, personality, learning, money, and information process.

[14] Chanawalla, S.A. and Sethia, K.C., *Foundations of Advertising Theory and Practice*, 1999, pp. 91-97.

5.6.3. Motivation and Involvement

Each of us is unique. We have a unique set of needs, aspirations, and motivations. Motivation is an internal force which stimulates action in response to some need, and sustain the same till the need is fulfilled. Physiological motivation satisfies social and prestige needs. Each one of us has both the physiological and psychological motivational force. We fulfil each of these motivations by different means. Someone seeks status by enrolling for an MBA programme, and someone else by acquiring membership of the best-known Club in the town. There may be someone who becomes a credit card holder to satisfy his need for status or may buy a Mercedes car to do so. We may satisfy our thirst by plain water or by mineral water or by a soft drink like Thums Up or Pepsi.

Differing motivations are a function of differing level of personal involvements. Involvement here means relevance or importance of a product perceived by the consumer in a given situation. For a professional musician, the choice of a music system is a situation of involvement, since it helps him immensely in his profession. He will be motivated, therefore, to buy the best state-of-the-art music system, irrespective of the price tag. For another consumer, a music system is just a means of recreation after office hours, and just about any system, which is convenient and moderately priced, might suffice his need.

High involvement leads to highly motivated state of mind. The behaviour process is distinctly different from that of low involvement and consequently low motivation.

5.6.4. Attitudes

Attitudes are predispositions towards people, objects, and events. They are learned. Our orientation towards people, objects, and events is guided by attitudes. Attitudes are learnt from our specialisation process. A large section of Indian population have a negative attitude towards non-vegetarian dishes. Attitudes may change, *e.g.*, we loved savings previously, but now prefer to splurge our income for a better lifestyle. Canned foods are frowned upon a few years ago. But now we have to come to accept them. Attitudes influence purchase decisions. Investment in stocks is preferred by risk-taking individuals.

5.6.5. Personality and Self-Concept

The sum total of unique individual characteristics makes up a personality. It is the framework within which a consistent behaviour is shown.

Self-image or self-concept is our perception of ourselves in social context. The products should match our self-concept. Product image should be close to self-image of target consumers, *e.g.*, royalty endorsing worsted suiting project, an image of class and exclusivity. This matches well with the self-concept of the target consumers.

5.6.6. Learning and Memory

In this age of information explosion, we tend to remember only relevant and important information. We tend to remember where we have a motivation to remember. Everyone is aware about the clutter of ads before Hindi Movie is shown on the TV. Now the husband remembers the ad of MRF tyres, the wife that of Dabur Amla Hair Oil and daughter that of Rasna Concentrate. This is because they all have a motivation for different products.

Attitudes, motives, personality acts as filters. They let in relevant information, keeping out the other information. Our retention is selective.

5.7 TYPES OF PURCHASE DECISION BEHAVIOUR

Consumer behaviour changes depending upon the nature or type of buying—a razor blade may be purchased without much fuss but a colour TV set purchase takes time and deliberations. The nature or type of purchase gives rise to three types of buyer behaviour.

(*a*) RR (routinised response) behaviour.

(*b*) LPS (limited problem solving) behaviour.

(*c*) EPS (extended problem solving) behaviour.

'RR' occurs where there is low product involvement, the consumer knows the brands available and criteria of choice, and the stakes are not so high in terms of price; *e.g.,* bread, soft drinks, pastes, soaps, etc. Here the customer expects a consistent quality in the products. New customers are drawn by sales promotion and product improvements.

'LPS' occurs when the consumer knows the brands available, but still needs additional information to make a correct choice especially when a new or unfamiliar brand confronts him. Thus, Ariel or Surf Ultra or Enzyme detergents must convince the housewife that they are superior to conventional detergents due to presence of enzymes and so the housewife feels the necessity of searching additional information. The marketer here has introduced a new brand in a well-known product category. The promotion here should explain complete features of the new brand, and build up consumer's confidence to facilitate the purchase decision.

'EPS' occurs when a new product category comes on the scene. Here extensive information is needed on both the product category and the brand being made available, *e.g.,* Microwave Owens introduced by Kelvinator first explain the concept of microwave cooking as distinguished from conventional cooking, and then sell the brand. Colour TVs as a product category, a particular brand of colour TV (Onida or Videocon) and a particular model (PIP: Picture-in-picture or Surround Sound system) do need information at these three levels, and especially how the advertised brand has a unique set of positive attributes. This concept is most applicable to new products, may be new to consumers. For a tribal, even purchase of toothpaste may involve EPS, whereas for us it is just RR.

5.8 MODEL OF BUYER BEHAVIOUR

Research workers have developed various models to explain the influences on buyer's behaviour of purchase. Howard-Sheth model, which has been developed by an Indian Jagdish Sheth in collaboration with Howard, explains the behaviour of an individual consumer. There are separate models for group consumer behaviour and organisational buying behaviour.

5.8.1. Howard-Sheth Model

The decision process is influenced by four major sets of variables, *e.g.*, (*i*) inputs, (*ii*) perceptual and learning constructs, (*iii*) outputs and (*iv*) external variables.

5.8.1.1. Inputs

These are stimuli to purchase decisions. Significative stimuli are tangible product characteristics provided by the marketer. Symbolic stimuli are intangible or perceptual characteristics of the product, *e.g.*, the overall quality. The actual price may be significative stimulus, and the price being on high or low side for the bargain in symbolic stimulus. Social groups like the family, reference groups and social class are the social stimuli.

5.8.1.2. Perceptual and Learning Constructs

These are psychological variables, *e.g.*, motivation, attitudes, and perceptions, affecting the buyer. The interpretation of the stimuli is influenced by stimulus ambiguity and perceptual bias. Ambiguity of stimulus means the consumer is not sure of the meaning of the stimulus and his response thereto. Perceptual bias makes him distort the information received to fit his previous experience and his established needs.

5.8.1.3. Outputs

The purchase decision itself is an output. Produced trial may give him satisfaction. It reinforces his positive attitude. Then there is reinforcement of purchase intent and brand. He is favourably inclined to receiving stimuli, which further improves his brand comprehensions. On getting dissatisfied with the product he may develop negative attitude, insensitivity to stimuli, poor brand comprehension and negative intention to purchase (Fig. 5.3).

5.8.1.4. External Variables

These are not part of the decision process in the model, but are improvement to the extent they influence a buyer. These differ from buyer to buyer and include, status, relevance of the product, social class, personality traits, etc.

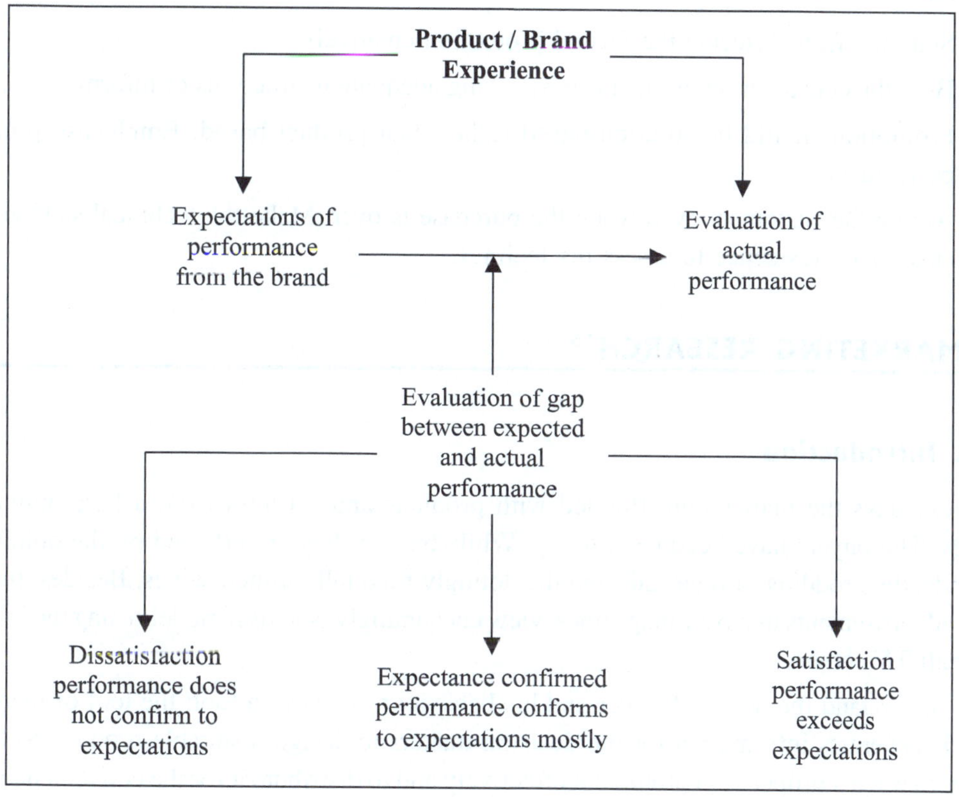

Fig. 5.3. Product/Brand Experience

5.9 POST-PURCHASE BEHAVIOUR

The desire to study the behaviour of consumers after the purchase has been made is a 'true' marketing orientation, identification with the consumers and seeing things from their perspective. Purchases are purposive and motivated. Post-purchase behaviour indicates to what extent these purposes have been met and motives achieved. Post-purchase activity gives an indication as to whether the customers are going to again patronise a firm in future, and also whether they will be in a mood to recommend a product to potential customers.

5.9.1. Formation of Satisfaction/Dissatisfaction

A purchase may lead either to satisfaction or dissatisfaction. Satisfaction is a result of expected outcome when the product meets our expectations. Dissatisfaction means it does not perform as per our expectations. Dissatisfied customers may discontinue their association with the company, may spread negative word of mouth, may send a formal complaint, or in extreme cases may sue the company. The communication strategy depends upon the expectation performance disparity.

5.9.2. Tips for Advertisements to Avoid Dissatisfaction

1. State the facts. Execute the factual promotion creatively.
2. Help the consumer on product use by giving adequate instructions or information.
3. Promotion should be solution-based rather than product-based. Emphasise product's performance.
4. Assure the customers even when the purchase is over. Make the technical staff visit the customer's residence to assess his feelings.

5.10 MARKETING RESEARCH[15]

5.10.1. Introduction

These days the markets are flooded with products and services from a large number of companies. The buyers have become choosey. While buying they are affected by the opinions of their friends, the prodding of their kids and the dotingly fond talk of their wives. Besides, they see glittering advertisements in glossy magazines, view enchantingly beautiful models using the products on the small TV screen.

To understand the needs of buyer and his behaviour, we have a tool; the tool of marketing research. It generates information for the decision-makers to design a suitable product, to further develop it, to price it properly, to promote it effectively and to distribute it for the convenience of the buyers. It helps the decision-maker to understand, to explain, to describe and to evaluate the marketing programme.

Against this background, we can say marketing research is research pertaining to any problem in the area of marketing.

5.10.2. Definitions

(*i*) "Marketing Research (MR) is the systematic, objective and exhaustive search for and study of the facts relevant to any problem in the field of marketing" (Crisp, R.D.).

(*ii*) MR is "the application of scientific method to the solution of marketing problems" (Luck, Wales and Taylor).

(*iii*) MR is "the systematic and objective search for the analysis of information relevant to the identification and solution of any problem in the field of marketing" (Green and Tull).

(*iv*) MR is "the systematic recording and analysis of data about problems relating to marketing" (American Marketing Association).

---

[15] Chunawalla, S.A. and Sethia, K.C., op. cit., pp. 769-773.

5.10.3. Salient Points of Marketing Research

1. **Marketing Research Consists of Findings based on Data:** These data relate to any area of marketing function—from a study of the market place to a study of buyer behaviour. They cover an expense of products, prices, distribution and promotion. The data collected are analysed and interpreted for the use of the decision makers.
2. **Systematic Collection of Data:** The data are collected by following a systematic procedure. First of all, a problem is identified. For example, the problem is that of declining sales. Perhaps on further examination we feel the declining sales are due to poor advertising. So, the real problem that emerges is that of measuring our ad effectiveness, and then if necessary to improve it. Keeping this problem in mind, research objectives are formulated and a sample selected to collect data, which are recorded, analysed and interpreted and presented in the form of a report.
3. **Marketing Research is Objective:** We do not pre-suppose things. We just put forth some hypotheses; collected data and either accept the hypotheses or reject it. While doing problem-oriented research also we do not allow subjective bias to creep in. The research is never carried out to support a pre-determined result.
4. **Marketing Research converts data into information:** Data as such are not meaningful. But on processing by systematic record, analysis and interpretation, they become useful information for the decision-maker.
5. **Marketing Research is a continuous process:** Since marketing activity is a continuous one where there are changes in product mix, promotion mix, distribution channels and prices, MR also is carried out on a continuous basis. Yes, one project of the MR is isolated. But in the light of changed environment, the data also changes, and so continuous monitoring is called for. These days the TV market and so also the toothpaste market have become so dynamic, that market shares of different brands do change month to month, and a constant MR is needed. In such cases, however, MR is integrated to Management Information System (MIS).
6. **Marketing Research is only a tool to the decision-maker:** MR does not supplant or replace decision-making process. It only serves as an input to the decision-making process. It is at best a tool that guides the decision-maker. However, certain other variables may make the decision-maker take a decision contrary to findings of MR, and he may like another MR study to be conducted for confirming or ruling out his decision. The judgement is always that of an executive.

Some typical questions that a marketing research study would be able to answer can be presented here to bring out the true nature of this subject:

(*i*) Which are those young ladies who prefer to apply lipstick and put nail-polish as a matter of routine in their lifestyle?

(*ii*) When most of the people are glued to their TV sets? Why do the programmes interest them?

(*iii*) Why some people avoid flying even when they are sufficiently rich to afford it?

(*iv*) Is Aamir Khan, the Coca Cola model creating enough of impact on the viewers when he says "Sirf Paanch"?

(*v*) Is the time right to launch a Hot-Shot like amateur camera when you just aim and shoot?

(*vi*) What are the occasions to use Vicks Herbal Drops?

(*vii*) Is Rasna properly positioned? Does it compete effectively with remote substitutes like tea and coffee?

(*viii*) What do people feel about public hospitals, airports and nationalised banks?

(*ix*) What are the prospects of exporting our handicraft items?

(*x*) Why our youngsters prefer romantic and/or thriller paperbacks?

These questions are related to marketing mix, sales, marketing environment, competition, market forecasting, buyer behaviour, etc. Marketing research does not answer technical/engineering questions like why this car is not fuel-efficient.

5.10.4. Need for Marketing Research

(*i*) There cannot be a real marketing activity without the backup of marketing research functions. It ultimately determines the customer's satisfaction.

(*ii*) Marketing research is a critical element that makes our marketing effort effective.

(*iii*) The transition from a seller's market to a buyer's market makes it necessary to have MR.

(*iv*) MR makes an organisation prepared to chasing turbulent business environment.

(*v*) As markets have expanded geographically there are attendant risks. So, MR comes handy to reduce these risks.

(*vi*) Product innovation, distribution, problems, price sensitive Indian market have all made MR essential.

5.10.5. Marketing Research Process

MR slowly acquires the status of a science. We call it a science for three reasons:

(*i*) It follows a systematised step-by-step method to study a given problem. It verifies the hypothesis in the light of the data.

(*ii*) It is an objective study, free from subjective bias. It sets out its objectives and methodology objectively. It presents its findings objectively after objective analysis of data.

(*iii*) It uses many sophisticated tools like Latin Squares, Markov Chairs, Likert and Thurstone Scales, Multidimensional Scaling like other sciences, which also use some of these tools.

In general, there are five major activities that collectively serve to define the marketing research procedure. Each stage consists of sub-activities to be performed and decision that need to be made.

Marketing problem or opportunity identification consists of several interrelated tasks and activities. It is perhaps the most crucial stage in the marketing research process. Identification of a marketing problem begins with a problem audit. It is comprehensive and systematic examination of a marketing problem with the objective of understanding its origin and nature. The keys to successful problem identification are creativity and flexibility.

If a problem audit and background analysis reveals that further marketing research is required, the marketing problems need to be translated into an operational marketing research task. This requires specifying research objectives, research questions, and research hypotheses.

(*i*) **Task:** Typically a marketing research task is expressed in terms of a specific set of marketing research objectives. These objectives delineate the scope of marketing research effort and specify what particular information needs are to be met by research results.

(*ii*) **Plan:** After the marketing research task has been determined, the next major activity stage in the marketing research process consists of developing a marketing research plan. This plan is formally termed as marketing research design. It systematically sets forth what research data are to be collected as well as how the data are to be collected and analysed.

(*iii*) **Data Collection:** The third activity stage, data collection, consists of physically collecting research data and includes sampling activities, and so forth.

(*iv*) **Analysis and Interpretation:** The fourth major activity stage is data analysis and interpretation. In this stage raw data from the third activity stage are analysed frequently by means of statistical techniques. The results of data analysing are then interpreted and inferences drawn as to the problem being researched.

(*v*) **Report:** The final activity stage consists of preparing and presenting a research report for managerial decision-making. This report summaries the particular marketing research process followed and contained research conclusion.

5.11 THE RATIONAL CONSUMER

The consumer is treated differently in microeconomics than macroeconomics. The nineteenth century classical economist propounding the microeconomic theory was of the view that man had complete knowledge of his wants and all the available means to satisfy these wants. Preferences were treated as independent of the environment of the time; and were treated as unlimited and non-satiable; and consistent. Thus, the choice or decision was one of the careful allocation of resources to maximise utility within the constraints of the financial budget. The consumer in this theory was treated as behaving rationally; and thus the motive for his behaviour was maximisation of utility. The classical economists mostly treated man as behaving in a mechanistic manner as they expected man to exhibit same reactions to given situations. But such a theory is not very much validated by present research findings. The Survey Research Centre of the University of Michigan has concluded from its researches that there is no invariable direct relation between willingness to purchase consumer goods and income. Besides, purchases of durable goods can decline during the periods of high and rising incomes.[16] But the nineteenth century economists cannot be blamed as those were the days of very little income and positively nowhere bear the present day affluent society. People had very little income during these days to spend on anything other than bare necessities of life.

In macroeconomic theory, however, the economist is not directly concerned with the individual buying choices. Instead, he is concerned with the choice patterns of large groups over time. He displays more interest in the patterns of behaviour pertaining to major decisions such as allocation of income to savings or investment in consumer durable goods It is argued that individual differences average out when a lot of people are covered under study; and thus individuals are of relatively lesser importance than other groups.

However, for the marketing man, a pure macroeconomic approach is untenable as the process of aggregation leads to the loss of important insights into buyer behaviour and thus hampering marketing planning. Although the macroeconomist does not involve himself in understanding the process of household decision-making, yet by establishing and clarifying statistical relations between purchase and underlying variables like income, and age, he contributes a lot to marketing thought. The consumer in marketing is viewed today as the blend of both the traditional pre-World War II concept as well as the modern post-World War II concept. The modern concept has the infusion of behavioural science theories, which were absent in the pre-War concepts of buyer behaviour.

In the traditional view of buyer motivation and behaviour, to explain why consumers do what they do, one term 'motive' has been viewed more than frequently to describe the causative variables in the black box. A leading psychologist has laid down almost thirty motives that were presumed to be common to all individuals.[17]

However, the most commonly appearing motives in the traditional views are (*i*) primary and selective; (*ii*) rational and emotional; (*iii*) patronage; and (*iv*) conscious and dormant.[18]

(*i*) **Primary and Selective Motives:** Primary motives are those, which guide us to the purchase or use of a class or service. The selective motives for buying are those, which influence the selection of a particular type of good from the rest of the class.

(*ii*) **Rational and Emotional Motives:** Purchase of rational motive is based on the objectivity measurable product features in contrast to personal feelings and opinions, which characterise emotional motives.

(*iii*) **Patronage Motive:** The source of purchase is determined by this motive.

---

16 Katona, G., The Powerful Consumer, McGraw Hill, New York, 1990.

17 Murray, H.A., Explorations in Personality, Oxford University Press, New York, 1938.

18 Engel, J.F., Kollat, D.T. and Blackwell, R.D., Consumer Behaviour, Holt, New York, p. 27.

(*iv*) **Conscious and Dormant Motives:** Conscious motives are those, which are felt and experienced and need not be aroused by any kind of marketing activity like advertising. Dormant motives, on the contrary, stay unrecognised and need to be aroused or brought to the attention of the buyer.

These traditional theories of motives have been found to be inconclusive and inadequate due to: (*i*) the lack of any empirical evidence to base on; (*ii*) the obscuring of other variables like personality traits, attitude, etc., which also affect the final outcome; and finally (*iii*) the fallacies of the rational emotional dichotomy; which an analysis shows that emotional motive of purchase can also be rational; and thus rational motive, the way it is connoted must be kept aside for reasons of safety. "It is necessary to restore the term motive to its rightful place as only one influence on consumer behaviour. Evaluative labels such as rational and emotional must be avoided. Consistent with contemporary psychological thought, therefore, this concept is not assigned the weight of explanation it has been traditionally given in marketing".[19]

"The motivation of human behaviour is exceedingly complex and is the result of myriad of influences and relationships. Therefore, it is necessary to present a model or representation of relationships among the factors underlying behaviour".[20]

5.12 PRESENTATION OF CONSUMER BEHAVIOUR IN MODELS

The sun-total of all the forces, which influences a man, is known as the psychological field. Under mentioned figure explains in detail:

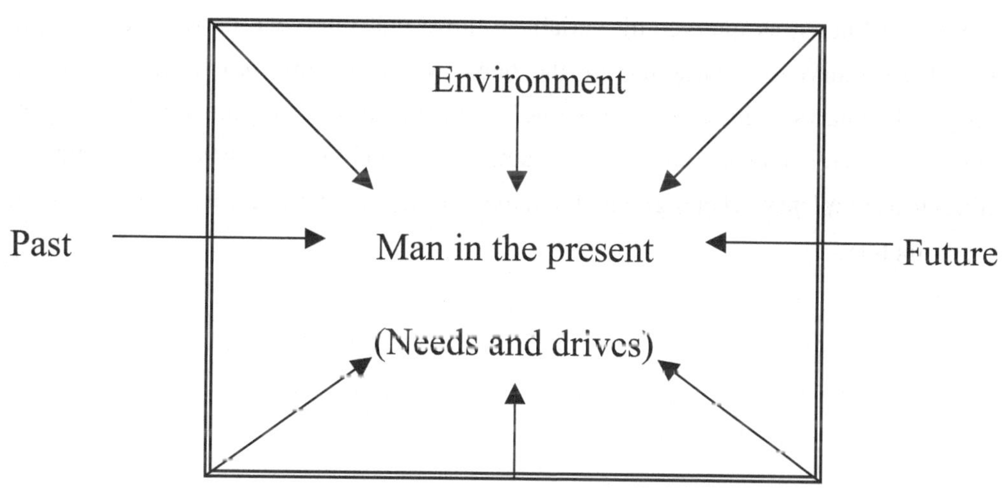

Fig. 5.4. Psychological Field Illustrated [21]

[19] *Ibid.*, p. 30.

[20] Ibid., p. 20.

[21] Ibid., pp. 5-6.

Unlike animals who are influenced basically by the present needs and drives apart from the environment of the present time, man is influenced by all of the above along with the consideration of past experiences and future anticipations. The sum-totality of all these is known as the psychological field of a man. Every individual adapts to his psychological field as this field is reality for him. Consumer analysis find it difficult to probe into the cause of human action because not only the psychological field poses a lot of complexities; but also the mental processes become virtually impregnable and cannot be directly observed. Mental processes are flanked by observable inputs and outputs from both the sides; but they themselves remain hidden forever from view inside the impenetrable "black box". Whenever explanation the analyst tries to give about what took place in the black box as a result of the input, can only be an inference made by him.

5.12.1. The Black Box Model

In the Black Box Model, the antecedents, which are inputs, are labelled as S (Stimulus) and the output behaviour as R (Response). The inference made regarding the influences on behaviour is indicated by the arrow in the model. As the model (Fig. 5.5 and 5.6) suggests, the stimuli and the responses are observable. From these observables, inference or inferences are made about what goes on or has gone on inside the impregnable black box resulting in the specific responses. To do this, the analysis relies on two kinds of relationships viz., Stimulus-Response (S-R) Relationships and Response-Response (R_R) Relationships. In the analyst's language, whatever goes on inside the black box are known as intervening variables, those that intervene between the stimuli and responses. These intervening variables are the ones; which are inferred from the associations established by the analysts either between stimulus and response or response and response. In a buying situation, such relationships are not only established for individuals; but also for groups ranging from families to a complete market segment. For a market forecast, a higher level of such aggregation becomes peremptory.

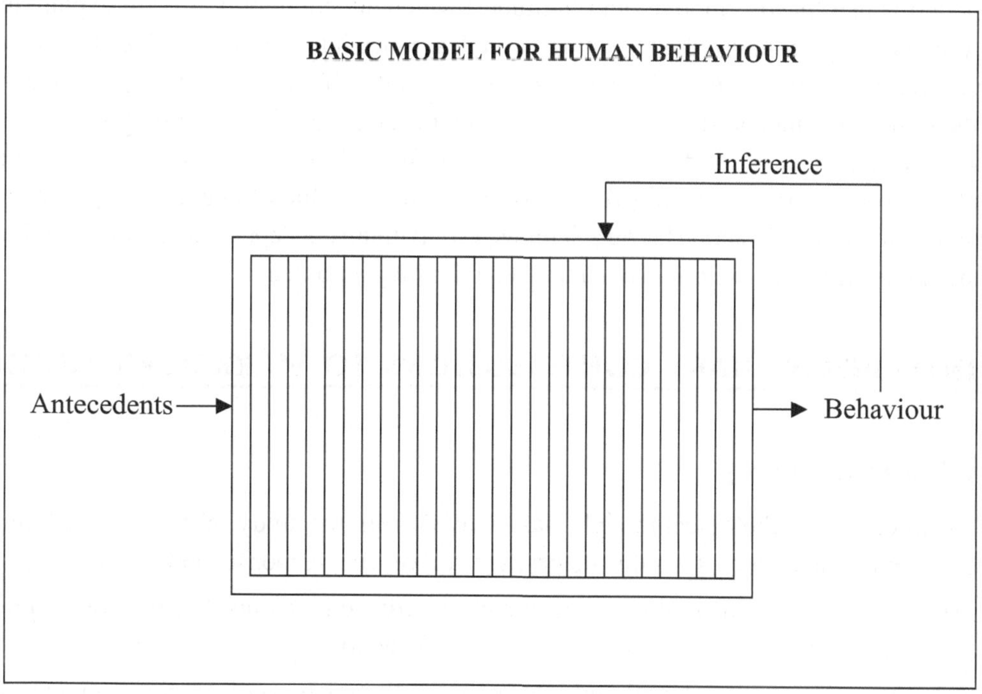

Fig. 5.5. Basic Model for Human Behaviour[22]

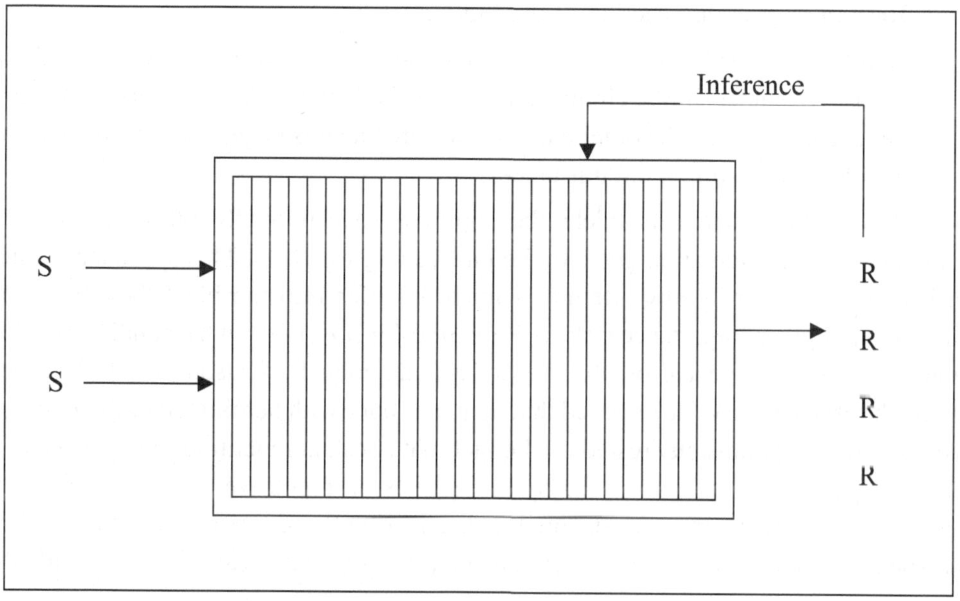

Fig. 5.6. Black Box Model[23]

---

[22] *Ibid.*, p. 6.

[23] *Ibid.*, pp. 5-6.

The terms like 'need', 'motive' and 'attitude'; which are commonly used to explain human behaviour are nothing but inferred intervening variables. Since intervening variables lack specified meanings, different analysts with different purposes describe different intervening variables while viewing the same phenomenon. This is a weakness with the analysis of mental processes. Inferences made about mental process can be genuinely meaningful and authentic only when intervening variables have specified meanings. It is the law of parsimony;[24] which can explain a psychological phenomenon with some satisfaction because it relies on maximum conceptual precision and minimum of assumptions while trying to explain a human behavioural phenomenon.

5.13 INTERDISCIPLINARY CONTRIBUTIONS TO MARKETING THOUGHT

5.13.1. Learning Theory

This aspect of psychological thought has evolved from the study of behaviour of animals. There are four important concepts in this theory, viz., drive, cue, response, and reinforcement.

(*i*) **Drive:** It is an internal stimulus, which is activated by a need or motive leading to a specific behaviour or promoting to a specific action.

(*ii*) **Cues:** These are external and internal stimuli, which go on to direct an appropriate response to satisfy the aroused need.

(*iii*) **Response:** It is the reaction of the individual.

(*iv*) **Reinforcement:** It occurs when the behaviour proves rewarding. When reinforcement is positive, under similar circumstances, it is likely that similar action or behaviour will be repeated. But on the other hand, if reinforcement is negative, similar action will be avoided under similar circumstances.

The S-R (Stimulus-Response) model is the empirical model normally followed in the Learning Theory with very little consideration given to the intervening variables. This approach is known as 'behaviourism' because hardly any attempt is made to infer into the black box from the S-R relationships. What is given importance is the S-R relationship, *i.e.*, under what conditions, what kind of behaviour is normally expected or observed of a man. John B. Watson based his concept of advertising on the above theory. He believed that man was born with nothing other than the capacity to learn. His advertising philosophy rested on the fact that constant repetition reinforced a response and lead to firm purchasing habits.[25] "Today's emphasis on repetitive advertising rests on this foundation as does advertising research devoted to discovering those appeals that stimulate the best short-run response".[26] However, behaviourism has no place for man's capacity to exclude through

[24] Engel, J.F., "Psychology and the Business Sciences", *Quarterly Journal of Economics and Business*, Vol. I, 1961, p. 78.

[25] Watson, J.B., *Behaviourism*, The People's Institute Publishing Co., New York, 1925.

[26] Engel, Kollat and Blackwell, *Consumer Behaviour*, op. cit., pp. 30-31.

selective perception or contain appeals that go contrary to his predispositions; and that is a weakness with pure behaviourism.

5.13.2. Clinical or Psychological Theory

This theory propounds the concept of intervening variables; and thus tries to improve upon the S-R model of behaviourism. The psychoanalytic theory owes its origin to Sigmond Freud. According to him child comes to the world with institutive needs, which he cannot gratify apart from others and systematically introduced social influence through the constraints exerted by the society on the human tendencies. Instinctive needs are governed by the ego when they are manifested. The ego serves as the intellectual mediator between unrestrained instincts and social constraints.[27] Freud also maintains that libido or sex is the most important of all instincts. Therefore, motives for most acts can be traced back to sexual drive manifested in unconscious and devious fashion. Another psychoanalyst, Adler, believed that power and the urge for it work as motivators for many human acts.[28]

5.13.3. Gestalt Model

Gestalt means form or configuration. According to this theory, individual stimuli are perceived and interpreted in relation to the organisation of one's experience.[29] Kurt Lewin propounded the theory that man lived in a complex psychological field composed of many influences. All these influences must be comprehended in a realistic theory of motivation.[30] Thus, behaviour of a man is motivated by the individual striving toward stable organisation of his psychological field through attempting to reduce tensions, reconcile conflicts, and make a sense out of the world in which he lives. Man is therefore, assumed to be goal oriented.[31] Man and the environment, he lives in are central to this model with emphasis on perception *i.e.,* reception of the stimuli through the five sensory organs and attribution of meaning to them.

5.13.4. Cognitive Theory

This is an extension of the Gestalt approach adopted by the social psychologists. In this the major focus is on the organisation of values, attitudes, and information started in an individual's memory.[32] An imbalance can be generated because of contradictory information from the environment or by non-fitting relationships in the structure itself. An imbalance occurs, a state of tension arises leading to the arousal of motivation that serves as a force for change of a structure from within to

---

27 Hall, C., A *Primer of Freudian Psychology*, Mentor, New York, 1954.

28 Adler, A., *The Science of Living, Greenberg*, New York, 1929.

29 Kohler, W., *Gestalt Psychology*, Liveright, New York, 1947.

30 Lewin, K., *Principles of Topological Psychology*, McGraw Hill, New York, 1936.

31 Engel, Kollat, and Blackwell, *Consumer Behaviour*, op. cit., p. 33.

32 Krech, D., Crutchfield, R.S. and Ballachey, E.L., *Individual in Society*, McGraw Hill, New York, 1962, Chapter - 2.

attain the balance or distorts the external input in some form for the same purpose. In this context it may be said that much of advertising and selling is undertaken to achieve attitude change.

However, none of the theories discussed above has tried sufficiently to probe into the psychological field of an individual with the consideration of the role of the social environment in it. The central concept of the social-psychological environment is the reference group or social entity within which an individual identifies and uses as a standard of behaviour. Besides, the sociology of the family as a concept aids to a great deal in understanding the household decision-making process.

5.14 MODELS OF BUYER BEHAVIOUR

Models represent various phenomena as replicas of the phenomena. They designate all the elements of the phenomena. Thus, a model is more like a map of the reality; and its study makes it possible to successfully predict the resulting behaviour or outcomes of the phenomena. The psychologist resorts to the mind or black box to analyse the human being with a system with outputs *i.e.*, behaviour in response to inputs. Through this he tries to gain knowledge about the human beings as a system of action by clarifying relationships among inputs, motivational determinants, and goal-oriented output.[33]

Models are beneficial in many ways:[34]

(*i*) They provide a frame of reference for research by describing the elements and their relationships; and thus identifying the gaps in information and potential areas for further inquiry.

(*ii*) When the entire process of consumer behaviour is put in the form of a model, the underlying relations of the various elements become visibly clear; which enables the researcher to utilise research findings from a variety of behavioural sciences with greater sophistication and precision.

(*iii*) Models can give researchable hypotheses basing on which knowledge can be extended; and thus theories can be constructed.

(*iv*) Models provide necessary explanations for performance of the system. More description of the motivational determinants of buyer action is hardly of any use to the researcher of buyer behaviour. On the contrary, relations among the various elements have to be necessarily established to be able to predict outcomes under varying sets of circumstances. Such a process is possible only when there is some sort of model.

5.14.1. The Nicosia Model

A leading scholar in the field of consumer motivation and behaviour, Francesco Nicosia has given one of the earliest comprehensive models, which is given in Fig. 5.7 in terms of its basic

---

33 Engel, Kollat and Blackwell, *Consumer Behaviour*, op. cit., p. 35.

34 *Ibid*., pp. 35-36.

components.[35] The model of Nicosia uses the computer flow charting method to designate the various elements and their relationships. Field one has two sub-fields. Sub-field one includes the firm sending the advertising message with its attributes on. The message is exposed before the consumer in sub-field two; which is received by the consumer in the way his psychological attributes or predispositions condition it. After the receipt of the message and reactions, an attitude towards the product is formed. Then in field two the advertised product is evaluated vis-à-vis the other available alternatives. In the process, a search for the same starts. Field two results in the output of negative or positive motivation to buy the advertised brand; which becomes input for field three. In field three, the decision is taken and the actual purchase action takes place as a result. Field four designates the stage of actual use of the product or its storage resulting in the experience with the product. This acts as a feedback to the consumer and is retained in his memory; which is sub-field two within the field one. The output of the sales result and purchasing behaviour is fed back to the firm; which aids it in designing its message as well as the product for future.

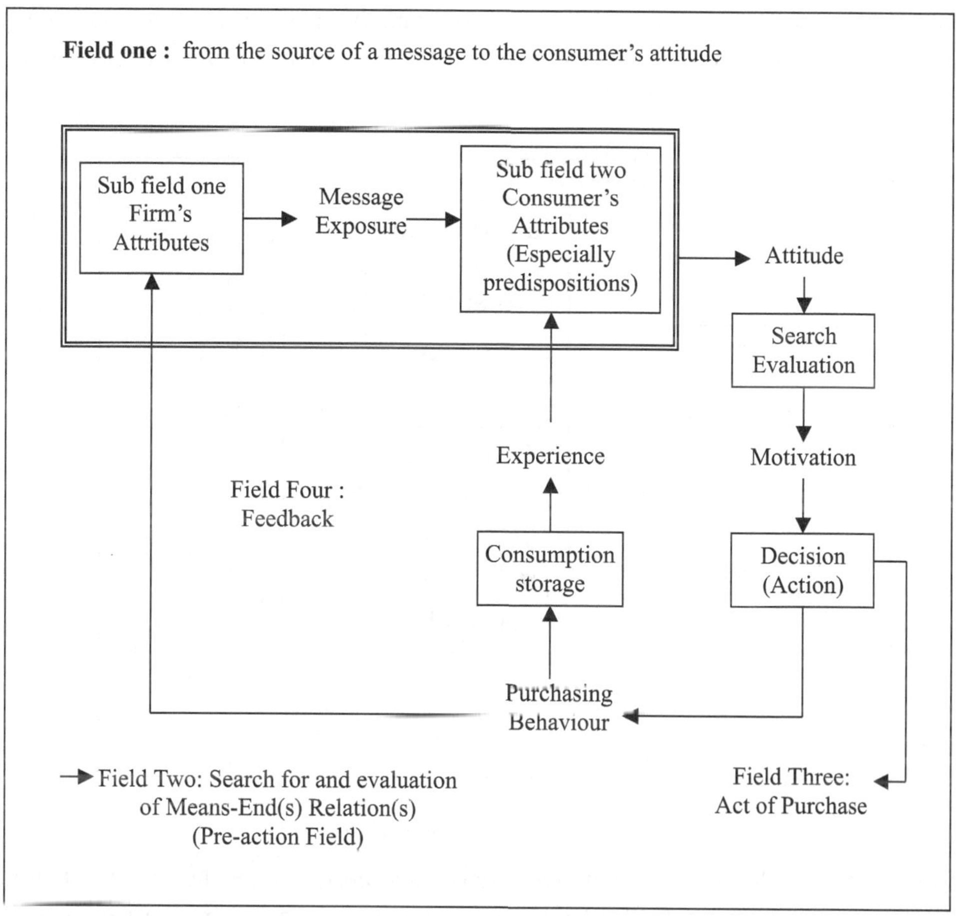

Fig. 5.7. The Nicosia Model

[35] Nicosia, F.M., *Summary Flow Chart of the Nicosia Model of Buyer Behaviour, Consumer Decision Process: Marketing and Advertising Implications*, Englewood Cliffs, N.J., Prentice Hall, 1966, p. 156.

5.14.2. Multimediation Model for Consumer Behaviour[36]

The decision-process approach to consumer behaviour discussed earlier presupposes the fact that consumer decision-making takes place in stages. It includes the stages that precede and follow the decision as well as the decision itself. The multimediation model is called so because many processes intervene or mediate between exposure to a stimulus and final outcomes of behaviour, which means many factors affect outcomes. However, no complex model can be proven or validated in the final sense. A model can be treated as a better one or a more acceptable one if it makes sense both in terms of intuition and existing knowledge, and if the predictions deduced from the model come true. No model can be termed as the best as a number of differing approaches can satisfy the same criteria.

Individual's Psychological Makeup[37]

An individual's "black box" is his or her psychological makeup; which is also known as the central control unit or the CCU. The CCU has memory and the facilities for thinking and directing behaviour. The components of the black box necessary to understand consumer behaviour are given in the Fig. 5.8.

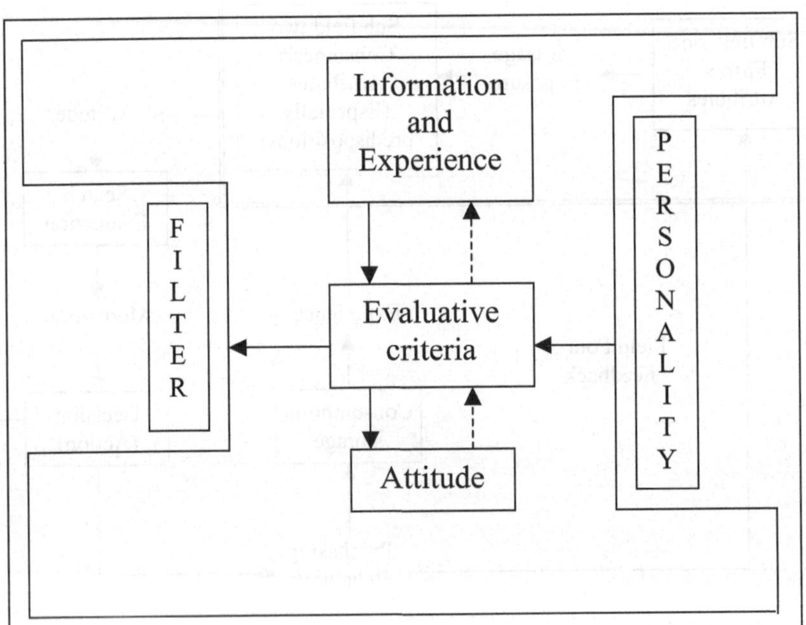

Fig. 5.8. Central Control Unit

Information and experience, evaluative criteria, and attitudes are the major components to understand consumer behaviour. Each of these components is affected by the personality of the

---

36 Engel, Kollat and Blackwell, Consumer Behaviour, op. cit., pp. 49-62.

36 Ibid., pp. 50-52.

individuals. Then these component variables interact to form a filter through which incoming stimuli are processed. But the components are individually integral in themselves and have their unique functions.

5.15 CULTURAL CONTEXT OF CONSUMER BEHAVIOUR

Culture is the underlying determinant of human decision-making.[38] Culture also explains as to why some choices are preferred over others. Smaller groups within the larger society also develop their own culture giving rise to the sub-culture effect on consumer buying decisions. "Culture means the complex values, ideas, attitudes, and other meaningful symbols created by man to shape human behaviour and the artefacts of that behaviour as they are transmitted from one generation to the next.[39] The process of learning culture, for a consumer in which he is raised is called socialisation or enculturation. The process of learning a new culture or sub-culture other than the one in which one is raised is called acculturation. Acculturation takes place when a person leaves a society to live in another. With time enculturation or acculturation of an individual goes on to become a part of the individual's central control unit. The phenomena of enculturation and acculturation are primarily affected by the family influence to start with. Reference groups such as work groups, grown-ups and friend circle for all ages also transmit culture. Racial and ethnic groups also transmit culture to an individual. This entire process of culture transmission through various media is known as cultural mediation.

5.16 CONSUMER BEHAVIOUR AND ADVERTISING

Marketing men have long recognised that if a product does not sell without advertising, it will not sell with advertising. For a product to sell at all, with or without advertising, it must appeal to, and satisfy, some needs and wants for some consumers at least as well as competing items. Advertising, in other words, possesses no magic capable of causing people to buy things they do not need or want; however, it may help them to rationalise purchases of products, they want but do not need in the strict economic sense. Who 'needs' custom-made shirts at double the price of readymade shirts? Only a small percentage of men of unusual sizes actually need custom-made shirts; but many men want them for prestigious reasons. Appeal to these other wants help consumers to rationalise uneconomic but satisfying wants. In appraising a product with regard to advertising opportunity, the really important questions to ask are: "Do potential buyers have needs or wants that this product or brand is capable of satisfying?" and "How important, or how strong, are these needs or wants?" If there are strong needs or wants for the product, the chances for its sale exist. If the product is capable of satisfying only the comparatively week and less basic needs or wants, there is not nearly so much advertising opportunity. The extent of the advertising opportunity varies with the strength of the basic underlying needs or wants that are satisfied by the product or brand.

---

[38] Engel, Kollat and Blackwell, *Consumer Behaviour*, op. cit., p. 71.

[39] Kroeber, A. and Parsons, T., "The Concepts of Culture and of Social System", *American Sociological Review*, Vol. 23, October 1958, p. 583.

Advertisers do not operate in secret; if their advertising remains hidden, then all is a waste. The advertisers identify and his objectives are both known to buyers. Unless communication is received and accepted by the audience for which it was intended, the communicator has failed. The advertising, which insults the intelligence of intellectuals, may not have been created to be sent to them; it may, however, be exactly the advertising necessary to communicate to the advertiser's intended audience. Advertising does not impose a scale of values or a set of motives on individuals.

The great majority of Indian consumers believe that each person should expand his needs and then gratify them. Parents want their children to enjoy more material comforts than the parents did. They want more material comforts for themselves too. Advertising should not be blamed because our society actively seeks more and better physical possessions. Materialism should not be an end - it should be a means to even better ends. Clearly, the purpose of advertising is to make ultimate consumers want to consume more. Persuasion and influence here are just as ethical as in politics, religion or education. The ultimate consumers want more than just bare functional utility from products. Each individual can be just as individualistic as he prefers. There are enough different goods and services to afford a wide range of choice. Public service advertising is significant both in impact and in volume in our country.

5.16.1. Definition

Consumer behaviour reflects the totality of consumer's decisions with respect to the acquisition and disposition of goods, services, time and ideas by (human) decision-making units [over time].[40]

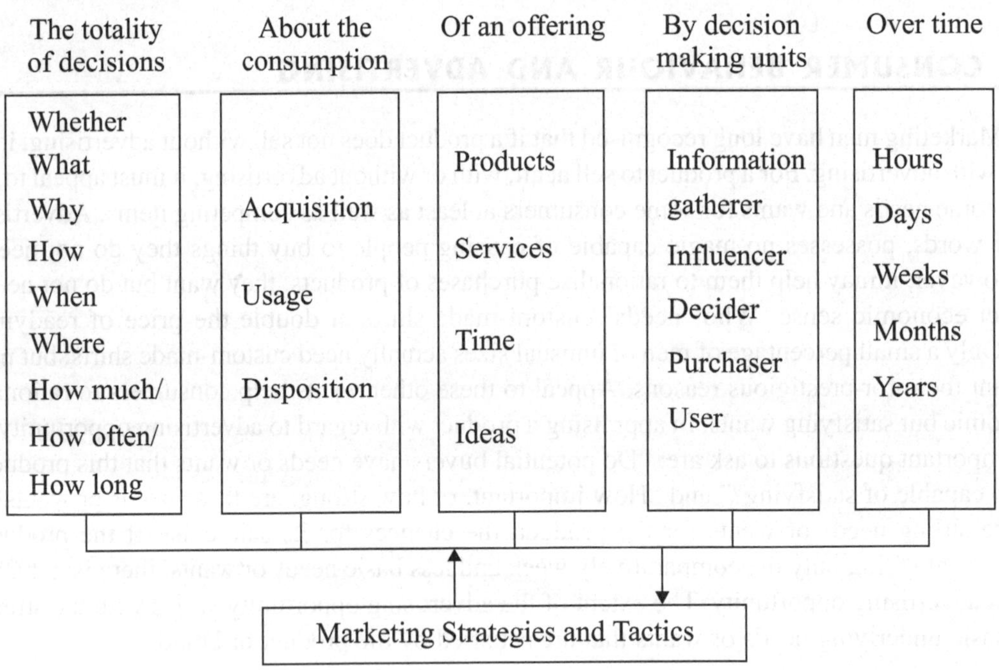

Fig. 5.9. Consumer Behaviour Reflects

[40] Jacob Jacoby, "Consumer Psychology: An Octennium", in Paul Mussen and Mark Rosenzweig (eds.), *Annual Review of Psychology*, 1976, pp. 331-358.

5.16.2. Consumer Behaviour Involves More than Just Buying

Consumer behaviour involves more than just buying (or purchasing). Although the manner in which consumers buy is extremely important to marketers, it is not the only thing of interest.

Acquiring: Buying represents one type of consumer acquisition behaviour. As we will see in greater detail later, acquisition includes other ways of obtaining products and services, such as leasing, trading or borrowing.

Using: After a product or service has been acquired it will typically be used in some manner. Although most consumer researchers have studied acquisition, usage is of the very care of consumer behaviour. First, usage has important symbolic implications for the consumer. The products we use may symbolise the importance of the event, how much we have worked to make a nice dinner, and how important our guests are to us. Second, understanding consumer's usage of products and services can guide marketing strategy and tactics. Usage can also influence other behaviours.

Disposing: Finally, consumer behaviour involves understanding consumer disposition behaviour, that is, how consumer get rid of an offering they have previously acquired.

5.16.3. Importance of Studying Consumer Behaviour

The study of consumer behaviour is important to at least four key constituents: marketing managers, ethicists, public policy makers and regulators, and consumers themselves.

5.16.4. Importance to Marketing Managers

"Marketing is the human activity directed at satisfying wants and needs through human exchange processes".[41]

According to this definition, to effectively market a product or service, marketing managers must clearly understand consumers' needs and wants. The study of consumer behaviour thus provides strategic information about what consumers need and want and how marketing programs should be designed to precipitate an exchange.

5.16.5. Market Segmentation

It is unlikely that all consumers in a market have the same needs and wants. Indeed, because consumers' worlds are affected by the myriad groups to which they belong, it is likely that marketers will find different groups or segments of consumers within a market, each with different needs and wants.

By understanding consumer behaviour, marketers can also determine how big various segments are. For example, markets have found that the biggest users of the prepaid calling card are immigrants and consumers who do not have residential phone service. Knowledge of segment size can be important because marketers can profit substantially by targeting large segments that competitions

[41] Philip Kotler, *Marketing Management Analysis, Planning and Control*, 4th Edition, Englewood Cliffs, N.J.: Prentice Hall, 1980.

have not similarly targeted. Consumer behaviour can also help marketers' identify underserved segments—segments of consumers who have clearly identifiable needs, but whose needs are not being met.

5.16.6. Target Market Selection

Understanding consumer behaviour also helps marketers determine who might represent the most viable target for marketing tactics. Knowledge of consumer behaviour also helps marketers identify all the individuals potentially involved in the acquisition, use and disposition process. Because consumer behaviour may involve multiple individuals fulfilling multiple roles, this knowledge can be quite important. To illustrate, condom marketers currently see tremendous growth in the purchase of condoms by women. Even though women do not actually use traditional condoms, they often buy them. Moreover, women are very influential in men's use of condoms. Recognising these gender effects, more marketers are explicitly targeting women.[42]

5.16.7. Positioning

One of the key goals of marketing strategy is to position a product or services in consumers' mind. In other words, marketers attempt to imbue the product with a certain image—an image that both reflects what the product is and how it is different from the competitors. Positioning decisions are critical to the success of an offering. Understanding consumer behaviour also helps marketers reposition existing products.

5.16.8. Product or Service Decisions

Developing products and services that satisfy consumers' wants and needs is a critical marketing decision. An understanding of consumer behaviour can provide useful information about several product decisions.

First, marketers need to design an offering that contains the benefits target consumers desire.

Second, marketers often do considerable consumer research to determine whether consumers are currently satisfied with aspects of a product.

Third, knowledge of consumer behaviour aids in the development of new products or services.

Fourth, understanding consumer behaviour also helps marketers know when products must be modified or tailored to meet the needs of new groups.

Finally, an understanding of consumer behaviour aids in decisions about other aspects of the product mix, such as the brand name, package, logo, and aspects of the extended product like warranties and guarantees.

---

[42] Fara Warner, " Condom Seller Lets Users Do the Talking", *Wall Street Journal*, March 22, 1955, pp. B3, B8.

5.16.9. Pricing Decisions

The price of a product or service is one of the most important variables influencing consumer decision-making. Therefore, an understanding of consumer behaviour is needed to predict how pricing strategies will affect purchase and sales.

5.16.10. Distribution Decision

Another important marketing decision involves the manner in which products or services are distributed. Consumer research has already shown that different distribution alternatives (*e.g.*, telephone sales, direct mail, face-to-face selling) have different images and that these images will affect consumers' perception of the offering.

5.16.11. Promotion Decision

Marketing decisions making also involves the use of a variety of promotional tools such as advertising, sales promotions, personal selling, and public relations. These tools often designed to influence consumers' acquisition, consumption, or disposition decisions and behaviours.

An understanding of consumer behaviour can help make a better environment for consumers themselves. Specifically, research on consumer behaviour has been instrumental in developing environments that help consumers make decisions.

An understanding of consumer behaviour has also led to product and service developments designed to protect certain segments of consumers. Finally, consumer research on disposition behaviour has the potential to affect programs that conserve natural resources. Consumer research was instrumental in testing the effectiveness of various alternatives, resulting in a more positive solution to the problem.

SUMMARY

The goal of this chapter is to introduce the topic of consumer behaviour and marketing research techniques. Specifically, it deals with identifying what consumers' behaviour is, what factors affect it and why this is to be studied. It is noted that, although the term consumer behaviour is often conceived rather narrowly as the study of what product a person buys, the study of consumer behaviour actually involves understanding of (1) the set of decisions (what, whether, why, when, how, where, how much, how often), (2) made about the acquisition, use, or disposition, (3) of products, services, ideas or time, (4) made by one or more decision-making entities and (5) over time.

This chapter also hinted at the multitude of factors that influence consumer behaviour. It is noted that, consumers' motivation, ability and opportunity affect their decisions. These factors influence what consumers are exposed to, what they attend to, and what they perceive, how they categorise or interpret information, how they form and change attitude, and how they form and retrieve memories.

Each of these aspects of the psychological core has a bearing on consumer decision-making process, and affects others' decisions as well as one's post-decision satisfaction level. And we revealed that consumer decisions are affected by the consumer's culture. We defined culture broadly as the myriad groups and social systems to which an individual belongs that bear on the values and beliefs they hold and the symbols they use to communicate group membership. This chapter also discussed how factors associated with the psychological core and the culture can influence several consumer behaviour outcomes, such as symbolic consumer behaviour and the diffusion of new consumer behaviours through a market.

Also discussed that, why it is important to study consumer behaviour. Knowledge of consumer behaviour can provide useful input to marketing strategies like market segmentation, target market selection, and positioning. It can also guide marketing tactics like product pricing, distribution and promotion decisions.

Chapter 6

ADVERTISING AND LIFESTYLE COMMUNICATION

6.1 INTRODUCTION

In the previous chapter, consumer behaviour, advertising and social-class lifestyle has been discussed in detail. The present chapter focuses on advertising and lifestyle communication in particular. It includes discussions on lifestyle communication, lifestyle marketing, lifestyle segmentation, social class lifestyles, social class and income related to lifestyle pattern, lifestyle advertising, application of lifestyle marketing; communication, types of communication and mass communication research.

The concept of lifestyles is, to a great extent, related to consumers' values and personality that represent internal states or characteristics. Lifestyles are manifestations or actual patterns of behaviour. In particular, they are represented by a consumer's activities, interests and opinions (AIOs). What one does in one's spare time is often a good indicator of one's lifestyles. One consumer might like to engage in activities such as camping or driving, whereas another might prefer to stay at home, read and listen to music. The basic idea in lifestyle is that consumers who engage in different activities and have different opinions and interests may represent distinct lifestyle segments.

Most often, lifestyle research is more specifically focusing on product usage and patterns. This enables marketers to gain a better understanding of how their product fits into the consumers' general patterns of behaviour. For example, a study of stomach remedies identified four main lifestyle segments: severe suffers, active medicators, hypochondriacs and practicalists. Also a study of fashion consumers found six major groups: older consumers, married households with college degree, fashion foregoers, social strivers, dutifuls with high-income high-quality buyers.[1]

Finally, consumers in different countries have characteristic lifestyles. One study found considerable lifestyle differences between Indian and American women.[2] Indian women are more home-focussed, less likely to visit restaurants, less price sensitive and less likely to drive or go to the movies. Given these orientations, we might surmise that Indian women would be more likely than American to spend time preparing meals at home and would therefore pay a premium for products that enhance the quality of the meal. Popular lifestyle activities among Russian consumers include going to cinema and theatre and playing sports like soccer, ice hockey and figure skating. Another research study found that watching sports on TV, going to movies, playing cards, reading a book and

---

[1] Piirto, *Beyond Mind Games*, March 1994, pp. 75-83.

[2] Onk Visit and Shaw, *International Marketing*, , p. 283.

playing the stereo are the favourite activities of the Chinese.[3] Consumer lifestyles can have important implications for communications, new product ideas and market segmentations.

6.2 LIFESTYLE AND COMMUNICATION

Advertising messages and promotions are often designed to appeal to certain lifestyles. The purpose of Reebok shoe campaign, for example, is to appeal to those with an active lifestyle in the "spirit of undefined performance". The same is true of Nike's "Just Do It" campaign. Likewise Aishwarya Rai's Coca Cola campaign "*Jo Chhahe Ho Jayee* - Coca Cola *Ho Jayee*" (Let's wish and get; let's get Coca Cola) featuring sports stars and famous athletes in ads is obviously designed to appeal to sports-related lifestyles. Lifestyles also have implications for the specific media consumers use. For example, because many fathers have changed their lifestyle to become more involved in childrearing, parenting magazines, which were traditionally a women's forum, are starting to focus more on male readers and male-oriented advertising. Also, many companies, including Holiday Inn, Universal Studios now try to communicate in Cyber space with consumers who like to surf the Internet.

Finally, media usage pattern may be related to lifestyles.[4] For example, most of the TV watchers tend to be unemployed, have low-prestige occupations and have a low interest in cultural matters. Magazine and newspaper reading on the other hand is positively related to education and occupational prestige, as well as community and political involvement.

6.2.1. New Product Ideas

Often marketers can develop new product and service ideas by uncovering unfulfilled needs of certain lifestyle segments. For example, marketers discovered that many workers who bring their lunch to work were tired of having sandwiches. In response to that, companies like Britannia, Nestle and Amul have developed "lunch kits" that are easy to carry offering varieties to the consumers.

Athletic shoe makers have realised that the footwear needs of consumers who engage in different sporting activities vary and this has led to the introduction of new offerings such as aerobic, tennis, walking and cross-training shoes. Active and affluent consumers have demonstrated an increasing desire for unique, high-quality products and services, leading to new brands of premium coffees and beers.

To appeal to frequent business flyers, some airlines are offering airport showers and hotel suits. In addition, Japan is a country where an increasing number of consumers like to eat and drink without "lifting a finger" and this has created a market for products like self-buffering bread, ready-mixed cocktails and spoonless gelatin.

---

[3] Sam Bradley, "Chinese Consumers Eyeing Hard Goods", *Brandweek,* June 12, 1995, p. 28.

[4] Jacob, Harnik and Schlinger, Mary Jane, "Allocation of Time to the Mass Media", *Journal of Consumer Research,* March 1981, pp. 343-355.

6.2.2. Market Segmentation

Lifestyles can be used to identify consumer segments for various offerings. For example, microwavable dinners, fast food, day care centres, and house cleaning services will obviously appeal more to consumers whose lifestyle demands convenience and saving time.[5] The popularity of fast food restaurants such as Mac Donald's Burger King, Pizza Hut and Dunkin's Donuts has been greatly increasing in India.

Lifestyle segmentation also has important cross-cultural implications. The recent economic changes have enabled Western hotel chains to offer services that are more pleasing to a typical traveller's lifestyle such as dry cleaning, room service, etc. Marketers often monitor lifestyle changes to identify new opportunities. For example, many companies now allow executives to dress more informally at work and treat it as a casual day like holiday. In response, many clothiers and retailers are giving more emphasis to casual items in their offerings. Home entertainment centres have also been popular among home-oriented consumers, who crave state-of-the-art technology.

6.3 VALUES AND LIFESTYLE SURVEY

One of the most widely known psychographic tools is called VALS (Values and Lifestyle Survey), which is conducted by Stanford Research Institute. A number of businesses uses VALS to identify potential target markets and to understand better as to how they should communicate with consumers. Researchers in the late 1980s began criticising VALS because it had become outdated and did not predict behaviour well. Changes due to the aging of the baby boom generation, the greater diversity of ethnic groups, greater media choices (especially TV and interactive media) and changes in values and lifestyles made VALS an invalid tool for describing consumers in the 21st century. In response to the criticisms, SRI developed VALS2. The newer survey includes only items that relate to consumer behaviour. It is, therefore, much more closely related to consumption than VALS.[6]

Table 6.1. Lifestyle Indicators

Activities	Interests	Opinions	Demographics
Work	Family	Social issues	Age
Hobbies	Home	Politics	Education
Social events	Job	Business	Income
Vacations	Community	Education	Occupation
Entertainment	Recreation	Economics	Family size
Club membership	Fashion	Products	Dwelling
Community	Food	Culture	Geography
Shopping	Media	Future	City size
Sports	Achievement		Life-cycle stage

[5] Cyndee Miller, "Study Dispels '80s Stereotypes of Women", *Marketing News*, May 22, 1995, p. 3.

[6] Martha, Fransworth Riche, "Psychographics for the 1990s", American Demographics, July 1989, pp. 24-54.

(Lifestyles are represented by consumer's activities, interests and opinions. Here are some major examples of each category.)

Source: Joseph T. Plummer, "The Concept and Application of Lifestyle Segmentation", *Journal of Marketing*, Jan. 1974, pp. 33-37.

6.4 SOCIAL CLASS LIFESTYLES

The significance of social stratification for the marketer is that there are differences in values, attitudes and behaviour of each of the classes. These differences provide a basis on which to segment markets and obtain an enhanced understanding of the behaviour of consumers. Some of the major findings from research on general social-class differences are summarised, which discusses class variations and lifestyle differences. As we describe the lifestyles of each of the major social class groups, it should be kept in mind that we are not implying that all members of the same class have homogeneous behaviour.[7]

6.4.1. Upper-Upper Class

This group is an interesting mix of many lifestyles: luxurious, counter cultural, conventional, intellectual, political and the like. They account for a smaller percentage, pay special attention to prestige brands. It is the smallest class group, international in residence, friendships and relationships. They are oriented toward living graciously; upholding the family reputation reflecting the excellence of one's breeding and displaying a sense of community responsibility.

6.4.2. Lower-Upper Class

This is the 'newly rich' class, composed of those who have recently arrived at their wealth and are not quite accepted by the upper-uppers. They are the "executive elite", founders of large businesses and wealthy doctors and lawyers. They have the highest incomes of all the classes and their goals are a blend of the upper-upper's pursuit of gracious living.

6.4.3. Upper-Middle Class

This class consists of moderately successful professional men and women, such as doctors, lawyers and professors, owners of medium-sized business and "organisation men" of the managerial level. It also includes younger men and women who are expected to reach those occupational status levels within a few years. Most members are college-educated; hence, this group is sometimes referred to as "the brains and eyes" of our society.

6.4.4. Middle Class

This class is at the top of the "common man" or "average man" level. It is composed of non-managerial workers, small-business owners, and highly paid blue-collars.

---

[7] Myers and Gutman, "Lifestyle", IMA, Chicago, 1987, pp. 253-254.

The key motivations for this group are "respectability" and "striving". Men and women want to be judged respectable in their personal behaviour by their fellow citizens; that is they desire to live in well-maintained homes which are neatly furnished and are located in neighbourhoods that are on the right side of the tracks.

This group is recognised as one in which people want to "do the right thing"and "buy what's popular". They are concerned with fashion and follow the recommendations of "experts" in the media.

6.4.5. Working Class

These are "poor but honest" and "family folks". The largest of all classes, it is composed of skilled and semiskilled workers and small business trades people. Working-class people are oriented toward living well and enjoying life from day to day rather than saving for the future or being concerned about what the middle classes think of them.

6.4.6. Upper-Lower Class

This class is the working poor who have not escaped the marginal sector of the labour market. Although above the poverty level, they cannot count on steady employment. Because they may have only some high school education, they are relegated low-paying, unskilled-labour positions. Unable to advance to the working class because of their low education level, they fear slipping of the lowest class.

6.4.7. Lower-Lower Class

Living below the poverty line, they receive most of their income from illegal activities or from welfare. They are fatalistic in their outlook. Unfortunately, they have a bad reputation among higher classes who view them as lazy, shiftless, against work and immoral.

6.5 SOCIAL CLASS AND INCOME RELATED TO LIFESTYLE PATTERNS[8]

(*a*) Many lifestyle items showed significant correlations with the index of social class, indicating definite but small differences between the social classes in terms of lifestyles.

(*b*) Some items showed a much greater correlation with social class than with income, suggesting that social class is a better predictor of consumer's living patterns than is income.

[8] Ibid., p. 252.

General lifestyle items that correlate well with product usage might well explain characteristics of the markets' activity, interest and opinions to the seller. Such findings could give the marketer some direction for product, promotion, channel and pricing-decisions. A preferred approach, however, would be to design a lifestyle study especially for the particular firm or its product line.

6.6 LIFESTYLE MARKETING[9]

Lifestyle analysis makes our understanding of demographic groups sharper. In India the marketers these days are tapping 'the young and upwardly mobile' group that cuts across many barriers. Many advertisement appeals are meant for this group. The behavioural differences do not come alive in demographic descriptions, but do show themselves in lifestyle patterns. Lifestyle is a group phenomenon, which pervades various aspects of life. It implies a central life interest such as family, leisure, religion, politics, sexual exploits, etc. and this interest fashions our interaction with the environment. Variations in lifestyles are a result of social change. Working women and working couples do have very distinct lifestyles. In India, one of the agencies is trying to build a psychographic profile of Indian children. Pathfinders have identified eight types of Indian housewives.

6.6.1. VALS System of Classification

Values and Lifestyle (VALS) classification was developed by Arnold Mitchell. The adults (18 plus) are classified into distinctive lifestyle groups. Each group has psychological needs (values) and behavioural response patterns (lifestyles). Much of VALS is based on Maslow's Need Hierarchy. VALS blends together demographics, attitudes, activities, consumption patterns, brand preferences and media graphics.

Four major groups in VALS are:

(*a*) Need-driven poor and uneducated,

(*b*) Outer-directed upper and middle class,

(*c*) Inner-directed due to inner motivation,

(*d*) Integrated—a combination of both outer and inner - directed values.

[9] Chunawalla, S.A. and Sethia, K.C., *Foundations of Advertising Theory and Practice*, 1999, pp. 102-103.

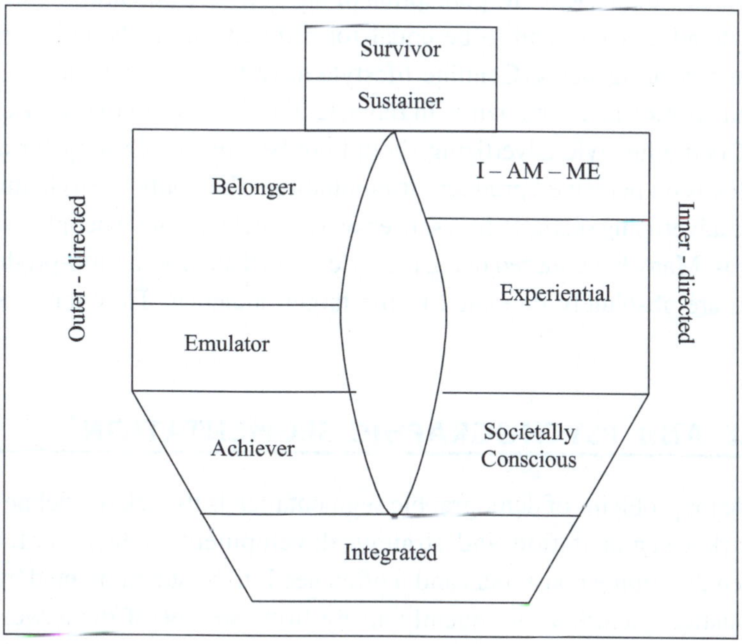

Fig. 6.1. Value and Lifestyle Classification

The above model of Thomas puts these groups into nine specific VALS segments.

Survivors are price-conscious and not very knowledgeable shoppers. Sustainers are swayed by brands and guarantees and are impulse-buyers. Emulators buy to impress others and to announce their status. Achievers buy high tech items and original top of the line products. Experiential buy for experimenting societally conscious want value for money.

Survivors are depressed; sustainers are strugglers. Belongers are conventional; emulators are status-conscious. Achievers are leaders and 'I-Am-Me' are young impulsive people. Experimental pursue a rich inner life and are interested in life's offerings. Societally conscious people are socially responsible and integrated, nature psychologically. Thus, an individual passes through several developmental stages. In India, we are now targeting at selected lifestyle groups for a suitable niche for our product.

6.6.2. Applications of Lifestyle Marketing

It is used for:

(*a*) positioning of new products

(*b*) repositioning of old/existing products

(*c*) developing new product inputs

(*d*) creating promotional strategies.

6.6.3. Lifestyle Advertising

A product which would add to the perception of one's life is a potential candidate for lifestyle advertising. Lifestyle advertising tend to be equal for different products and to break this parity requires time and effort of agencies. Genuine lifestyle advertising makes an aspect of a lifestyle intrinsic to the brand position and personality. In India, textile firms resort to lifestyle advertising that is not distinctive. Good elite-style advertising should not become advertising for a good elite. We should, therefore, focus on perceived product differentiation. Then only lifestyle imagery works. In most cases, lifestyle advertising seems to be a safe easy way out by creative people, without bothering to think of fresh ideas. Many have started using lifestyle advertising for me-too-products. Sometimes lifestyles portrayed are absolutely unrelated to the target audience. They tend to become visual clichés.

6.7 LIFESTYLE AND PSYCHOGRAPHIC SEGMENTATION[10]

One of the major problems of demographic segmentation is its lack of 'richness' in describing consumers for market segmentation and strategy development. It lacks colour, texture and dimensionality when describing consumers and it often needs to be supplemented by something that fills in the bare statistical picture. Consequently, many firms are one of the newest, most exciting and promising approaches to select target markets is lifestyle and psychographic segmentation. Although the concepts of lifestyles and psychographics are often used interchangeably, they are not equivalent but are complementary.

The term "lifestyle" is not new, but its application to marketing has been rather recent. Alfred Adler coined the phrase "style of life" over fifty years ago to refer to the goal of a person for himself and the ways he uses to reach it. From this perspective, lifestyle can be viewed as a unique pattern of living which influences and is reflected by one's consumer behaviour. Therefore, the way in which marketers facilitate the expression of an individual's lifestyle is by "providing customers with parts of a potential mosaic from which they, as artists of their own lifestyles, can pick and choose to develop the composition that for the time seems best. Many products today are "lifestyle" products, that is, they portray a style of life sought by potential users.

A very fundamental question, that strikes the mind about how does the concept of psychographics relate to lifestyles? Unfortunately, it is not an easy matter to define psychographics because there is no general agreement as to exactly what it is. It has to do with mental ("psycho") profiles or the profiling of consumer's psychological processes and properties. Thus, it pertains to the consumer's cognitive style. One of the more precise statements about its nature is the following: Psychographics is the systematic use of relevant activity, interest and opinion constructs to quantitatively explore and explain the communicating, purchasing and consuming behaviours of persons for brands, products and clusters of products.

---

[10] Louden, D.L. and Della Bitta, A.J., *Consumer Behaviour*, 4th Edition, pp. 71-74.

Thus, psychographics may be viewed as the method of defining lifestyles in measurable terms. It should be noted, however, that there is some question about the use of psychographic instruments as a precise measure of the lifestyles of the individual consumer. Nevertheless the basic premise underlying lifestyle research is that the more marketers understand their customers, the more effectively they can communicate and market to them. In many cases the primary targets of such marketing efforts are heavy users. Heavy users have traditionally been looked at demographically but by incorporating lifestyle characteristics the marketer obtains a better, more true-to-life picture of such customers.

6.7.1. The Techniques of Lifestyle Segmentation[11]

Lifestyle segmentation research measures:

(*a*) How people spend their time engaging in activities;

(*b*) What is most interest or importance to them in their immediate surrounding; and

(*c*) Their opinions and views about themselves and the world around them.

Together, these three areas are generally referred to as Activities, Interests and Opinions, or simply AIOs.

In a typical large-scale lifestyle research project, questionnaires are mailed to members of a nationwide consumer panel. The questionnaires solicit traditional demographic information, average usage rates for as many as 100 different products, media habits and respondents activities, interests and opinions. Approximately 300 AIO statements may be included, to which respondents indicate the extent of their agreement or disagreement on six-point Likert scales ranging from "definitely disagree" to "definitely agree".

Generally, the process of lifestyle segmentation involves two steps. First, a determination is made of which lifestyle segments will efficiently produce the greater number of profitable consumers. Often heavy users are sought, but as we have seen, other segments also have potential. The second step involves defining and describing the selected target customers in more depth to understand how they may be attracted and communicated with more efficiently and relevantly. One danger of relying on psychographic models, even when they are appropriate, is that marketers may risk alienating groups with a low index of usage, who make-up a much larger proportion of the population. For example, Yogurt consumption is one psychographic segment may be 20 per cent better than average, but if they only comprise, say 3 per cent of the market, their usage really does not compare to that of another psychographic group representing 40 per cent of the market, who although only average *Yoghurt* eaters, may account for one-third of all the *Yoghurt* sold. How to appeal successfully to each different psychographic group is an extremely challenging issue to marketers.

---

[11] *Ibid.*, pp. 60-61.

6.7.2. Application of Lifestyle Segmentation[12]

Lifestyle may be used as a basis for segmentation in several ways. In one approach, the marketer seems to classify the consumer population into groups based on general lifestyle characteristics, so that consumers within the groups have similar lifestyles. Using the research approach described above, a representative sample of consumers responds to a questionnaire containing *AIOs, product usage, media consumption and demographic items*. Through statistical routines (clustering and others) the marketer attempts to find out if people can be grouped together into distinct groups. Each group represents a different pattern of needs for and consumption of products and services. Once these groups are identified, the communicator is able to direct his product to appeal to one or several segments.

Another segmentation approach often used by communicators is based on product or brand usage by consumers. Usage segmentation can take a number of directions. For example, the communicator/ marketer may want to identify various segments of users for a particular product category or users of the company's brand. In other cases, one may want to segment users into those who buy frequently versus those who only buy occasionally (either product or brand) or into those users who usually purchase just one brand versus those who switch from brand to brand. It may also be useful for the marketer to understand how segments arise based on different product-usage situations. Any usage segmentation approach needs to specify the relevant dimensions of interest.

6.7.3. Lifestyle Profiles of the Social Classes[13]

Consumer research has found evidence that within each of the social classes, there is a constellation of specific lifestyle factors (shared beliefs, attitudes, activities and behaviours) that tend to distinguish the members of each class from the members of all other social classes.

To capture the lifestyle composition of the various social class groupings, Table 6.2, presents a consolidated portrait, pieced together from numerous sources, of the members of the following six social classes; upper-upper class, lower-upper class, upper-middle class, lower-middle class, upper-lower class and lower-lower class. Each of these profiles is only a generalised picture of the class. People in any class may possess values, attitudes and behavioural patterns that are a hybrid of two or more classes.

Lifestyle differences should be considered when choosing appropriate appeals to communicate with the core members of any social-class group. For example, Table 6.3 provides lifestyle information regarding consumer 65 years and above, with annual incomes of at least 30 lakhs. It shows that, compared with national averages, these affluent older consumers are three times more likely to own a vacation home, taken more than three times as many foreign trips, are nearly twice as involved in news and current affairs and are wine, tennis and golf enthusiasts. The table also indicates other types of lifestyle activities valued by these older affluent consumers.

---

12 *Ibid.*, pp. 62-63.

13 Schiffman, L.G. and Kanuk, L.L., *Consumer Behaviour*, Sixth Edition, p. 387.

Table 6.2. Social Class Profiles

The Upper-Upper Class—Country Club Establishment
• Small number of well-established families • Belong to best country clubs and sponsor major charity events. • Serve as trustees for local colleges and hospitals. • Prominent physicians and lawyers • May be heads of major financial institutions, owners of major long-established firms. • Accustomed to wealth, so do not spend money conspicuously.
The Lower-Upper Class—New Wealth
• Not quite accepted by the upper crust of society. • Represent "new money". • Successful business executives • Conspicuous users of their new wealth.
The Upper-Middle Class—Achieving Professionals
• Have neither family status nor unusual wealth. • Career-oriented. • Young successful professionals, corporate managers and business owners. • Most are college graduates, many with advanced degrees. • Active in professional, community and social activities. • Have a keen interest in obtaining the "better things in life". • Their homes serve as symbols of their achievements. • Consumption is often conspicuous. • Very child-oriented.
The Lower-Middle Class—Faithful Followers
• Primarily non-managerial white-collar workers and highly paid blue-collar workers. • Want to achieve "respectability" and be accepted as good citizens. • Want their children to be well behaved. • Tend to be churchgoers and are often involved in church-sponsored activities. • Prefer a neat and clean appearance and tend to avoid faddish or highly styled clothing. • Constitute a major market for do-it-yourself products.
The Upper-Lower Class—Security-Minded Majority
• The largest social segment • Solidly blue-collar • Strive for security (sometimes gained from union membership)

• View work as a means to "buy" enjoyment • Want children to behave properly • High wage earned by this group may spend impulsively • Interested in items that enhance their leisure time (*e.g.,* TV sets, hunting equipment) • Husbands typically have a strong "macho" self-image. • Males are sports fans, heavy smokers, beer drinkers.
The Lower-Lower Class—Rock Bottom
• Poorly educated, unskilled labourers • Often out of work • Children are often poorly treated • Tend to live a day-to-day existence.

Table 6.3. Segment Profile: 65 Years and Over, Income 30 lakhs above

The Top Ten Lifestyles	**Great Outdoors**
• Stock/Bond Investments • Supports Health Charities • Own a Vacation Home/Property • Grandchildren • Real Estate Investment • Military Veteran in Household • Foreign Travel • Current Affairs/Politics • Frequent Flyer • Attend Cultural/Arts Events	• Boating/Sailing • Camping/Hiking • Fishing Frequently • Hunting/Shooting • Motorcycles • Recreational Vehicles • Wildlife/Environmental
Homelife	**Sports, Fitness and Health Households**
• Avid Book Reading • Bible/Devotional Reading • Gardening • Grandchildren • Home Furnishing/Decorating • House Plants • Own a Cat • Own a Dog • Subscribe to Cable TV • Vegetable Gardening	• Bicycling Frequently • Dieting/Weight Control • Golf • Health/Natural Foods • Improving your Health • Physical Fitness/Exercise • Running/Jogging • Snow Skiing Frequently • Tennis Frequently • Walking for Health • Watching Sports on TV

Good-life	Hobbies and Interests
• Attend Cultural/Arts Events	• Automotive Work
• Fashion Clothing	• Buy Pre-recorded Videos
• Fine Arts	• Career-Oriented Activities
• Foreign Travel	• Current Affairs/Politics
• Frequent Flyer	• Sewing
• Travel for Pleasure	• Home Workshop
• Wines	• Supports Health Charities
• Own a Vacation Home	• Coin/Stamp Collection
Investing & Money	**High-tech Activities**
• Casino Gambling	• Home Vide Games
• Entering Sweepstakes	• Own a CD Player
• Moneymaking Opportunities	• Science/New Technology
• Real Estate Investments	• Use a Personal Computer
• Stock/Bond Investment	• VCR Recording

6.8 EFFECTS OF ADVERTISING ON LIFESTYLES[14]

Advertising by its very nature receives wide exposure. Furthermore, it presumably has an effect on what people buy and thus on their activities. Because of this exposure and of its role as a persuasive vehicle, it is argued that it has an impact on the values and lifestyles of society and that this impact has its negative as well as positive side. Richard Pollay, in an article titled "Quality of Life in the Padded Sell...", for example states that appeals to mass markets tend to promote conformity; appeals to status promote envy, pride and social competitiveness; appeals to fears promote anxiety; appeals newness promote disrespect for tradition durability, experience, or history; appeals to youth promote reduced family authority; and appeals to sexuality promote promiscuity.

The key issues are which value and lifestyles are to be encouraged as healthy, which are to be avoided and what relative impact or influence advertising has on them. Despite their difficulty and their relationship to deep philosophical questions, they are well worth addressing to illuminate judgements and assumptions about our market system and society that are too often glossed over.

It is interesting that the issues are hotly debated at the international level and those countries, particularly third world countries, are vitally interested in them. The 'United Nations' UNESCO organisation, for example, put together a sixteen-member commission to study the **"totality of communication problems in modern society"**. The Commission's report, which became known as the "MacBride Report" produced eighty-two recommendations directed largely at the potential

[14] Batra, R., Myers, J.G. and Aaker, D.A., *Advertising Management*, Fifth Edition, pp.679-682.

dangers of advertising and the needs for controls on advertising practices. As might be expected, reactions to the report were highly polarized with support largely coming from third world countries and opposition coming from industry representatives in developed countries.

Three issues that have attracted particular attention are:

(*i*) the relationship of advertising to materialism;

(*ii*) the role, advertising has played in creating harmful stereotypes of women and ethnic minorities; and

(*iii*) the possible contribution of advertising in promoting harmful products.

6.8.1. Materialism

Materialism is defined as the tendency to give undue importance to material interests. Presumably, there is a corresponding lessening of importance to non-material interests such as love, freedom and intellectual pursuits.

'Bauer and Greyser' argue, however, that although people do spend their resources on material things, they do so in the pursuit of non-material goals. They buy camping equipment to achieve a communion with nature, music systems to understand the classic composers and an automobile for social status. The distinctive aspect of our society is not the possession of national goods, but the extent to which material goods are used to attain non-material goods.

Does advertising create or foster materialism or merely reflect values and attitudes that are created by more significant sociological force? Mary Gardiner Jones develops the argument that advertising, especially television advertising is a contributing force.

The conscious appeal in the television commercial ... is essentially materialistic. Central to the message of the television consumer is the premise that it is the acquisition of things, which will gratify our basic inner needs and aspirations. It is the message of the commercial that all of the major problems confronting an individual can be instantly eliminated by the application of some external force—the use of a product. Externally derived solutions are thus made the prescription for life's difficulties... In the world of television commercials all of life's problems are difficulties, all of our individual yearnings, hopes and fears can yield instantly to a material solution and are which can work instantly without any effort, skill or trouble on our part.

The issues to which the topic concern is the role of advertising in creating harmful stereotypes and in promoting harmful products.

6.8.2. Promoting Stereotypes

The accusation that advertising has contributed to the role stereotyping of women and ethnic minorities has been supported by several studies. A host of questions are raised. Does role stereotyping continue in advertising? What negative impact does advertising have in creating stereotypes or what positive forces does it have in breaking them down? In the absence of definitive answers to these questions, what should the advertiser's position be? Should countering role stereotypes be one objective of advertising? It is known that portrayals of women in advertising which are consistent with the roles played by women in the viewing audience is more effective than when the roles are inconsistent.

Thus, advertising showing women in traditional roles is less effective with an audience of professional women and vice versa.

6.8.3. Promoting Harmful Products

There is a national concern with the problems of alcohol and cigarettes. Local legislators have increased taxes to around 45 per cent of total alcohol sales and toughened drunk-driving laws.

Concerning alcohol, a group calling itself SMART (Stop Merchandising Alcohol on Radio and Television) has proposed a ban on wine and beer advertising. There have been other less severe proposals as well. Some have suggested counter ads, which would dramatically "advertise" the health disadvantages of drinking. Similar movements against cigarettes were effective and led to the banning of cigarette advertising on television. Others have proposed that beer advertising (like wine advertising) stop using sports figures in their advertising. There is already a ban on the use of active athletes and actual drinking in beer commercials.

The basic argument is that alcohol, like cigarettes is a "harmful" product. Alcohol is unhealthy for the individual and is indirectly responsible for injuries and deaths resulting from drunk drivers. Why encourage people to use alcohol via advertising? The use of sports stars whom kids admire suggests that alcohol is not only harmless but that it is associated with fun-loving, healthy people.

There are a variety of counter-arguments. First, there is no evidence that advertising, which is geared toward brand choice rather than increasing consumption, affects total alcohol consumption. Multi-countries studies do not indicate that those countries, which already banned alcohol advertising on television, have lower consumption than other countries, which do not. Over time, observations are similar. Beer advertising has increased substantially in the first half of the 1980s, while sales dropped during the same period. On the other hand, per capita alcohol consumption has risen during the past thirty years at the same rate as in Western Europe, without, of course, any advertising. In addition to this basic counter arguments, there is also the suggestion that:

1. A ban on advertising would prohibit product innovation that may be helpful. For example, firms have introduced products such as the wine coolers and the low-alcohol beers.
2. The real goal is to return to alcohol prohibition, which did not work—it only created a revenue source for gangsters and made lawbreakers of the rank and file.
3. Many other products could be criticised on similar grounds. Should advertising for automobiles be banned when high performance and sportiness is stressed since that could contribute to reckless driving?

An interesting study by Camille Schuster and Christine Powell[15] showed that the Sloan-Ketting report linking cancer and smoking, warning labels on cigarettes and implementation of the Fairness Doctrine, which gave equal time to antismoking messages in the 1950s and 1960s, all resulted in declines in cigarette consumption. However, in all cases, the declines were short-lived and consumption would generally recover and continue upward a year or so after the announcements. In contrast, the outright banning of cigarette advertising on radio and television in 1970s had little negative impact on cigarette consumption. In fact, consumption increased after the ban was put into

---

[15] Mohan Manendra, *Advertising Management*, p. 683.

effect. Thus, outlawing advertising in the case of either cigarettes or alcohol may not be the most effective way of handling the problem.

6.9 COMMUNICATION AND ATTITUDE CHANGE[16]

In modern marketing, persuasive communication plays probably the most vital role in facilitating the flow of goods from the manufacturers or producer to the ultimate consumer or user. Persuasive communication occurs most conspicuously through mass communication in the world of market, which the layman understands as advertising. Mass communication is unique in significance as,

(*i*) it is the major means of consumer persuasion as it is evidenced by the mammoth investment made in commercial advertising.

(*ii*) it draws more attention and is subject to discussions and criticism because of its conspicuousness over face-to-face persuasion.

(*iii*) it transmits messages to the mass; and thus can be readily screened out by the recipient. This means great difficulties for managers.

6.9.1. The Nature of Communication

In communication, a message is transmitted by the sender or source; and the receiver receives it by grasping the intended point. There is communus or commonness between the sender's message and the interpretation of the same by the receiver after receiving it.

6.9.2. Interpersonal Communication

When there is communication between two persons, the process at its simplest form takes place in the following manner.[17]

Figure 6.2 suggests that a communication between two persons takes place when there is a sender or communicator who encodes the ideas he wants to communicate either in the medium of a language, signs, written or verbal; and sends through a channel(s) to a receiver or communicatee who in turn deciphers or decodes the encoded message *i.e.*, interprets the ideas of the sender in the same way. The decoded messages by the communicatee are fed-back to the communicator to complete the communication by either a proper action or another communication to reciprocate it.

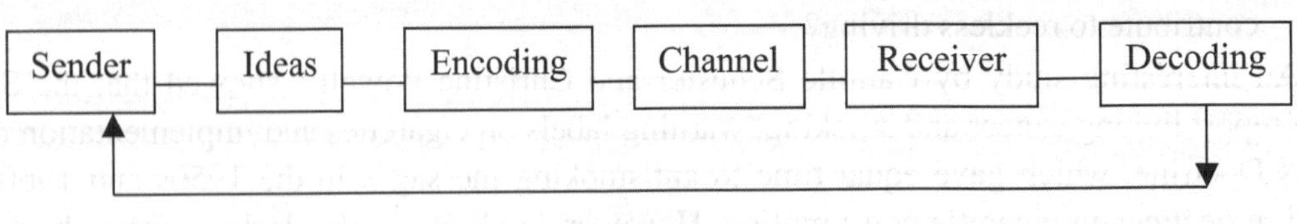

Fig. 6.2. Interpersonal Communication

[16] Engel, Kollat and Blackwell, *op. cit.*, pp. 308-347.

[17] Prasad, L.M., *Principles and Practice of Management*, Sultan Chand & Sons, New Delhi, p. 490.

Communication can only be complete or proper when there is commonness of understanding between the communicator and communicatee. The message communicator sends must be received by the latter in the same way intended by the former. Any lapse in any of the steps described above can only be tantamount to miscommunication or no-communication. Going a step further, interpersonal communication can further be represented in the Figures 6.3 and 6.4.

In Figure 6.3[18] the concept of noise is introduced, which is a common factor to all the steps of communication including feedback. Noise is the reason of distortion of the message of all the stages as it travels from the source and comes back to the source through the feedback system from the receiver. Figure 6.4[19] also basically has the same structure and same elements. As per this model, the communicator has both an intended content and an intended effect for the message. In order to encode the intent, the communicator must place himself in the shoes of the communicatee or the receiver through the process of empathy, which starts right from childhood. As a child grows, he is introduced to the expectations of those around him. This helps him in acquiring a common set of meanings and definitions, which helps him in communicating to the others. The intent is encoded into a message through the use of signs, signals, or symbols. Symbols become language when they become commonly understood by many, signifying particular referents. Thus words are used as symbols for external objects or reference even when they are absent or non-existent. The medium through an interpersonal message sent is known as the channel. It can be spoken words as in the case of a verbal communication, or gestures and posture as in the case of non-verbal communication.

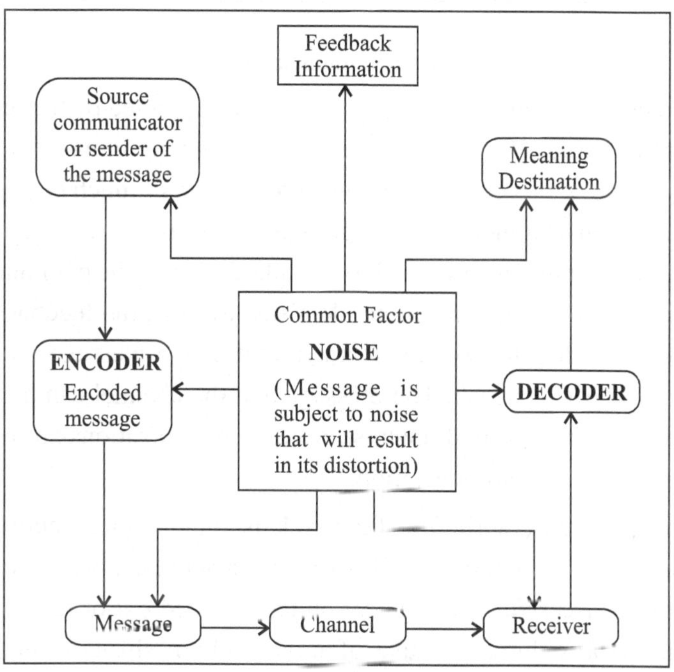

Fig. 6.3. The Communication Model

[18] Sherlekar and Sherlekar, *Principles of Business Management*, Himalaya Publishing House, Bombay, p. 309.

[19] Engel, Kollat and Blackwell, *Consumer Behaviour*, op. cit., p. 309.

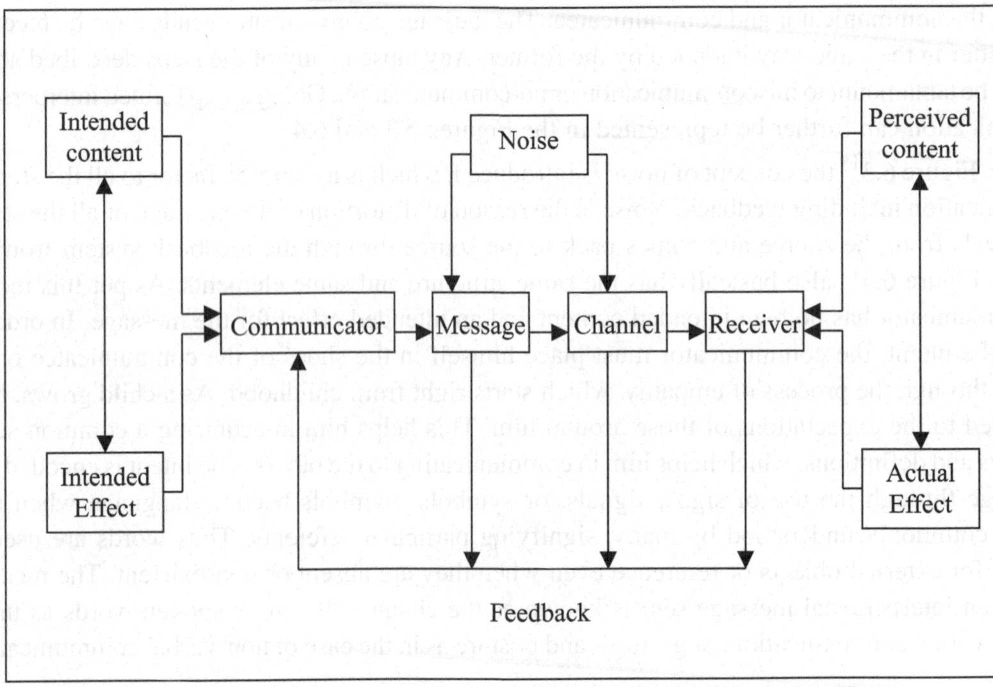

Fig. 6.4. The Communication Model

Communication occurs when the content of the message pressed by the receiver corresponds to that which was transmitted. Because of the common phenomena of selective attention, comprehension and retention, a successful communication will very much be dependent on the fact whether receiver's motivational influences are regarded or not. If the motivational influences are positive for the receiver, the communication will be completed. If not, the communication may fail in most cases. A successful communication can be identified through the feedback coming from the receiver. In case of poor results, the communicator modifies the message and tries the steps of communication to get a proper feedback. The message and the channel can be distorted by noise, which arises if the receiver's background, interest, needs and dispositions are not properly heeded before getting into the process of communication.

Two-way communication with free feedback is much more accurate in developing understanding than one-way communication with zero feedback. Feedback is essential in some or other form to find out if a successful communication has resulted out of the process. A chance of miscommunication is always there because of noise, which shrouds the entire process of communication like an umbrella. Noise is any kind of interference in interpersonal and organisational communication reducing the accuracy of communication. Noise can be disturbing in a communication in its internal sense; but the other kinds of disturbances like errors in writing or mechanical failures can also be termed as noise. The office grapevine *i.e.,* informal communication can also work as noise in the case of formal communication.

6.10. TYPES OF COMMUNICATION[20]

6.10.1. Formal Communication

Such communication takes place between superiors and subordinates as per the defined structure of the organisation for the smooth conduct of business. Formal communication is an open form of communication.

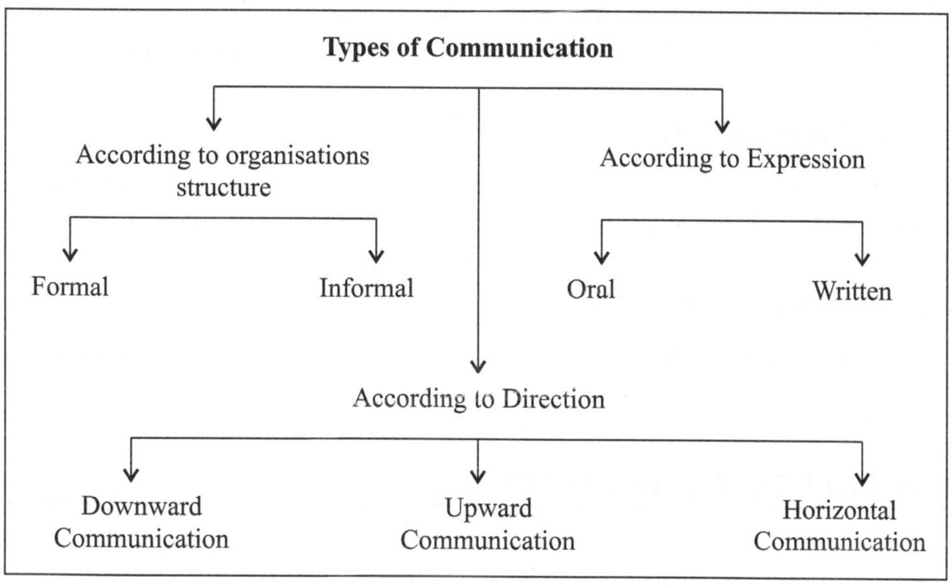

Fig. 6.5. Types of Communication

6.10.2. Informal Communication

It is also known as grapevine; and is free from all formalities. It arises in organisations due to informal relationships between various people in various levels of the human relationships rather than formal relationships prescribed by the structure. The advantage with this is that certain information, which one cannot be transmitted through official channels, can be disseminated through the grapevine. On the contrary, grapevine can also cause noise in informal communication.

6.10.3. Downward Communication

Flow of communication from superior to subordinates is downward communication in an organisation.

[20] Gupta, R.S., Sharma, B.D. and Bhalla, N.S., *Business Management*, Kalyani Publishers, New Delhi, pp. 143-148.

6.10.4. Upward Communication

It is the reverse of downward communication, where subordinates are allowed to communicate back to their superiors. Such a state exists mostly in free-form organisations where two-way communication is a normal occurrence. Upward communication may not get distorted as an employee may not communicate to his superior in an honest manner, to keep him happy and impressed.

6.10.5. Horizontal Communication

It is the communication between people in the same level in an organisation. It is a peer communication, which provides social need satisfaction and leads to coordination.

6.10.6. Oral Communication

It is a direct face-to-face communication between two individuals. It can also take place in meetings, conferences, lectures and interviews.

6.10.7. Written Communication

Circulars, magazines, notes and manuals are some forms of written communication in organisations.

6.11 BARRIERS TO COMMUNICATION

6.11.1. Constructive Barriers[21]

A completely free system of communication in an organisation leads to chaos many times. Therefore, some barriers are intentionally established to inhibit the free flow of communications. It is sometimes argued that the effectiveness of communication is dependent more on the right selection of the transmission rather than the free flow of all communications. Thus, filtration in organisational communications is normally a constructive barrier. But sometimes it may lead to overdoing of it to hide one's weakness, especially when it is an upward communication.

6.11.2. Non-Constructive Barriers[22]

(*i*) Unsound objectives of the organisations lead to the failures in communication by creating barriers with respect to organisation-wide communication programmes. This happens because the organisations in pursuit of the unsound objectives (*e.g.* dividing the workers, influencing them against union leaders, etc.) try to either misinform or hide information proper from being communicated.

---

21 McFarland, D.E., *Management Principles and Practices*, pp. 572-573.

22 *Ibid.*, pp. 573-578.

(*ii*) Organisational blocks are created on the way of free communication flow when a rigid structural channel of communication is prescribed to be followed in the organisation. This system prohibits the subordinate to communicate to any one other than his immediate subordinate. But it can be said that a good communication system prevails when in an organisation, one is free to communicate to any other member who can help him with his problems.[23] But such a system should be prohibited when the superior is forced into a compromising situation.

(*iii*) Semantic blocks can be created when the meaning intended by the sender may vary greatly from the meaning understood by the receiver. This happens because words have varied meanings depending on one's behaviour and experience. To be more precise, it is not only the words but actions, implications and the entire situational content that produce misunderstandings.

(*iv*) Human relations and positions also create barriers on the way of effective communication. Status is the degree of importance others attach to the position or to the individual occupying it. Thus, status can impede the communication process, especially in case of upward flow since subordinates quite often feel that they do not speak the same language as their superiors. A considerable amount of unwanted filtration occurs in such cases.

6.11.3. Other Barriers of Communication[24]

(*i*) Management is lack of attention to the interests of the people with whom it intends to communicate, frequently creates a barrier to effective communication. This is so because the management is attentive to listen to only that, which is in line with its interest.

(*ii*) Emotional attitudes of the sender and receiver also create barriers to communication. Quick-tempered superiors are avoided by the subordinates for this reason.

(*iii*) Half-listening or lack of patience to listen carefully also causes barriers to effective communication.

(*iv*) Perception of the world by one in terms of one's needs, level of education, cultural factors, social environments, etc. also creates barrier to communication. Everyone tries to interpret and understand the information communicated to him from his own viewpoint.

(*v*) There are also other barriers to communication, which are situational or arise from specific situation or context. Examples of these are lack of ability to communicate, inattention by the receiver, unclarified assumptions by the sender and receiver, noise, etc.

---

[23] Learned, E.P., Ulrich, U.N. and Booz, D.R., *Executive Action*, Boston Division Research Graduate School of Business Administration, Harvard University, 1951, pp. 111-113.

[24] Gupta, R.S., Sharma, B.D. and Bhallan, N.S., *op. cit.*, p. 150-151.

6.11.4. Ways to Effective Communication

(*i*) Communicator must be clear in his mind about the information to be communicated. It must be communicated in a language easily understandable by both the communicator and the communicatee.

(*ii*) Message to be communicated must be adequate and complete in all respects to avoid any kind of misinformation or under-information.

(*iii*) Self-contradictory messages create chaos and confusion and thus, should be avoided.

(*iv*) Feedback in words or actions is all important to ensure a proper communication, expressions or emotions on the receiver's face also work as feedback of effective communication.

(*v*) The receiver must be understood by the communicator with respect to the environment in all respects before engaging in communication. What, when and in what manner the communicator would like to be communicated in a similar environment and position should be the question posed to himself by the communicator. Then only he can well realise the position of the receiver and understand him better to have an effective communication.

(*vi*) In an organisation, consultation with others before communication provides objectivity to the message and more insight into it.

(*vii*) Selection of the right medium for communication whether oral or written, is equally important for effective communication.

(*viii*) The language, tone, expression and emotion of the communicator - all play a definite role in good communication.

(*ix*) Timing and timeliness of communication is an important as anything else.

(*x*) Communication supported by action of the communicator leads to effective communication.

(*xi*) Patient listening also leads to better communication.

(*xii*) When there is an environment of trust and confidence in an organisation, honest reporting takes place, which amounts to effective communication.

(*xiii*) Communication system in an organisation should be kept open and alive all round the year. It should not be made a one-time event or practised for a brief period.

6.12 MASS COMMUNICATION[25]

In such communications, a message is transmitted to a group of individuals roughly at the same time. In mass communication, the communicator normally is not an individual, but the output of many individuals in an organisation. This means simply that mass communication is undertaken by

[25] Engel, Kollat and Blackwell, *Consumer Behaviour*, op. cit., pp. 311-313.

the organisations, as in the case of advertisements by business organisations or messages transmitted by educational, religious and government agencies. In all such instances, no one individual coins the message to be communicated to the mass. It is the interaction of many individuals in the organisations, which gives birth to the message to be communicated. Since such interaction is a precondition for the determination of the message content, the speed of communication is drastically reduced. Collective decision on the message content is a pre-requisite in most cases of mass communication.

The message here is impersonal in nature, unlike the face-to-face interpersonal communications. The target in mass communication is a group of individuals, which makes the content of the message very difficult to be oriented to have the right impact on a given individual. Message alteration flexibility is absent in mass communication when it comes to creae the optimum impact on individuals of a group. Thus, just the way the communicator is the output of many individuals in an organisation, the communicatees are also many in mass communication. The mass communication model[26] given in Figure 6.6 elaborates the theory in detail.

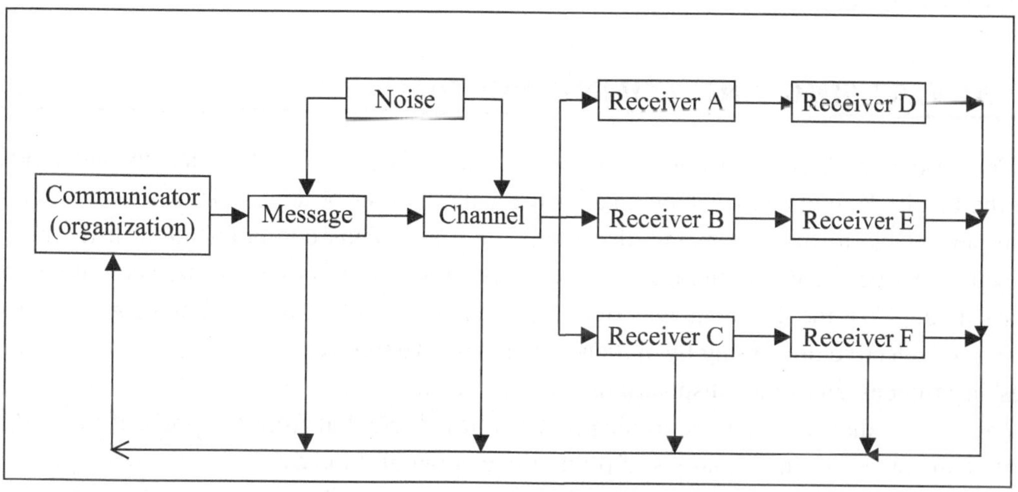

Fig. 6.6. Model of Mass Communication

The roles of the communicator and the receivers are pretty much clear from the discussions made above in the light of the model of mass communication. The channels in such communications are mainly the mass media like television, radio, magazines, newspapers, etc. All these media are either printed or aired at regular intervals, which further reduces speed and flexibility of communication. Because of the media used, communication necessarily becomes indirect since the communicator and the recipient are not simultaneously present in time or space. The greatest advantage with this kind of communication is, however, that a large group can be reached relatively economically.

Receivers are in groups in mass communication. Each individual receiver in the group selectively responds to the message. All such messages aim at creating a pronounced situation of selective

[26] Engel, J.F., Wales, H.G. and Warshaw, M.R., *Mass Communication, Promotional Strategy,* revised edition, Homewood, Irwin, 1971, p. 24.

attention, comprehension and retention so that all the individuals of the group receive the message in the way it is intended. But the probability of reaching all the recipients of a target, with one message successfully is much lower. This is the greatest problem with the mass media. Besides, the effect of mass communication of the message is very much influenced by the word-of-mouth interpersonal communication of the members of the target audience. A positive word-of-mouth filler by members of the target audience about a mass media message, can have a positive effect on another member of the same target group, when he himself is exposed to the message through the mass media. An unfavourable word-of-mouth contact, however, can cause a negative effect in the same manner. Unlike interpersonal communication, feedback in mass communication is a very difficult proposition. On the same token, feedback if at all obtained is considerably delayed in case of the latter. Because feedback in the latter is obtainable only by direct survey of the audience, which is time consuming. Besides, due to the late availability of feedback, no change or alteration in the message is possible at the time of communication to have the right effect. However, feedback helps in planning out future strategies for messages.

6.13 ADVERTISING AND COMMUNICATION

Person-to-person communication, as is in the case of personal selling, has the advantage of getting the feedback right away, which enables the seller to alter or adjust his message on the spot in a way acceptable to the buyer; and also motivating him. Thus communication difficulties are minimised in interpersonal communication; and are less than those present in mass communication. The mass media have the disadvantages of delayed feedback, inflexibility of message and greater probability of selective processing by audience members. Therefore, it is difficult to achieve major changes in attitudes and other dispositions. Despite all these weaknesses, mass media allow to reach a massive audience rather economically, when it is looked at from the point of view of cost per individual contacted. In all matters of promotional strategies in advertising the best approach is to make trade-off between communication effectiveness *i.e.,* flexibility and case of feedback; and cost per individual reached.

6.13.1. Using the Mass Media[27]

Consumer information processing consists of the four stages—exposure, attention, comprehension and retention. Expanded information processing model has three broad phases, viz., (1) exposure, (2) reception (attention, comprehension and retention) and (3) attitude/ behaviour modification. Each stage is necessary for the next stage to occur; but a state is not a sufficient condition to guarantee the occurrence of the next stage. To be more precise, only a segment of the total audience is likely to be exposed to a communication message. Even though there is exposure, it is only probable that the message will be received and processed. And even though it is processed, it is again, only probable that it will lead to any attitude or behaviour modification. However, it is

[27] Engel, Kollat and Blackwell, *Consumer Behaviour*, op. cit., pp. 313-318.

noteworthy that if attitude or behaviour change has come, then the message must have been received and processed. In the same token, if the message has been received and processed, the exposure to the message must have been preceded.

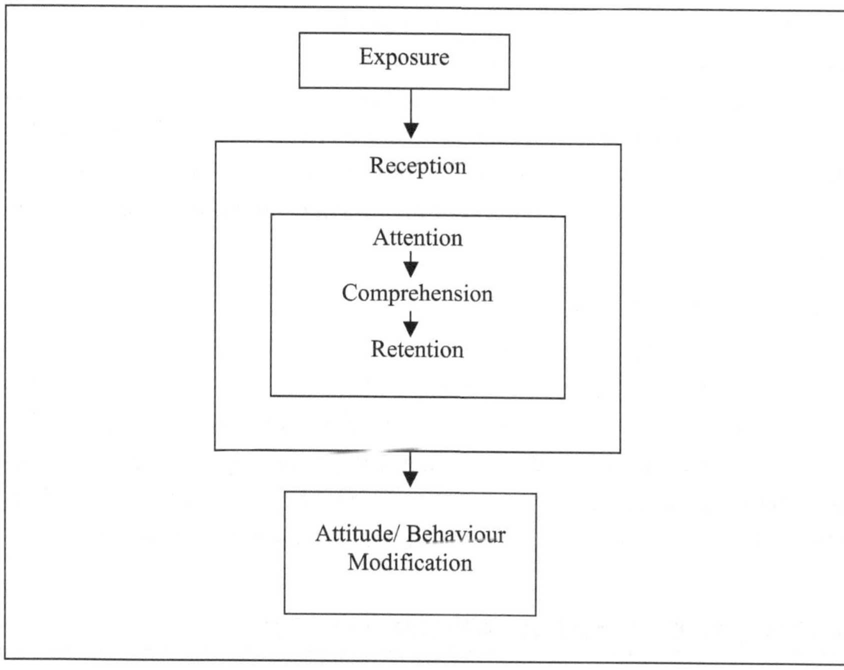

Fig. 6.7. Expanded Information Processing Model[28]

6.13.1.1. Exposure

Its success very much depends on the proper selection of the media. The right selection of media is dependent on the following factors. Audiences gave to the defined in precise demographic terms first. Then using the media audiences data, those media are selected for transmission of the message; which most closely reach the target groups.

6.13.1.2. Reception

The concept reception is being delineated in the above model, consists of three stages of attention, comprehension and retention. Attention occurs when there is a focus within the central control unit of an incoming stimulus. Once the stimulus is attended to by the central control unit, the stimulus is then processed for meaning. The response of the individual when presented with a new stimulus is termed as the orientation reaction.[29] This response mobilises the central nervous system in the form of arousal. The stimulation of orientation response can be done more effectively by using stimulus patterns like novelty and surprise, intensity, colour and conditioned stimuli. The conditional stimuli are those for which a previously learned pattern of response is called forth. When the stimulus

[28] *Ibid.*, p. 314.

[29] Lyan, R. *Attention, Arousal and the Orientation Reaction*, Oxford, Pergamon, 1966.

gets habituated, the ability to generate orientation reaction fades. Habituation is brought about by lower stimulus intensity, longer duration of stimulus, easy grasp of stimulus details, lesser duration between exposures, etc. But when a stimulus has become conditioned so that it is not personal significance to the recipient, despite repetitions, will not be habituated. Habituation is a great problem for the advertisers as they always intend the orientation reaction of the recipient to be alive and active for the message. But this is a very difficult task because most products are highly familiar, and hardly can anything be said in a message that is truly novel or new. Besides, the noise barrier created by the glut of competing messages, makes it very difficult for one message to break through and capture attention. Therefore, advertisers resort to devices like novelty and contrast, manipulation of intensity through variation of size and position of the message, and use of colour to bring about the orientation reaction.

6.13.1.3. Novelty and contrast

Contrast is frequently used in advertising messages to make them effective by making them look novel. In the midst of many colour messages, a black and white advertisement featuring an unusual amount of white space with no print or illustration can stand out clearly. An unusually-shaped container or package captures attention when it is put among products in the usual-shaped containers or packages. An announcers' voice can be used as a sharp contrast if a product is advertised during the breaks between programmes like classical music or ballets etc.

6.14 ADVERTISING COMMUNICATION SYSTEM[30]

The most important factor to be considered in planning advertising, in addition to the marketing plan, is an understanding of the communication and persuasion process. Although much has been researched and written about the effects of advertising and how it works, it is important to appreciate that this is a subject about which there are few definite answers. There are perhaps as many theories about how advertising "works" as there are people who work in advertising and it is impossible to discuss them all here. An appreciation from the process by which advertising works is of great value in designing advertising plans - plans that maximise the advertisement's impact on the consumer.

Figure mentioned below shows one simple model of the advertising communication system. Advertising communication always involves a perception process and four of the elements shown in the model:

- the source;
- a message;
- a communication channel; and
- a receiver.

In addition, the receiver will sometimes become a source of information by talking to friends or associates. This type of communication is termed word-of-mouth communication and it involves

[30] Botra, R., Myers, J.G. and Aaker, D.A., *Advertising Management*, pp. 45-48.

social interactions between two or more people and the important ideas of group influence and the diffusion of information.

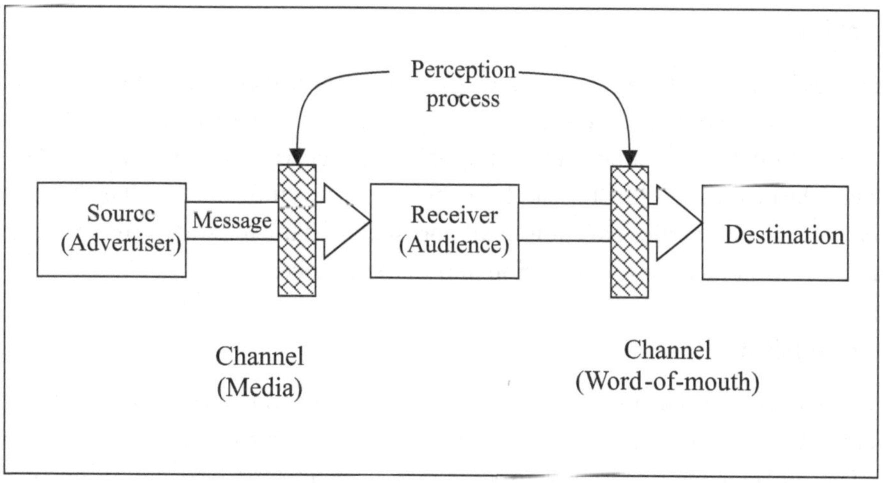

Fig. 6.8. Model of the Advertising Communication System

6.14.1. Source

The source of a message in the advertising communication system is the point of which the message originates. There are many types of "sources" in the context of advertising, such as the company offering the product, the particular brand or the spokesperson used. The various dimensions of source effects such as credibility and attractiveness are of obvious importance in deciding how best and through whom to communicate the advertising message.

6.14.2. Message

The message refers to both the content and execution of the advertisement. It is the totality of what is perceived by the receiver of the message. The message can be executed in a great variety of ways and can include, for example, the use of humour and fear.

6.14.3. Channel

The message is transmitted through some channel from the source to the receiver. The channel is an advertising communication system consists of one or more kinds of media, such as radio, television, newspapers, magazines, billboards, point-of-purchase displays and so on. The impact of communication can be different for different media. Word-of-mouth communication, as mentioned above, represents another channel that is of special interest because it can sometimes play a key role in an advertising campaign. It should be noted that any communication system has a channel capacity. There is only so much information that can be moved through it and only so much that a receiver will be motivated to receive and capable of processing. For example, there is a physical limit to the number of advertisements that can be shown on prime time. Shortage of available advertising time can be a real problem.

6.14.4. Receiver

The receiver in an advertising communication system is also called the target audience. Thus, the receiver can be described in terms of audience segmentation variables, lifestyle, benefits sought, demographics and so on. Of particular interest might be the receiver's involvement in the product ad the extent to which he or she is willing to search for and/or process information. It is the characteristics of the receiver - the demographic, psychological and social characteristics - that provide the basis for understanding communications, persuasion and market process.

6.14.5. Destination

The communication model in Fig. 6.8 does not stop at the receiver but allows for the possibility that the initial receiver might engage in word-of-mouth communication to the ultimate destination of the message. The receiver then becomes an interim source and the destination becomes another receiver. As mentioned earlier, word-of-mouth communication resulting from advertising can be a critical part of a campaign. The reality is that for some products the absence of word-of-mouth communication can be fatal. It is only the word-of-mouth communication that has the credibility, comprehensiveness, and impact to affect the ultimate behaviour of a portion of the audience. Furthermore, advertising can actually stimulate word-of-mouth activity. Even when it cannot stimulate it, a knowledge of its appropriateness and power can be very helpful.

An advertising message can have a variety of effects upon the receiver. It can:

- create awareness;
- communicate information about attributes and benefits;
- develop or change an image or personality;
- associate a brand with feelings and emotions;
- create group norms;
- precipitate behaviour.

6.15 ADVERTISING EXPOSURE MODEL

Figure 6.9 mentioned below presents another model of the communication and persuasion process that shows the various processes that can occur after consumers are exposed to an advertisement. **First,** exposure to the advertisement can create awareness about the brand, leading to a feeling of familiarity with it. **Second,** information about the brand's benefits and the attributes on which the benefits are based can register with the consumer can also result from exposure to the ad. **Third,** advertisements can also generate feelings in an audience that they begin to associate with the brand or its consumption. **Fourth,** though the choice of the spokesperson and various executional devices the advertisement can lead to the creation of an image for the brand, often called "brand personality". **Fifth,** the advertisement can create the impression that the brand is favoured by the consumer's pecrs, or experts - individuals and groups, the consumer likes to emulate. This is often, how products and brands are presented as being fashionable. These five elements can create a favourable liking, or attitude, toward the brand, which in turn should lead to purchase action. Sometimes the advertiser will attempt to spur purchasing action directly by providing a reminder or by attacking reasons why the consumer may be postponing that action.

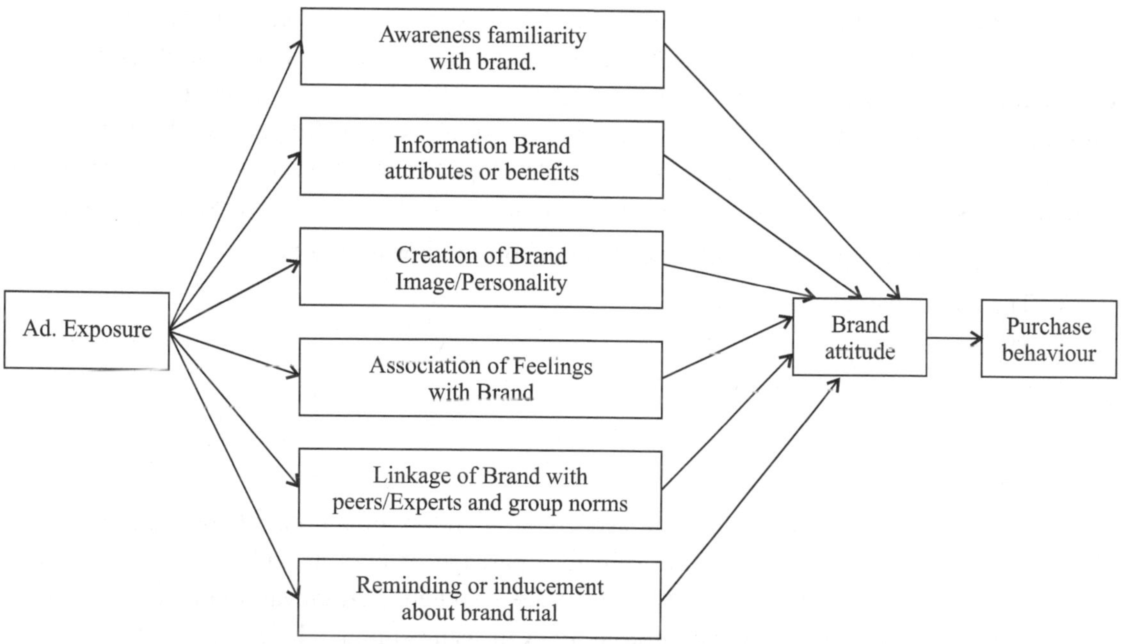

Fig. 6.9. A model of communication/persuasion process

These two models help us to understand how and why consumers acquire, process and use advertising information. It is also important at the planning stage to develop a good understanding of where advertising fits into the total pool of information and influence sources to which a consumer is exposed.

Understanding information processing invariably leads to the need for understanding a wide range of other important psychological constructs, such as perception, learning, attitude formation and change, source effects, brand personality and image, cognitive and affective response and social factors such as group influence.

6.16 MASS COMMUNICATION RESEARCH

The greatest of all difficulties in mass communication is that the message gets screened out by the recipients. At that point there is no way of modifying and retransmitting the message. Therefore, great care is taken at the stage of message design. The probability of communication failure is also reduced through the use of research undertaken before the final message is sent. Such research is known as pre-testing.

6.16.1. Measurement of Attention Attraction

Measuring exposure on a pre-test basis is not possible as the message has to be placed in the actual media and on-the-spot monitoring on the recipient's behaviour has also got to be made. Thus, the first stage that can be pre-tested usually is attraction of attention. The procedure followed for pre-testing normally is that a sample of prospects is exposed to one or more messages under conditions ranging from presentation of three or four test advertisements in some type of booklet to full-scale exposure to an actual television or radio show or print publication. Sometime after exposure, the sample of prospects is asked to, recall or recognise the messages that they can, after re-exposure to the same message. Although this is a method to pre-test attraction of attention, yet it seems more like a test for retention. This is a test conducted on the basis of verbal response; and therefore, is not a full-proof test of attention. Instead, it becomes more a test of retention. To get over the weaknesses of such tests, many laboratory measures have been developed in recent years to focus on attention without resorting to verbal response.[31] A few of such measures which have attained prominence are:

1. Galvanic skin response (GSR) and Pupil dilation response (PDR)
2. The eye movement of camera
3. The tachistoscope, and
4. Binocular rivalry.

6.16.2. GSR and PDR

These two measures reflect different aspects of attention attraction.[32] GSR measures (1) a decline in the electrical resistance of the skin to a passage of current and (2) a change in the potential difference between two areas of body surface.[33] When GSR elevates upon exposure to a stimulus, it gives an accurate measure of arousal. PDR measures minute differences in pupil size as it dilates and contracts. It is a sensitive measure of the amount of information or load processed within the central control unit with the incoming stimulus. PDR measures effective or emotional response to a stimulus.[34] As per the Ohio State University research report, when GSR and PDR are both high, the stimulus in question generates good short-term and long-term retention. In other words, a high score on attention attraction is reflected by a corresponding high score on retention. This indicates that the stimulus has not been screened out in information processing.[35]

---

[31] Hensel, J.S. and Kollat, D.T., "Present and Projected Uses of Laboratory Equipment for Marketing and Advertising Research", paper presented at the American Marketing Association, Sept. 1970.

[32] Hensel, J.H., "Psychological Measures of Advertising Effectiveness, A Theoretical and Experimental Investigation", Doctoral Dissertation, Columbus, Ohio, Ohio State University, 1970.

[33] Blackwell, R.D., Hensel, J.S., Philips, M.D. and Sternthal, B., *Laboratory Equipment for Marketing Research*, Dubuque, Iowa, Kendal Hunt Publ. Co., 1970, p. 42.

[34] Hess, E.H. and Polt, J.M., "Pupil Size as Related to Interest Value of Visual Stimuli", vol. 132, 1990, p. 349-350.

[35] Engel, Kollat and Blackwell, *Consumer Behaviour*, op. cit., p. 320.

6.16.3. The Eye Movement Camera

This is a cumbersome process as viewing has to be done under unnatural conditions with the help of awkward equipment. In this method, eye movements the advertising copy is tracked with the aid of a specially designed camera. With this method it is possible to find out the parts of the message that capture and holds attention. Besides, it can also be found out if or not various elements are perceived in the intended order.

6.16.4. The Tachistoscope

This is basically a slide projector with attachments, which enable the researcher to present stimuli under varying conditions of speed and illumination. It can be used to access the rate at which a message conveys information.[36] The speed of response is recorded for various elements like illustration, product or brand name that comes through the message. Researchers show that high readership across usually correlate with the speed of recognition of the elements under analysis.

6.16.5. Binocular Rivalry

This method measures, which of the two competing stimuli first attracts attention.[37] In this technique, the stimuli are viewed through a stereoscopic device with an eyepiece. A different stimulus is projected to each eye. In this way the stimulus with the greater potential for attention attraction can be found out.[38]

6.17 ATTITUDE MODIFICATION

High retention and comprehension are not sufficient indication of communication success. The effect on attitude has got to be measured since high retention does not necessarily imply that there will be an eventual behavioural change. Of course, some disagree with this position and stop measurement at the recall stage. However, the others assess attitude change in the same manner as comprehension and recall. This is done by asking a group of respondents to rate the brand advertised, which it is exposed to, along with competitive brands using a number of evaluative criteria. Attitude scores before exposure to the advertised brand from a matched group are also collected. These two groups are selected in way that they do not differ significantly in the initial positions. The ratings of both the groups are then compared to give a measure of the attitude shift. Another pre-test method is to assess attitude change through the evaluation of the effects on counter-argumentation. Attitude change appears to take place as the recipient sub-vocally responds to the message. Attitudes can also be changed through somehow overcoming or suppressing counterarguments.

---

[36] Leavitt, C., "Intrigue in Advertising - The Motivational Effects of Visual Organisation", *Proceedings, 7th Annual Conference*, New York, Advertising Research Foundation, 1998, pp. 19-24.

[37] Caffyn, J.M., "Psychological Laboratory Techniques in Copy Research", *Journal of Advertising Research*, vol. 4, 1994, p. 48.

[38] *Ibid.*, p. 49.

6.18 BEHAVIOURAL CHANGE

This is very difficult to be evaluated without a full-scale field test. If any test has to be conducted, it has to be conducted in some type of forced choice situation. An example may be that consumers are asked to choose products to be given away through lottery. After their choices are made, they are exposed to advertisements made for this purpose in a theatre. Now they are asked to rate the products again as per their choice. The shift that can be observed can help in measuring choice with respect to behavioural change. However, despite the various methods discussed, it can be concluded that at the present time, there is no way to provide a definite indication that a message will be successful in generating attention, comprehension, recall and response.

6.19 COMPREHENSION AND RECALL TESTS

The method of doing it is to place the test message in a magazine or television programme and ask the respondent to be exposed to the messages under completely natural conditions. Recall or, recognition is then assessed at some period after exposure, usually within 24 hours. The assessment can be done aided or unaided by the assessor. The readers or viewers are then reassessed with reference to their recall ability of the brand advertised either through the aid of the assessor or without the aid. Their identification of the brand is further strengthened if they are able to pay back the message to some extent. Through these tests, comprehension and impact of the messages can also be assessed if the readers or viewers are able to state correctly the actual intended content of the copy. Although attention, attraction, retention and comprehension can be tested to a great extent by the recall and recognition tests, yet pre-tests cannot provide a definite measure of attitude or behavioural change. Attitude or behaviour change can only be measured by actually running the message in one or more test markets and later evaluating the results. But such experiments incur prohibitive costs and time requirement is too high.

6.20 ATTITUDE CHANGE[39]

Human beings resist a challenge to their attitudes, especially if the attitude is held strongly. But attitude is not impermeable all together. Lifestyle communication and persuasion is undertaken to change preferences, in the hope that behaviour will exhibit similar change. Mass communication is also undertaken with the same purpose in mind. This is done by emphasising on three areas. The areas are:

(*i*) Discrepancy between attitudes of members of the target audience and the position advocated by the message,

(*ii*) Variations in message content, and

(*iii*) Variations in message structure.

---

[39] Engel, Kollat and Blackwell, *Consumer Behaviour, op. cit.*, pp. 325-347.

(*i*) **Discrepancy between Recipients' Attitudes and the Message**

A lot of early researchers tried to prove that the more the message deviates from the recipient's own position, the greater the likelihood of attitude change in the desired direction. But later studies on the same issue found a lot of contradictory results. However, they all agree that after a certain point is reached, increasing discrepancy only reduces attitude change. This points out to the fact that discrepancy limit has to be determined beyond which it should not be pursued. So that the message stays within limit; and the required level of attitude change is achieved.

(*ii*) **The Source Credibility**

In general, there is a positive linear relationship between message discrepancy and attitude change, especially when it comes from a highly credible source. This is probably credible sources of message has led to the contradictions most likely. Receivers continue to accept arguments even if they forget the source if the source is credible. This is known as 'sleeper effect'. People tend to place greater confidence in a trustworthy source; and are quite receptive to the message delivered by him, even though the message is a substantial deviation from their own position. This way an attitude change is a most likely event. In the same token, a source with moderate or low credibility leads to non-acceptance of the discrepant message. It is however, very difficult to make an advertisement credible. Because its intention is very obvious; which is nothing but to persuade. A message, which deviates to a great extent from the recipient's own position, is likely to be screened out as he processes the stimulus. Repeated attempts to find out an acceptable level of discrepancy have failed.

Source credibility in advertisements is very difficult to create as such sources are not plentifully available in the commercial world. Those who are treated as credible sources do not like to lend their names to commercial advertisements. Nevertheless, a properly trained salesman can be used as a credible source of information in personal selling situations.

(*iii*) **The Effect of Ego Involvement**

The clash between an individual's own point of view and some voluntarily perceived information gives rise to an uncomfortable state of dissonance. This can be reduced by changing either one's own position or by downgrading the credibility of the source. It is easier to change attitude than to downgrade credibility. Therefore, for an advertiser, the best strategy is to induce high dissonance by a wide discrepancy. As per this theory, advertisement of a brand should deviate substantially from the recipients' attitude towards that brand. However, the opposing views about the individuals position affecting attitude (that is, agree strongly or disagree strongly) is not necessarily an indication of a person's commitment to position. In fact, a more appropriate measure is the number of divergent positions he will accept *i.e.*, the latitude of acceptance, against the ones he will reject *i.e.,* the latitude of rejection, or those towards which he will remain neutral *i.e.,* latitude of non-commitment.

A broad latitude of acceptance is the result of low commitment. In such cases, there can be a wide discrepancy between the position of the recipient and the position of the communication without engaging selective exposure, distortion and retention. On the contrary, if a message falls into the latitude of rejection, attitude change will not occur. Instead, selective perception will be engaged. Thus increase in discrepancy produces attitude change as long as it does not exceed the latitude or acceptance.

When a communication is written within the latitude of acceptance, assimilation effect is likely to take place; which means the communication appears to be closer to the subject's own position than it actually is. On the contrary, if the point of view of the communication falls within the latitude of rejection *i.e.,* the communication will be perceived farther away than it actually is, from the person's position. Therefore, source credibility and ego involvement moderate effects of message discrepancy on attitude change. It is important to note that the marketing communication are not viewed as highly credible. In view of that, the message should deviate only to a small extent from the attitude position of members of a target audience. Attitude change is best achieved by successive exposures, each of which should encompass only a small discrepancy. This is very important especially when the recipient's attitudes are based on ego involvement.

SUMMARY

Lifestyle, communication, persuasion and attitude change are essentially pursued in advertising. Consumer behaviour researches into these aspects in detail. Consumer behaviour is the acts of individuals directly involved in obtaining and using economic goods and services; and the decision processes that precede and determine these acts. It normally deals with the consumer buying rather than the consumption act.

A product, which would add to the presentation of one's life, is a potential candidate for lifestyle advertising. Lifestyle advertising tend to be equal for different products and to break this parity requires time and effort of agencies. Genuine lifestyle advertising makes an aspect of a lifestyle intrinsic to the brand position and personality. In India, textile firms resort to lifestyle advertising that is not distinctive. Good elite-style advertising should not become advertising for a good elite. We should, therefore, focus on perceived product differentiation. In most cases, lifestyle advertising seems to be a safe easy way out by creative people, without bothering to think of fresh ideas. Many have started using lifestyle advertising for me-too-products. Sometimes lifestyles portrayed are absolutely unrelated to the target audience. They tend to become visual clichés.

Buying behaviour does not include only the processes that an individual has to go through before a purchase act, it also includes the family decision-making process that leads to the individual's buying act.

Thus, advertisers have to heed these processes in order to influence the buying behaviour of the consumers to their favour. The decision-process approaches to analyse consumer behaviour includes the analysis of the events that precede and follow the purchase itself. Such analysis helps in understanding the purchase. Advertising, in today's world, the TV commercials, is probably one of the most vital and important events that precede the purchase and influence the decision-process for the purchase of the advertised product.

Consumer analysis is essential in evaluating and understanding the new market opportunities, choosing market segments, increasing efficiency of marketing strategy and tactics and improving retailing performance. The three approaches used to study consumer behaviour empirically are: (*a*) the distributive approach focusing on behavioural outcomes, (*b*) the morphological approach dealing with the way a decision is made and (*c*) the analytical approach, which is similar to the above but also assesses the impact of various influences like that of advertisements or displays on purchases. Due to the similarities between morphological approach and analytical approach, they are frequently referred to as the decision-process approach.

Lifestyle analysis makes our understanding of demographic groups sharper. In India the markets these days are tapping 'the young and upwardly mobile' group that cuts across many barriers. Many advertisement appeals are meant for this group. Lifestyle is a group phenomenon, which pervades various aspects of life. It implies a central life interest such as family, leisure, religion, politics, sexual exploits, etc. and this interest fashions our interaction with the environment. Variations in lifestyles are a result of social change. Working women and working couples do have very distinct lifestyles.

Values and lifestyle classification (VALS) blends together demographics, attitudes, activities, consumption patterns, brand preferences and media graphics. Lifestyles can be used to identify consumer segments for various offerings, such as microwavable dinners, fast food, day care centres and house cleaning services, which obviously appeal more to consumers whose lifestyle demands convenience and saving time. Advertising messages and promotions are often designed to appeal to certain lifestyles. Lifestyles also have implications for the specific media consumers use. For example, because many factors have changed their lifestyle to become more involved in childrearing, parenting, magazines, which were traditionally a women's forum, are starting to focus more on male readers and male-oriented advertising. Lifestyle segmentation also has important cross-cultural implications. Marketers often monitor lifestyle changes to identify new opportunities.

Human behaviour is the result of myriads of influences and relationships, which can be represented in the form of models. There are various models, which are used to explain consumer behaviour. Human mind, the seat of the decision-making process, is termed as an impregnable black box with the past or antecedents working as the stimuli impinging on it; and the result (s) coming out of the mind because of the stimuli are responses manifested in the consumer's actions. This theory being the basis, a model has been developed to explain consumer behaviour. A model is more like a map of the reality; and its study makes it possible to successfully predict the resulting behaviour of consumer put in a certain situation.

Lifestyle communication, persuasion and attitude change are dealt with in detail with consumer behaviour, which in essence what advertising stands for. Both interpersonal communication and mass communication come under the domain of consumer behaviour research. Advertising basically deals with mass communication whereas personal selling uses the finer aspects of interpersonal communication. Mass media are used for mass communication by the advertisers.

Mass communication research, which essentially is advertising research from the viewpoints of the consumer recipients' psychological make-up is studied in depth in consumer behaviour. Mass communication research intending to measure the effectiveness of communication to very large group undertakes various techniques to measure attention attraction in pre-testing. GSR (Galvanic Skin Response), PDR (Pupil Dilation Response), the eye movement camera, the tachistoscope and the binocular rivalry are a few of the pre-testing measures used in laboratory conditions to measure attention attraction of the consumer recipients before actually putting the message in the mass media chosen for the purpose.

Attitude change is a very important aspect of consumer behaviour, which is the prime objective of advertising. The consumer's attitude has to be favourably changed towards the advertiser's products. Consumer behaviour research tells how it can be achieved through the stages of message reception, retention and attitude change.

Chapter 7 IMPACT OF ADVERTISING ON CONSUMER BEHAVIOUR

7.1 INTRODUCTION

The present chapter attempts to examine the impact of media advertisement on consumer behaviour. It deals with effectiveness of media advertising, its influence on consumer behaviour and how it has succeeded in changing consumer's lifestyle pattern. For the purpose of analysis, a random sample of 252 respondents have been taken and information from them collected through administration of a well structured as well as pre-tested questionnaire, that have been analysed here question by question to study vividly.

7.2 MAGAZINE/NEWSPAPER READERSHIP

The respondents were asked to indicate their views towards magazine/newspaper reading. Table 7.1 summarises the respondents' opinion in this matter.

Table 7.1. Magazine/Newspaper Readership

Response	No. of Respondents	Percentage
Yes	252	100
No	Nil	Nil
Total	**252**	**100.00**

The above table reveals that all the respondents favour reading magazines/newspapers.

Table 7.2. Choice of Magazine/Newspaper Readership

Response	No. of Respondents	Percentage
Most often	102	40.47
Sometimes	60	23.81
Seldom	20	7.94
Always	70	27.78
Total	**252**	**100.00**

The above table shows that majority of the respondents, irrespective of age, sex, education, occupation and income go through newspapers and magazines.

7.3 TELEVISION WATCHING PATTERN

Television has the distinction of being the fastest growing medium in history. The tabular presentation below indicates the nature of respondents' television watching behaviour.

Table 7.3. Television Watching

Response	No. of Respondents	Percentage
Yes	252	100.00
No	Nil	Nil
Total	**252**	**100.00**

The above table shows that all the respondents watch television.

7.3.1. Television Viewing Pattern

A summarised response of the sample indicates that slightly higher than 52 per cent of the population devote two to four hours in a day for watching television, while about 32 per cent of the sample watch less than two hours and about 16 per cent watch more than four hours a day.

Table 7.4. Duration of Television Viewing

Time	Aggregate Sample		Male		Female	
	No. of Respondents	Percentage	No. of Respondents	Percentage	No. of Respondents	Percentage
Less than 2 hrs	80	31.75	50	30.86	20	22.23
2 to 4 hrs	132	52.38	86	53.08	55	61.11
Above 4 hrs	40	15.87	26	16.06	15	16.66
Total	**252**	**100.00**	**162**	**100.00**	**90**	**100.00**

A sex wise classification of the sample and their respective television-viewing pattern reveals that about 53.08 per cent of the male and 61.11 per cent female watch television for two to four hours, while 31.75 per cent male, 22.23 per cent female respondents watch television for less than two hours respectively. Likewise, an identical 16.06 per cent male and female watch television for more than four hours. Thus it is clear from the above analysis that females are devoting more time for viewing television than the male respondents.

7.4 POPULAR PROGRAMMES IN TELEVISION

Television programmes and advertisements are complementary to each other. Television programmes are usually sponsored by advertisers, who always are in search of such programmes, which are watched by majority of the viewers. Against such a backdrop, the viewing pattern of the sample is examined. For this purpose, the television programmes are broadly divided into five categories such as film based programme, mega serials, sports, news and others which include the patriotic programmes, social problem related programmes like dowry, child marriage, child labour, illiteracy, environment and so on.

Table 7.5. Ratings of Programmes in Television

Prog.	Aggregate Sample		Male		Female	
	No. of Respondents	Percentage	No. of Respondents	Percentage	No. of Respondents	Percentage
Film based	81	32.14	53	32.71	33	36.67
Maga Serials	87	34.52	57	35.18	35	38.89
Sports	36	14.29	20	12.35	10	11.11
News	38	15.08	26	16.06	10	11.11
Others	10	3.97	6	3.70	02	2.22
Total	**252**	**100.00**	**162**	**100.00**	**90**	**100.00**

The above table summarises the response of the sample which indicates that among the different categories of television programmes, viewership of mega serial is the largest. A sex-wise classification points out that in both the categories, mega serial viewers are highest in number. However, in case of female respondents, the relative percentage of watching mega serials is higher than their counterpart. The second preferred programme with the sample is the film-based programme. An identical ranking is also observed in case of both the male and female segments of the sample. The third preferable programme with the sample is the news and sports. In case of male and female, an identical choice is observed. The category of programmes which are termed as 'others' has the lowest viewership.

This analysis clearly indicates that both male and female respondents agree that the mega serials are more interesting than any other television programmes and in this context females are more interested in them than the males. As far as film based programmes are concerned, female viewers are found to be more inclined than the males. However in case of sports and news, an identical trend is observed. In 'others' category of programme, there remains marginal difference between the male and female sample groups.

7.5 EXPOSURE TO ADVERTISEMENT

Table 7.6 shows the exposure of the respondents to advertisement.

Table 7.6. Exposure to Advertisement

Responses	No. of Respondents	Percentage
Yes	252	100.00
No	—	—
Total	**252**	**100.00**

The table indicate that all the respondents are exposed to advertisement through various media.

7.6 VIEWING PATTERN OF TELEVISION/MAGAZINE/NEWSPAPER ADVERTISING

Television advertising with the judicious combination of moving images, sound and colour is able to allure the audience throughout the globe. As such advertising through television has enormous impact on the viewers. The advertisements being aired through television mostly are recurrent in nature. Therefore, it is quite obvious that they are greatly persuasive in nature leaving impression on the viewers. Advertisement through magazine and newspapers are also widely circulated.

As indicated in the table, as high as 52 per cent of the respondents are of the opinion that they watch the advertisements carefully, and analyse the massage content. Respondents who simply watch/read the advertisements which appear in television/magazine or newspapers, comprise 39.68 per cent. Whereas 5.16 per cent of the total respondents did not provide their opinion in the matter.

Table 7.7. Viewing Pattern of Television/Magazine/Newspaper Advertising

Response	No. of Respondents	Percentage
Simply ignore it	13	5.16
Watch/read it	100	39.68
Watch / read it carefully and analyse the message content	132	52.38
Non Response	07	2.78
Total	**252**	**100.00**

7.7 USEFULNESS OF ADVERTISING

Consumers are generally interested to know about the quality, price and nature of the product/ Service, which they intend to buy in near future. The ultimate purpose underlying all advertising is increased awareness. Since the basic aim of advertising is to inform consumers about the various aspects of products and services, consumers most often depend upon advertising for its information value. Against such a theoretical assertion, the respondents were asked to indicate their views regarding the usefulness of advertising. Table 7.8 summarises the respondents' opinion in the matter.

Table 7.8. Usefulness of Advertising

Response	No. of Respondents	Percentage
Yes	252	100
No	0	0
Total	**252**	**100**

From the above table, it can be seen that advertising is found to be quite useful for all the respondents for buying products and services from the modern day competitive market. All the respondents in fact, accepted advertising being quite useful in the exchange process that takes place between the buyer and the seller.

In order to further probe into the matter, the respondents were asked as to what extent, advertising is useful.

Table 7.9. Extent of Usefulness

Response	No. of Respondents	Percentage
To some extent	53	21.03
Very much	199	78.97
Total	**252**	**100.00**

The above table shows that for majority of the respondents advertising is very much useful.

7.8 TRUTHFULNESS IN ADVERTISING

In today's world, advertising forms an integral part of our social and economic system. Advertising though commercial in nature is supposed to present a true picture of the products or services by which the consumer's confidence is gained and retained about such products and services.

Table 7.10. Truthfulness of Advertising

Response	No. of Respondents	Percentage
True picture of the products	132	52.39
An exaggerate picture	42	16.66
Both fact and fantasies	60	23.80
None of the above	18	7.15
Total	**252**	**100.00**

As per the above table more than half of the respondents believe that advertising gives the true picture of the products and quite good number of people think it to be facts exaggerated and fantasized.

7.9 INFLUENCING BUYING DECISION

The following table indicate factors influencing the buyer's purchasing decision the most.

Table 7.11. Ranking of Factors Influencing Buying Decision

Response	No. of Respondents	Percentage	Rank
Advertisements	139	55.15	1
Friends and neighbours	61	24.21	2
Relatives	32	12.70	3
The reference group	30	11.91	4

From the above table it is clear that advertisement ranks number one in the list for influencing consumer's buying decisions, while friends and neighbours rank second, Family and relatives ranks third and the reference group ranks fourth in the table. Hence it is advertising, which is widely acceptable in influencing buyer's decision-making while purchasing a commodity.

7.10 NATURE OF ADVERTISEMENT

The following table depicts the nature of advertisement according to the respondents.

Table 7.12. Nature of Advertisement

Response	Preference of the Respondents	Percentage
Informative	143	56.75
Entertaining	56	22.22
Educative	40	15.87
Manipulative	26	10.32

In response to the nature of advertising, 56.75 per cent of the respondents accepted advertisement as informative, while 22.22 per cent believed advertising as entertaining and 15.87 per cent accepted advertising as educative. A minimum of 10.32 per cent termed advertising as manipulative.

Irrespective of age, sex, education, occupation and income, majority of the respondents accept advertisement as an informative medium to the consumer segment.

7.11 PREFERABLE MEDIUM OF ADVERTISING

There are numerous media through which advertising is undertaken. For the purpose of analysis, media of advertising are broadly classified in to three categories. They are print media, *i.e.,* newspapers and magazines, broadcasting media *i.e.,* television and radio, and outdoor media *i.e.* hoarding, billboards, wall writings and transit media.

Advertisers are always in search of an effective medium so that they can get the best out of their advertising programme. Therefore, any study in regard to advertise effectiveness seems incomplete without identifying the most effective medium of advertising. Accordingly, the respondents were asked to identify the most effective medium among the leading media like, radio, television, newspaper, magazine, hoarding, bill board and wall writing and rank them in descending order. The summarised response and the ranking of various media by the sample are presented in the following table.

Table 7.13. Ranking of various Media by the Respondents

Rank Media	W1 x7	W2 x6	W3 x5	W4 x4	W5 x3	W6 x2	W7 x1	Total (Σ WX)	Weighted Average (Σ WX / Σ W)	Ranks
Magazines	0 (0)	63 (378)	90 (450)	63 (252)	18 (54)	9 (18)	9 (9)	1161	41.46	3
Newspapers	27 (184)	99 (594)	63 (315)	54 (216)	9 (27)	0 (0)	0 (0)	1341	47.89	2
Television	225 (1575)	27 (162)	0 (0)	0 (0)	0 (0)	0 (0)	0 (0)	1737	62.04	1
Radio	0 (0)	54 (324)	63 (315)	72 (288)	45 (135)	9 (18)	9 (9)	1089	38.89	4
Hoarding	0 (0)	0 (0)	18 (90)	18 (72)	90 (270)	54 (108)	72 (92)	612	21.86	5

Billboards	0 (0)	9 (54)	0 (0)	18 (72)	63 (189)	99 (198)	63 (63)	576	20.50	6
Wall writings	0 (0)	0 (0)	18 (90)	27 (108)	27 (81)	81 (162)	99 (99)	540	19.29	7
Total (Σx)	**252**	**252**	**252**	**252**	**252**	**252**	**252**			

The table above clearly points out that television is accepted as the first choice medium of advertising by the sample irrespective of the age groups having the highest average ranking of 62.04 among all the respondents. The next preference by the sample goes to newspaper having a weighted average of 47.89 while magazines occupy the third place as a preferred advertising medium having a weighted mean of 41.46. Radio, hoarding, billboard and wall writing occupy fourth, fifth and sixth and seventh positions respectively by the sample as a preferred medium of advertising.

Thus, the television emerges as the most effective medium of advertising according to the respondents.

7.12 ADVERTISING IN SHAPING BRAND IMAGE

"Brand will only succeed in as much as they build relationships with the consumer. It is no longer a question of functional or even emotional relation with the brand. It has to be a more comprehensive relationship, which will have to be based on understanding of the way consumers are. As choices of the consumer increase, it will be increasingly a buyer's market". (Khanna, M., 1994).

With a view to find out the views of respondents, the sample has been asked to opine whether advertisement helps the company in building the brand image as well as the brand loyalty. Table presented below summarises the view of the sample in the matter.

Table 7.14. Advertising and Brand Image

Opinion	Aggregate		Male		Female	
	No. of Respondents	Percentage	No. of Respondents	Percentage	No. of Respondents	Percentage
Agree	225	89.28	148	91.36	59	65.55
Disagree	27	10.72	14	8.64	31	34.45
Total	**252**	**100.00**	**162**	**100.00**	**90**	**100.00**

Summing up the responses of the sample indicates, that an overwhelming majority of 89.28 per cent agree that advertising really helps the company in building brand image whereas only 10.72 per cent of the respondents don't agree with the statement. When the above sample is stratified on the basis of sex *i.e.,* male and female, about 91.36 per cent male respondents agree that advertising really helps build up brand image of the organisation. Similarly, 65.55 per cent of the female respondents agree that advertising helps the company in building brand image of products and services, whereas the rest 14 per cent male and 31 per cent female respondents disagree with such view.

7.13 ADVERTISING RESULTING IN INCREMENTAL COST OF PRODUCTS AND SERVICES

Advertising acts as a solution to the problems of the prospective buyer by providing necessary information needed by them. At the same time, sellers who provide all these information in the forms of advertisements have to incur some expenditure, which ultimately are included in the cost of the products and services thereby increasing their final price for the consumers. Therefore it is almost often argued that advertisement makes the products/ services costlier as advertising expenditure constitutes an element of total cost of such products /services. However, few argue that such a conclusion is not justified, since advertising in the modern business world is most essential and without the same, products and services would remain unsold.

Though advertisement is believed to increase the cost of products/services, it is not true in most of the cases. There are some charitable organisations or some societies like oil conservation society, family planning organisation, pollution control organisation, childcare organisation etc., who undertake advertising, but the cost of the same is not passed to the consumers. They advertise for the benefit and service for the people. Similarly, most advertisements are informative and have educational value. Therefore, when cost of advertisements is compared with their utility value, the former becomes negligible.

The view of the respondents in the matter was solicited and presented in the table below. As indicated, 84 per cent of the respondents confirm the widely held view that advertisement really increases the cost of products & services. However, only a marginal respondents disagree to the same. Thus, advertisement contributing to cost escalation of products and services finds large-scale acceptance by the sample.

Table 7.15. Advertisement Contributing to Cost Escalation

Response	No. of Respondents	Percentage
Yes	211	83.73
No	41	16.27
Total	**252**	**100.00**

In the light of above trend, we find further that in the age-wise classification, majority of the respondents belonging to all the four age groups are of the opinion that advertising increases the cost of products/services. Table mentioned below indicates that 95.23 per cent of the sample respondents belonging to teen age group, accept that advertisement increases the cost of the products whereas only 4.77 per cent discard such a contention.

Table 7.16. Advertisement Contributing to Cost Escalation
(Age-wise Classification)

Responses	Teen		Young		Middle		Old	
	No. of resp.	Percent-age	No. of resp.	Percent-age	No. of resp.	Percent-age	No. of resp.	Percent-age
Yes	40	95.23	130	96.30	58	82.86	04	80.00
No	02	4.77	05	3.70	12	17.14	01	20.00
Total	**42**	**100.00**	**135**	**100.00**	**70**	**100.00**	**05**	**100.00**

In the young and middle-aged group about 96.30 per cent and 82.86 per cent respondents accept the increasing cost point, whereas 3.70 per cent and 17.14 per cent rejected the claim. In case of old age group, 80 per cent supported the increasing cost concept, while 20 per cent rejected the claim.

In view of the aforesaid age-wise opinion of the sample regarding advertising, it can be safely concluded that people belonging to all ages, from Teen to Old think advertisement costs are included in the total cost thereby increasing the cost of the product and services.

7.14 INFORMATIVE VALUE OF TELEVISION ADVERTISING

In order to examine further the range superiority of television advertising over other medium, the sample have been asked to indicate how far television advertising is being considered superior or otherwise.

Table 7.17. Information Value of Television Advertising

Response	No. of Respondents	Percentage
Very much	160	63.50
Moderately	55	21.82
Not so much	10	3.97
Non Response	27	10.71
Total	**252**	**100.00**

The respondents' opinion regarding the relative significance of television advertisements clearly discerns that a majority of the respondents (63.50 per cent) accept that television advertising is more informative than other medium of advertising. About 22 per cent respondents moderately agree about its relative superiority over other medium, whereas insignificant percentage of respondents (about four percent) opened that information-value of television advertisement is not so much. A slightly higher than 10 per cent respondents are non-committed to the relative significance of television advertising.

7.15 INFLUENCE OF TELEVISION ON CONSUMER BEHAVIOUR AND LIFESTYLE

Television advertising, whether social or commercial since its appearance has been able to change the consumers' lifestyle and their consumption pattern in a big way. Perhaps few of the new inventions would not have been instant success in the market and would not have received wide spread market acceptance but for television advertising.

Table 7.18. Influence of Television on Consumer behaviour and Lifestyle

Response	No. of Respondents	Percentage
Agree	174	69.90
Disagree	78	30.10
Total	**252**	**100.00**

The above table reveals that 60.90 per cent of respondents have agreed that television advertising indeed influences the consumers' behaviour and their needs as well as choices. This implies that people in general life are influenced by television advertising to a significant extent.

7.16 TELEVISION ADVERTISING AND PURCHASE BEHAVIOUR

Admittedly, television advertising has significantly influenced the purchase behaviour of consumers through moulding the attitude in favour of products, services and ideas. In many cases, it has resulted in shifting the brand loyalty from one product/service to another. Brand switching instances are galore in the Indian market, which is the net outcome of aggressive television advertising campaigns undertaken by the marketer or otherwise.

Table 7.19. Television Advertising and change in Purchase Behaviour

Response	No. of Respondents	Percentage
Yes	179	71.03
No	73	28.97
Total	**252**	**100.00**

In order to examine whether the respondents have experienced any major attitudinal change in their purchase behaviour after the advent of television advertisement in different channels in a big way, they have been asked to express precisely their opinion in 'yes' or 'no' form. Table mentioned above indicates that 71.03 per cent of the respondents agreed that television advertisements have changed their buying behaviour whereas 28.97 per cent respondents do not agree to the statement. This amply demonstrates the all-pervasive capacity of television advertising over the viewers. It also affirms that television advertisement undertaken on scientific lines have the inherent capacity of moulding the consumer behaviour in a particular manner.

7.17 TELEVISION ADVERTISING AND BRAND SWITCHING

Having come to know about the influencing behaviour of television advertising, further attempts have been made to pinpoint the nature of change caused by such advertising by asking the sample to identify the products which they have purchased in recent past, mainly influenced by television advertising. However, for the purpose of analysis all such products have been classified as convenience goods have greater vulnerability. Under this category are tea, toothpaste, toiletries and other similar products.

Table 7.20. Television Advertising and Brand Switching

Types of Goods	No. of Respondents	Percentage
a. Consumers Convenience goods	102	40.50
b. Consumers Soft goods	68	27.00
c. Durable goods	52	20.60
d. Other social advertising	23	9.12
e. Non Response	7	2.78
Total	**252**	**100.00**

As can be seen from the above table, 40.50 per cent of the samples have switched their loyalty in the convenience goods category chiefly influenced by television advertising. Likewise 27 per cent respondents conceded that they have changed their loyalty in case of soft goods. About 21 per cent of the sample agreed that television advertising has altered their choice in the durable goods category and 9.12 per cent respondents acknowledged that their behaviour and action have changed by viewing the social advertisements and other public interest commercials. In view of such findings, it can be surmised that television commercials have mostly succeeded in influencing the purchasing pattern of the respondents because of its unique audio-video features. The sample switched over their loyalty largely in case of consumer convenience, soft and durable goods chiefly influenced by television advertising.

7.18 CELL PHONE USER

In the present research study, an effort has been made to find out how advertising influences lifestyles and to assess the impact of media for moulding consumer behaviour. As cell phone becomes a part and parcel of lifestyle and everyday there are number of advertisements placed in the media targeted for the consumers. Recently a catchy slogan introduced by Reliance cellular phone service titled. 'Mobile phones are more affordable than mangoes', appealed consumer's attention. The table mentioned below explain in detail about the use patterns and nature of using Cell phone.

Table 7.21. Cell Phone User

A. Cell Phone User			**B. Cell Phone User**		
Response	**No. of respondents**	**Percentage**	**Response**	**No. of respondents**	**Percentage**
Yes	154	61.11	(*a*) It is Unnecessary	22	22.45
No	98	38.89	(*b*) You cannot afford it	36	36.73
			(c) Both (a) and (b)	40	40.82
Total	**252**	**100.00**	**Total**	**98**	**100.00**

The tabular presentation reveals that, out of 252 respondents, 61.11 per cent respondents gave positive response of using cell phone, whereas 38.89 per cent respondent said 'No' to use cell phone. From the above table it is clear that majority of the respondents are using cell phone.

Table 7.21 also explains the reason, for which 38.89 per cent of the total respondents say 'No' to cell phone use. Out of the total 98 respondents, 40.82 per cent respondent say that, the use of cell phone is unnecessary and also they cannot afford to purchase a cell phone. On the other hand 36.73 per cent respondents answered the question by saying that their economic status does not permit them to purchase cell phone, even if they desire to possess the same. As many as 22.45 per cent respondents categorically rejected the use of the cell phone by saying that it is totally unnecessary.

Some of the respondents who are unable to purchase cell phone have a desire to possess the same.

Table 7.22. Use of Cell Phone

Response	**No. of Respondents**	**Percentage**
Fashion/Style	61	24.21
Need	123	48.81
Status symbol	60	23.81
Disturbance	08	03.17
Total	**252**	**100.00**

The above table reveals the reason as to why people opt for cell phone. Nearly half the respondents feel that the use of cell phone is a need today. Almost one fourth of them call it as fashion and style, while almost the same number of people call it as status symbol. Only a minimal few consider it a disturbance.

7.18.1. Sex-wise Analysis

Table 7.23 depicts a detailed sex-wise analysis about the use of cell phone.

Table 7.23. Sex-wise Analysis

Response	Male		Female	
	No. of Respondents	Percentage	No. of Respondents	Percentage
Fashion/Style	30	18.51	31	34.45
Need	91	56.17	32	35.55
Status symbol	36	22.22	24	26.66
Disturbance	05	3.10	03	3.34
Total	**162**	**100.00**	**90**	**100.00**

The table shows that more than half of the male and 36 per cent female respondent termed cell phone as a need of the hour, while the rest of the total say it as a fashion and status symbol.

7.18.2. Age-wise Analysis

The following table shows the cell phone usership among different age groups. The age group is divided into four major segments such as teen age, young age, middle age and old age people.

Table 7.24. Age-wise Analysis

Response	Teen		Young		Middle		Old	
	No. of resp.	Percent-age	No. of resp.	Percent-age	No. of resp.	Percent-age	No. of resp.	Percent-age
Fashion/ Style	30	71.44	20	14.81	11	15.71	Nil	Nil
Need	06	14.28	65	48.15	49	70.00	03	60.00
Status Symbol	06	14.28	44	32.60	10	14.20	Nil	Nil
Disturbance	Nil	Nil	06	4.44	Nil	Nil	02	40.00
Total	**42**	**100.00**	**135**	**100.00**	**70**	**100.00**	**05**	**100.00**

In short, we arrive at the following conclusions:

(*i*) Cell phone is widely used as a need, irrespective of age group.

(*ii*) Next to need comes fashion and style.

(*iii*) It is also considered as a status symbol by all except the old age group.

(*iv*) Only a minimal few consider cell phone to be a disturbance.

7.19 FREQUENCY OF INTERNET CHATTING

Table below reveals the respondents' frequency of Internet chatting.

Table 7.25. Frequency of Internet Chatting

Response	No. of Respondents	Percentage
a. Frequently	59	23.41
b. Occasionally	119	47.22
c. Rarely	55	21.83
d. Never	19	7.54
Total	**252**	**100.00**

It shows that nearly half of the respondents *i.e.,* 47.22 per cent chat Internet occasionally, while 23.41 per cent chat frequently, 21.83 per cent rarely and only 7.54 per cent never chat Internet. In fine, the table depicts that Internet chatting has almost become a way of life.

7.19.1. Sex-wise Analysis

Table 7.26 shows frequency of Internet chatting among male and female respondents.

Table 7.26. Frequency of Internet Chatting (Sex-wise Analysis)

Response	Male		Female	
	No. of Respondents	Percentage	No. of Respondents	Percentage
(*a*) Frequently	29	17.90	30	33.33
(*b*) Occasionally	68	41.98	51	56.67
(*c*) Rarely	46	28.39	09	10.00
(*d*) Never	19	11.73	-	-
Total	**162**	**100.00**	**90**	**100.00**

The male and female classification shows that majority of them chats Internet occasionally. Only a minimal few never chats Internet. Thus to conclude, Internet chatting has become a way of their lifestyle.

7.19.2. Age-wise Analysis

Table 7.27. Frequency of Internet Chatting (Age-wise Analysis)

Responses	Teen		Young		Middle		Old	
	No. of resp.	Percent-age	No. of resp.	Percent-age	No. of resp.	Percent-age	No. of resp.	Percent-age
a. Frequently	8	19.05	30	22.22	21	30.00	Nil	Nil
b. Occasionally	30	71.43	70	51.85	16	22.86	03	60.00
c. Rarely	04	9.52	25	18.52	24	34.28	02	40.00
d. Never	Nil	Nil	10	7.41	09	12.86	Nil	Nil
Total	**42**	**100.00**	**135**	**100.00**	**70**	**100.00**	**05**	**100.00**

An age-wise analysis of Internet users explained with the help of table above. On a careful study of the table, we arrive at the conclusion that majority of all the age group chats Internet whereas a few of them never chat.

7.20 FEELING TOWARDS INTERNET CHATTING

Table 7.28 reveals respondents feeling towards Internet chatting.

Table 7.28. Feeling towards Internet Chatting Habit

Response	No. of Respondents	Percentage
Interesting & relaxing	94	37.30
Wastage of time	Nil	Nil
Need of the hour	82	32.54
A way of acquiring Friends	76	30.16
Total	**252**	**100.00**

A majority of the respondents (37.30 %) responded Internet chatting as interesting and relaxing whereas 32.54 per cent termed it as need of the hour. About one-third of the total respondent felt chatting as a way of acquiring friends. It is significant to note that, none of the respondents termed Internet chatting as wastage of time. Thus for majority of the respondents, Internet chatting has become a part of their lifestyle.

7.20.1. Sex-wise Analysis

Table 7.29 shows a sex-wise analysis of Internet chatting habit.

Table 7.29. Feeling towards Internet Chatting habit (Sex-wise Analysis)

Response	Male		Female	
	No. of Respondents	Percentage	No. of Respondents	Percentage
Interesting & relaxing	60	37.04	34	37.78
Wastage of time	Nil	Nil	Nil	Nil
Need of the hour	71	43.83	40	44.45
A way of acquiring friends	31	19.13	16	17.77
Total	**162**	**100.00**	**90**	**100.00**

On a careful study of the above table it is to be concluded that, majority of the respondents termed Internet chatting as interesting & relaxing plus need of the hour. Hence to have an equal footing with the modern lifestyle, Internet chatting plays a vital role. Therefore, irrespective of sex, age, education, occupation and income almost all the respondents support Internet chatting as a part of their modern lifestyle.

7.21 BROWSING PORNO WEB-SITE ON INTERNET/READING PORNOGRAPHIC MAGAZINE

Table 7.30 shows respondents' reaction towards browsing porno website on Internet and reading pornographic magazine.

Table 7.30. Browsing Porno Website on Internet/ Reading Pornographic Magazine

Response	No. of Respondents	Percentage
Strongly agree	11	4.36
Agree	59	23.41
Disagree	168	66.67
Strongly Disagree	14	5.56
Total	**252**	**100.00**

The permissiveness of browsing or reading porno is explained in the above table. It is significant to note that, a preponderant majority of the respondents disagreed with browsing pornographic website and reading porno magazines.

7.21.1. Sex-wise Analysis

Table 7.31 shows a sex-wise analysis about the permissiveness of browsing pornographic website and reading pornographic magazine.

Table 7.31 Browsing Porno Website on Internet/ Reading Pornographic Magazine (Sex-wise Analysis)

Response	Male		Female	
	No. of Respondents	Percentage	No. of Respondents	Percentage
Strongly agree	11	6.79	Nil	Nil
Agree	38	23.45	21	23.33
Disagree	107	66.05	61	67.78
Strongly Disagree	06	3.71	08	8.89
Total	**162**	**100.00**	**90**	**100.00**

Table above reveals that despite modernity in lifestyles and advanced way of life, majority of the male and female respondents do not permit unethical, illegal website browsing or reading pornographic magazines. Irrespective of age, sex, occupation, education and income, it is unanimously disagreed opinion for illegal browsing or reading porno magazines.

7.22 COMPUTER USE

Table mentioned below reveals respondents' response towards computer use.

Table 7.32. Computer Users

Response	No. of Respondents	Percentage
Yes	232	92.06
No	20	7.94
Total	**252**	**100.00**

From the table, it is crystal clear that a significant majority of the respondents (92.06 %) are using computer, while a barely few says 'No' to Computer use. Hence, it is clear that majority of the respondents accepted computer as an essential element of their modern lifestyle.

7.23 TELE SHOPPING/ONLINE SHOPPING

Tele shopping / sky shopping / online shopping is a modern concept and a developed marketing tool available to the consumers in the present day lifestyle. Tele shopping or online shopping becomes an important part of their life. Table no. 7.33 shows people's response towards tele shopping.

Table 7.33. Tele Shopping/Online Shopping

Response	No. of Respondents	Percentage
Yes	90	35.71
No	162	64.29
Total	**252**	**100.00**

It is clear from the table that, majority of the respondents (64.29 %) say 'No' to Tele shopping or on line shopping due to the fact that, either they are ignorant, do not have direct access to those services or in some cases they lack in knowledge. On the other hand, 35.71 per cent said 'yes' for Tele shopping/on line shopping. It is evident from the table that, people are gradually accepting the modern marketing tool in their day-to-day life.

7.24 READYMADE DRESS BUYING

A question was asked to know about respondents' reaction towards readymade dress buying. The response of the same is tabled in the following.

Table 7.34. Readymade Dress Buying

Response	No. of Respondents	Percentage
a. Brand image	107	42.46
b. They have a style	53	21.03
c. Convenient to purchase	60	23.81
d. Combine all the above	32	12.70
Total	**252**	**100.00**

From the table it is clear that majority of the respondents purchase readymade garments because it is convenient, having stylish format and a class brand image.

7.24.1. Sex-wise Analysis

Table 7.35. Readymade Dress Buying (Sex-wise Analysis)

Response	Male		Female	
	No. of Respondents	**Percentage**	**No. of Respondents**	**Percentage**
a. Brand image	77	47.53	30	33.33
b. They have a style	20	12.35	33	36.67
c. Convenient to purchase	39	24.07	21	23.33
d. Combine all the above	26	16.05	06	6.67
Total	**162**	**100.00**	**90**	**100.00**

Table 7.35 shows sex-wise analysis of consumers' readymade dress buying behaviour. Majority of the male and female respondents prefer brand image and stylish content of the readymade garments. Thus to conclude, respondents from all the categories support readymade dress buying due to its brand image, convenience to purchase and stylish presentation.

7.25 PURCHASE OF CAR AND MOTORBIKE

Purchasing new brands of car and motorbike, agreeably a symbol of leading modern lifestyle. Mostly in such cases advertising plays a significant role for the same. Table 7.36 reveals the purchasing behaviour while buying car and motorbike.

Table 7.36. Purchase of Car and Motorbike

Response	No. of Respondents	Percentage
Fuel efficient	28	11.11
Costly	25	9.92
Latest in Style	169	67.06
They Combine all	·30	11.91
Total	**252**	**100.00**

From the above table it is clear that a significant majority of the respondent prefers latest style while purchasing car and motorbike.

7.25.1. Sex-wise Classification

Table 7.37 shows the sex-wise classification of respondents' response.

Table 7.37. Purchase of Car and Motorbike (Sex-wise Classification)

Response	Male		Female	
	No. of Respondents	Percentage	No. of Respondents	Percentage
Fuel efficient	18	11.11	10	11.11
Costly	10	6.17	15	16.67
Latest in style	114	70.37	55	61.11
They combine all	20	12.35	10	11.11
Total	**162**	**100.00**	**90**	**100.00**

The table above reveals that majority of both female and male, respondents prefer car and motorbike with latest style. It is known that advertisement plays a vital role for informing the latest available car and motorbike information to the respondents.

7.26 CONSUMPTION OF COLD DRINKS AND FAST FOOD

Consumption of cold drink and fast food becomes an important element in day-to-day lifestyles. Table 7.38 shows respondents reaction on that.

Table 7.38. Consumption of Cold drinks and Fast food

Response	Aggregate		Sex-wise analysis			
	No. of Respondents	Percentage	Male	Percentage	Female	Percentage
a. Almost regularly	30	11.90	20	12.34	10	11.11
b. Sometimes	51	20.24	26	16.05	25	27.78
c. Occasionally	165	65.48	113	69.76	52	57.78
d. Not at all	06	2.38	03	1.85	03	3.33
Total	**252**	**100.00**	**162**	**100.00**	**90**	**100.00**

Table 7.38 reveals that, a majority (65.48 %) respondents consume cold drink and fast food occasionally while 20.24 per cent sometimes, 11.90 per cent almost regularly and a barely 2.38 per cent never consume either of the two. The result signifies that respondents adapt to the changing

habits of taking food or drink. From a sex-wise analysis it is clear that a majority of both male and female respondents prefer to take cold drink and fast food.

7.27 DRINKING WATER PREFERENCE

The table mentioned below explains respondents' reaction towards their drink preference.

Table 7.39. Drink Preference

Response	No. of Respondents	Percentage
Mineral Water	43	17.06
Filtered Water	189	75.00
Tap Water	20	7.94
Total	**252**	**100.00**

The table shows that a majority of the respondents prefer to take filtered water whereas a very minimal few are interested for tap water. This signifies that from media advertisement, people are cautious in their drinking approach.

7.28 PARTICIPATION IN SOCIAL DRINK

Organising cocktail party, attending club and social drinks are modern means of advanced lifestyles. A sincere attempt has been made to know about respondents' reaction towards social drink. Table 7.40 reveals respondents' opinion in the following.

Table 7.40. Participation in Social Drink

Response	Aggregate		Sex-wise analysis			
	No. of Respondents	Percentage	Male	Percentage	Female	Percentage
a. Regularly	16	6.35	16	9.87	Nil	Nil
b. Occasionally	89	35.32	68	41.98	21	23.33
c. Sometimes	84	33.33	78	48.15	06	6.67
d. Not at all	63	25.00	Nil	Nil	63	70.00
Total	**252**	**100.00**	**162**	**100.00**	**90**	**100.00**

The above tabular presentation clearly indicates that majority of the respondents' enjoy social drink occasionally, sometimes and regularly whereas a few among the whole never like to drink. From a sex-wise analysis of the above, it is clear that most of the male drink occasionally while majority of the female never take drinks. It is an agreeable fact that media advertisement on alcoholic drink often influences the respondents' attitude and their lifestyle.

This symbolizes a changing lifestyle of the society.

7.29 INVITATION FOR DRINK

Organizing social drinks and extending invitation for drinks become a new means of high-class lifestyle. The tabular presentation intends to find out the habit of the respondents.

Table 7.41. Invitation for Drinks

Response	Aggregate		Sex-wise analysis			
	No. of Respondents	**Percentage**	**Male**	**Percentage**	**Female**	**Percentage**
a. Regularly	02	0.79	02	1.23	Nil	Nil
b. Occasionally	98	38.89	83	51.24	15	16.67
c. Some times	89	35.32	77	47.53	12	13.33
d. Not at all	63	25.00	Nil	Nil	63	70.00
Total	**252**	**100.00**	**162**	**100.00**	**90**	**100.00**

The table shows that a significant majority of the total respondent prefers to invite other either regularly, occasionally or sometimes to participate social drinks. The sex-wise analysis reveals that majority of the male prefers to invite for drink while more than of the female reacted negatively to this. Thus to conclude majority of the respondents occasionally and sometimes celebrate get-together drinks.

7.30 PARTICIPATION IN DISCO DANCING

Participating in disco dance, attending nightclub and bar have become a fashion. Most-often, the stylish presentation of club life, bar life and disco dance on television or other advertising media draws viewers' attention and at times they are carried away.

Table 7.42. Participation in Disco Dancing

Response	No. of Respondents	Percentage
a. Whenever opportunity comes	57	22.62
b. Almost regularly	04	1.59
c. Occasionally	59	23.41
d. Not at all	132	52.38
Total	**252**	**100.00**

The table shows that majority of the respondents are averse to participate disco dancing. The tabular presentation further indicates that respondents even though small in number are either occasionally or on an opportunity basis participates disco dancing. The modern life towards disco dancing is gaining momentum nowadays.

7.30.1. Sex-wise Analysis

Table 7.43 reveals sex-wise analysis about participation in disco dancing.

Table 7.43. Participation in Disco Dancing (Sex-wise Analysis)

Response	Male		Female	
	No. of Respondents	Percentage	No. of Respondents	Percentage
a. Whenever opportunity comes	54	33.33	03	3.33
b. Almost regularly	04	2.47	Nil	Nil
c. Occasionally	50	30.86	9	10.00
d. Not at all	54	33.34	78	86.67
Total	**162**	**100.00**	**90**	**100.00**

From the above table, it is crystal clear that two third of the total male respondent prefers to participate disco dancing either occasionally, regularly or on an opportunity basis whereas one third respondent reacts negatively to the same. On the other hand maximum number of female never participates disco dancing.

7.30.2. Age-wise Analysis

The table below closely observes an age-wise analysis of the same.

Table 7.44. Participation in Disco dancing (Age-wise Analysis)

Responses	Teen		Young		Middle		Old	
	No. of resp.	Percent-age	No. of resp.	Perce-ntage	No. of resp.	Perce-ntage	No. of resp.	Percen-tage
a. Whenever opportunity comes	04	9.53	20	14.81	33	47.14	Nil	Nil
b. Almost regularly	02	4.76	Nil	Nil	02	2.86	Nil	Nil
c. Occasionally	06	14.28	40	29.63	13	18.57	Nil	Nil
d. Not at all	30	71.43	75	55.56	22	31.43	05	100.00
Total	**42**	**100.00**	**135**	**100.00**	**70**	**100.00**	**05**	**100.00**

The above tabular presentation reveals that most of the respondent from different age groups opined negatively to disco dancing. On the other hand a negligible portion of the total respondent prefers to disco occasionally, regularly and on an opportunity basis.

7.31 APPEARANCE OF GIRLS WITH TIGHT JEANS AND SKIMPY DRESSES

Table below reveals respondents reaction towards girl with tight jeans and skimpy dresses.

Table 7.45. Girls on tight jeans and skimpy dresses appearing on Television

Response	Aggregate		Sex-wise analysis			
	No. of Respondents	Percentage	Male	Percentage	Female	Percentage
a. Modern and up-to-date	179	71.03	93	57.41	86	95.55
b. Lacking in traditional Indian values	38	15.08	34	20.99	04	4.45
c. Immoral and promiscuous	35	13.89	35	21.60	Nil	Nil
Total	**252**	**100.00**	**162**	**100.00**	**90**	**100.00**

From the above table it is clear that about two-third of the total respondent opined in favour of tight jeans with skimpy dressed girl as modern and up to date. On the other hand nearly one-sixth of the respondent said that it lacks traditional Indian values. From a sex-wise analysis, majority of the male and female respondent supports jeans and skimpy dressed girl as modern and up to date.

7.31.1. Education-wise Analysis

Table 7.46 reveals in detail the response of the respondents in accordance to different educational groups.

Table 7.46. Girls on tight jeans and skimpy dresses appearing on Television

Responses	Education-wise Analysis							
	Under graduate	**Percent-age**	**Graduate**	**Perce-ntage**	**Post graduate**	**Perce-ntage**	**Professional degree**	**Percen-tage**
a. Modern and up-to-date.	20	47.61	49	81.67	90	72.00	20	80.00
b. Lacking in traditional Indian values	17	40.48	08	13.33	10	8.00	03	12.00
c. Immoral and promiscuous	05	11.91	03	5.00	25	20.00	02	8.00
Total	**42**	**100.00**	**60**	**100.00**	**125**	**100.00**	**25**	**100.00**

From the above table it is clear that most of the respondents from different educational group favours modern and up to date culture where as a negligible percentage reacts negatively by saying that such type of modern girl lacks traditional Indian values.

7.31.2. Age-wise Analysis

An age-wise analysis of the same depicts in Table 7.47. The table shows that majority of the respondents from different age groups except the old age group support jeans and skimpy dressed girl as modern and up to date. They look well dressed and well equipped with the modern lifestyles.

Table 7.47. Girls on tight jeans and skimpy dresses appearing on Television (Age-wise Analysis)

Response	Teen		Young		Middle		Old	
	No. of resp.	Percent-age	No. of resp.	Perce-ntage	No. of resp.	Perce-ntage	No. of resp.	Percen-tage
a. Modern and up to date.	40	95.24	100	74.07	39	55.71	Nil	Nil
b. Lacking in traditional Indian values	02	4.76	12	8.89	20	28.57	04	80.00
c. Immoral and promiscuous	Nil	Nil	23	17.04	11	15.72	01	20.00
Total	**42**	**100.00**	**135**	**100.00**	**70**	**100.00**	**05**	**100.00**

7.32 BEAUTY CONTEST

Beauty contest nowadays has been accepted as a popular culture everywhere. It becomes a part and parcel of modern lifestyle. Table presented below intends to reflect respondents' reaction towards beauty contest.

Table 7.48. Beauty Contest

Response	Aggregate		Sex-wise analysis			
	No. of Respondents	Percentage	Male	Percentage	Female	Percentage
a. Pleasant figure	159	63.09	125	77.16	34	37.78
b. Dressing Style	78	30.96	29	17.90	49	54.44
c. Message	11	4.36	04	2.47	07	7.78
d. None	04	1.59	04	2.47	Nil	Nil
Total	**252**	**100.00**	**162**	**100.00**	**90**	**100.00**

This may be seen from the above table that majority respondents like pleasant figure of the beauty queens whereas about one third of the total respondents are very much attracted towards their dressing style. Barely a minimal few are interested for the message.

Sex-wise analysis shows that a significant majority of males prefer pleasant figure while more than half of the female like dress style of the beauty queen.

7.33 CONDOM ADVERTISEMENT ON AIDS

An attempt has been made to know about respondents' reaction towards condom advertisement on AIDS. The table below explains in the following.

Table 7.49. Condom Advertisement on AIDS

Response	No. of Respondents	Percentage
a. Multiple Sex life	12	4.76
b. Safe Sex	240	95.24
c. None of the above	Nil	Nil
Total	**252**	**100.00**

It is crystal clear from the above table that a thumping majority of the total respondents prefer condom advertisement on AIDS for safe sex whereas a negligible majority favours multiple sex life.

7.33.1. Sex-wise Analysis

Table below reveals sex-wise analysis of the above.

Table 7.50. Condom Advertisement on AIDS (Sex-wise Analysis)

Response	Male		Female	
	No. of Respondents	Percentage	No. of Respondents	Percentage
a. Multiple Sex life	12	7.40	-	-
b. Safe Sex	150	92.60	90	100.00
c. None of the above	-	-	-	-
Total	**162**	**100.00**	**90**	**100.00**

The table above shows that almost all the male respondents to feel that condom advertisement suggests safe sex whereas cent percent female respondents support condom advertisement for safe sex. Thus the trend shows that both male and female respondents are very much conscious about health and their sex life.

7.34 ADVERTISEMENT OF SANITARY NAPKINS

Use of sanitary napkin or its advertisement through various media is completely a modern concept. As it is a very delicate issue, an attempt has been made to know about respondents' reaction towards such advertisement. Table 7.51 explains the following.

Table 7.51. Advertisement of Sanitary Napkins

Response	No. of Respondents	Percentage
a. Offends the viewers.	04	1.59
b. Informs the target group	190	75.40
c. Health awareness	58	23.01
Total	**252**	**100.00**

From the tabular presentation, it is found that a significant majority of the respondents say that sanitary napkin advertisement informs the target group while one-fifth of the total sample favour such ad for health awareness.

7.34.1. Sex-wise Analysis

Table below explains in detail the sex-wise analysis of sanitary napkin advertisement through media.

Table 7.52. Advertisement of Sanitary Napkins (Sex-wise Analysis)

Response	Male		Female	
	No. of Respondents	Percentage	No. of Respondents	Percentage
a. Offends the viewers	04	2.47	Nil	Nil
b. Informs the target group	136	83.95	54	60.00
c. Health awareness	22	13.58	36	40.00
Total	**162**	**100.00**	**90**	**100.00**

From the above table it is clear that almost all the male respondent support sanitary napkin advertisement by saying that it informs the target group. On the other hand more than half of the female respondent said that such type of ad informs the target group while one-third of them supports health awareness. Thus to conclude, a significant majority from both the group supports napkins advertisement through various media.

7.35 PRODUCTS/SERVICES WITHOUT ADVERTISEMENT

Product or service needs to be advertised to draw consumer attention. In the competitive market scenario, there are number of goods and services available with different brand name in the market. Therefore, it often creates confusion in the mind of the consumers to judge the right quality of the product. In such cases, it is advertisement, which supports consumer as a guiding tool to select the right things. An attempt has been made to know about consumers' reaction towards non-advertised goods/services.

Table 7.53. Product/Services without Advertisement

Response	Aggregate		Sex-wise analysis			
	No. of Respondents	Percentage	Male	Percentage	Female	Percentage
a. The life style will be narrow	148	58.73	96	59.26	52	57.78
b. Life will be rather dull	14	5.56	04	2.47	10	11.11
c. Progress will be in Jeopardy	75	29.76	51	31.48	24	26.67
d. Nothing will happen	15	5.95	11	6.79	04	4.44
Total	**252**	**100.00**	**162**	**100.00**	**90**	**100.00**

The tabular presentation shows that more than half of the total respondents feel that if goods and services are not advertised, the lifestyle will be narrow whereas about one-third of the total sample feels that progress will be in jeopardy if advertisement does not take place. On the other hand the sex-wise analysis shows more than half of the male and female respondents supports the statement that without advertisement lifestyle will be narrow. Thus to conclude, advertised goods and services are highly preferred by the respondents as they help enhance consumers' lifestyle and contribute to the progress of the society.

7.36 ADVERTISEMENT AND ITS IMPACT ON YOUNGER GENERATION

Younger generation on a large scale are influenced by media advertisement. An attempt has been made to find out consumers reaction towards advertisement and its impact on younger generation. The response of the same is reflected through the following tabular presentation.

Table 7.54. Does Advertisement Corrupt Young Generation?

Response	No. of Respondents	Percentage
Yes	43	17.06
No	209	82.94
Total	**252**	**100.00**

The table shows that almost all the respondent said no by favouring advertisement and its positive impact on younger generation. On the other hand a minimal few reacts against advertisement and its impact. Thus, the trend shows that a significant majority of the total respondent supports advertisement and for its positive impact on the younger generation.

7.37 AN OPINION ON BREAK TIME FOR ADVERTISEMENT

The research study made an attempt to know about respondents' attitude towards break time for advertisement. The summarized responses are framed in the following table.

Table 7.55. Opinion on Break Time for Advertisement

Response	Aggregate		Sex-wise analysis			
	No. of Respondents	Percentage	Male	Percentage	Female	Percentage
a. Hindrance and disturbance	79	31.35	51	31.48	28	31.11
b. If not welcome, useful for self & family	102	40.48	60	37.04	42	46.67
c. Sometimes tolerable	46	18.25	31	19.14	15	16.67
d. Annoying and undesirable	25	9.92	20	12.34	05	5.55
Total	**252**	**100.00**	**162**	**100.00**	**90**	**100.00**

This is evident from the table that, nearly half of the respondents support break time. Even though break time is not welcome but is useful for self and family members, they opined. On the other hand about one-third of the total sample say advertising as a hindrance and disturbance. Nearly one-fifth of the total sample feel advertisement sometimes tolerable. The trend shows that a significant majority support advertisement break time due to its informative and entertaining nature.

A sex-wise analysis of the same shows that nearly one-third of the male and half of the female respondents favour advertising for its usefulness to self and family members.

7.38 CELEBRITY ENDORSEMENT OF PRODUCTS AND CONSUMER PREFERENCE

Goods and services need to be advertised on large scale. Advertised goods and services have mass consumer appeal, as almost all the respondent supports advertised goods. But to make the advertisement more attentive and attractive, advertisers now a days are using celebrity such as film star, sports star and from other walks of life. The researcher made an attempt to know about respondents' reaction towards celebrity endorsement of product and their preference. A summarized response of the same is presented in the following table.

Table 7.56. Celebrity Endorsement of Product and Consumer Preference

Response	Aggregate		Sex-wise analysis			
	No. of Respondents	Percentage	Male	Percentage	Female	Percentage
a. Yes, very much	137	54.36	88	54.32	49	54.44
b. No. not at all	05	1.98	02	1.24	03	3.33
c. To some extent	72	28.58	52	32.09	20	22.23
d. Makes no difference	38	15.08	20	12.35	18	20.00
Total	**252**	**100.00**	**162**	**100.00**	**90**	**100.00**

The table mentioned above reveals that more than half of the respondents support celebrity endorsement of product to the maximum possible extent, while nearly one-third of them favour to some extent. A sex-wise analysis of the same shows that majority of both male and female respondents like celebrity endorsement of product. Thus, to conclude, irrespective of age, sex, education, income and occupation, almost all the respondents prefer celebrity-endorsed products.

7.39 INFLUENCING FACTOR FOR LEADING MODERN LIFESTYLE

An attempt has been made to know about the various influencing factor that mould respondents' attitude towards leading a modern lifestyle. The summarised response of the respondents is presented in the following table.

Table 7.57. Influencing factor for Leading Modern Lifestyle

Response	Aggregate		Sex-wise analysis			
	No. of Respondents	Percentage	Male	Percentage	Female	Percentage
a. Friends only	27	10.72	15	9.26	12	12.33
b. Family and relatives	31	12.30	23	14.20	8	8.89
c. Media only	151	59.92	91	56.17	60	66.67
d. All of them	43	17.06	33	20.37	10	11.11
Total	**252**	**100.00**	**162**	**100.00**	**92**	**100.00**

The above table reveals that more than half of the respondents hold media as an active influencing factor, which shaped their attitude towards leading a modern lifestyle. On the other hand, one-fifth of them support friend, family and relatives as their influencing tool for leading a modern lifestyle. Nearly, one-sixth of the total respondents support all the above-mentioned elements responsible for moulding their behaviour towards leading a modern lifestyle. A sex-wise analysis of the same clearly says that a significant majority of both male and female respondents support media as their influencing factor. Thus, to conclude, a preponderant majority of the total sample favour media as one of the most influencing factors in moulding their attitude towards leading a modern lifestyle.

7.39.1. Age-wise Analysis

An age-wise analysis of the same is depicted in the following table.

Table 7.58. Influencing factor for Leading Modern Lifestyle

(Age-wise Analysis)

Responses	Teen		Young		Middle		Old	
	No. of resp.	Percent-age	No. of resp.	Perce-ntage	No. of resp.	Perce-ntage	No. of resp.	Percen-tage
a. Friends only	06	14.28	10	7.41	11	15.71	Nil	Nil
b. Family and relatives	02	4.76	12	8.89	15	21.43	02	40.00
c. Media only	30	71.43	78	57.78	40	57.15	03	60.00
d. All of them	04	9.53	35	25.92	04	5.71	Nil	Nil
Total	**42**	**100.00**	**135**	**100.00**	**70**	**100.00**	**05**	**100.00**

From the above table it is clear that irrespective of the age group, a significant majority respondents supports the role of media as an influencing factor which moulds their behavioural attitude towards leading modern lifestyle.

7.39.2. Education-wise Analysis

An education-wise analysis of the same is presented in the Table 7.59. From the table, it is pointedly clear that, irrespective of the education groups, a significant majority of the total sample supports the role of media as an influencing tool in moulding their attitude towards leading a modern lifestyle.

Table 7.59. Influencing factor for Leading Modern Lifestyle
(Education-wise Analysis)

Responses	Under-Graduate		Graduate		Post-Graduate		Professional degree holder	
	No. of respon-dents	**Percent-age**	**No. of respon-dents**	**Percent-age**	**No. of respon-dents**	**Percent-age**	**No. of respon-dents**	**Percen-tage**
a. Friends only	06	14.28	08	13.33	07	5.60	06	24.00
b. Family and relatives	10	23.81	02	3.33	09	7.20	10	40.00
c. Media only	24	57.14	39	65.00	79	63.20	09	36.00
d. All of them	02	4.77	11	18.34	30	24.00	Nil	Nil
Total	**42**	**100.00**	**60**	**100.00**	**125**	**100.00**	**25**	**100.00**

To conclude, majority of the respondents unanimously support the role of media as a significant influencing force, which mould consumers' behavioural attitude towards leading a modern lifestyle.

7.40 DEVELOPMENT OF A MODEL FOR CONSUMER BEHAVIOUR

In the present chapter sincere attempt has been made to develop a consumer behaviour model to exhibit the purchasing behaviour of an individual consumer. For this purpose, the findings from Chapter VII (Impact of advertising on consumer behaviour) and the knowledge of consumer behaviour models from Chapter V of this study have been incorporated together.

The model presented in Fig. 7.1 has been developed by studying the impact of TV advertisement on the purchasing behaviour of the individual consumers of Berhampur.

In case of TV advertisements, the stimuli generated go through the step of exposure into the Central Control Unit (CCU) or the mind of an individual buyer/consumer. There is interaction at that level between the CCU and exposure. When the exposure is acceptable to the CCU, it generates attention for the exposure. At this level, if there is a lack of the right amount of interest, the consumer

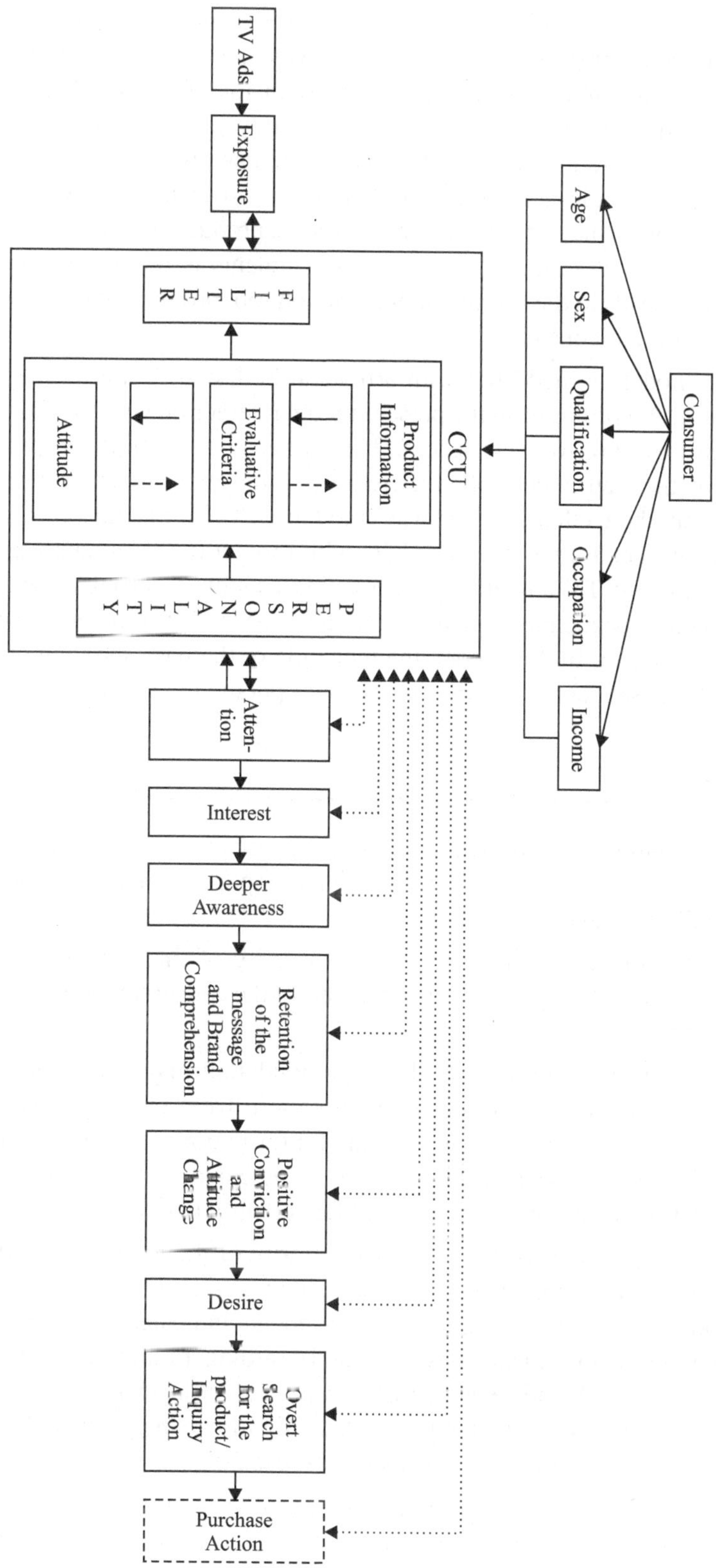

Fig. 7.1. Model developed for the Impact of Media (Television) Advertisement on the Consumers

is aware of the commercial. In the present case, the interest generated has to be considered as substantial in the commercials leading to the next step of deeper awareness. The deeper awareness leads to the retention of the message and comprehension of the brand advertised in a strong manner. Such a state, as has been found out in the present study, leads to a state of positive conviction and an attitude change in favour of the product. This state usually creates a desire in the consumer about either possessing or at least learning more about the advertised product. The obvious next step the consumer gets into, is the state of overt search for the product or inquiring action. With the completion of this state, the positive impact of TV advertisements is proved; but in many cases the step of inquiring action leads to the actual purchase action too, proving again the very strong impact of TV advertisement on the consumers.

In the model, dashed lines with arrows at both ends point to interaction through feedback from both ends. Accordingly, in the present model interaction with the CCU is observed at each step starting from exposure to overt search. This is because the ultimate processing and rejection or acceptance of the step is controlled there *i.e.*, in the mind of the consumer. However, after the purchase action, the feedback is one way into the CCU for the reason of post purchase evaluation. A dissonance or a consonance in the CCU with respect to the purchase gets stored in it for future response by it to the TV advertisements coming as stimuli through exposure. The environmental influences such as occupation, qualification, age, sex and income also exert their influence on the CCU of the consumer. In this model, the rectangle or the base showing purchase action is given in dotted lines because a consumer may or may not pursue the purchase action after the overt search.

SUMMARY

This research work has been confined to magazine and television as the two different advertising media. A majority of the respondents support both the print and electronic media as their favourite media for advertisement.

The analysis clearly indicates that a majority of the respondents accept advertising as a helping hand in formulating the buying decisions of the consumer indicating its pervasive presence in their daily lives.

It is observed from the study that a preponderant majority accept that advertising is solely responsible for change in their consumption pattern from one brand to another. Advertisements generally are aimed at providing a good deal of information regarding the products or services to the prospective buyers. In the present survey it is revealed that more than half of the respondents believe advertising as it presents a true and fair picture, where as a minimal few discarded it.

In the survey analysis it is seen that majority of the total respondents agreed advertising as informative, while a negligible percentage agreed by saying that, advertising is manipulative to some extent. Ranking of various media by the respondents indicates that, television placed at the top of table, whereas newspaper, magazines, radio and hoarding, billboards and wall writing placed second, third, fourth, fifth, sixth and seventh respectively. Advertisement leads to cost enhancement of the product/services. Survey analysis indicates that a significant majority of the total respondents favours more by saying that advertisement leads to cost escalation.

Television programme and the advertisements are complementary to each other. Thus, it is necessary to know about interesting programme, which are watched most by the viewers. It is clear from the survey that mega serials are the most popular programmes followed by film-based programmes. A sex wise classification points out that mega serials and film-based programmes are mostly watched by females than their male counterparts. Television advertisements are mostly accepted by all the viewers due to its audio-video feature. In the present survey almost all the respondents indicate that they watch/read advertisements both in television and magazines/ newspapers. An analysis of the watching/reading pattern of television/magazine indicates that a majority of 52.38 per cent respondents watch/read the advertisements carefully and analyse the message content there of. Undoubtedly, television advertising is more informative than other media, which is clearly proved through the present survey since 89 per cent respondents accept that television advertising is more informative than other due to its visual effects and other features. Television advertising helps brand switching and thus it plays an important role in moulding the attitude of consumers.

Survey analysis shows that, majority of the respondents use cell phone for the sake of need, fashion, style and status symbol. To make life up to date, fast and dynamic, majority of the respondents are using Internet chatting. A significant majority of the respondents show disinterest for browsing porno website on Internet and also for reading pornographic magazines. A significant majority of the respondents use computer for better lifestyle and knowledge dissemination. More than half of the respondents say no to sky shopping/tele shopping or online shopping. Majority of respondents purchase readymade dress for the sake of quality brand image and for latest fashion. For the sake of status symbol and better lifestyle, majority of the respondents prefer to purchase car and motor bike which are latest in style. The survey analysis shows that majority of the respondents prefer occasional consumption of cold drinks and fast food. A simple majority of respondents participate in disco dancing. A thumping majority of respondents say that, girls on tight jeans and skimpy dresses who appear on television screen are modern and up to date.

On beauty contest, majority of the respondents irrespective of age, sex, education, occupation and income favour their pleasant figure and dressing style. A majority respondents favour advertisement of sanitary napkins on various media. Almost all the respondents are of unanimous view towards advertised goods and services. Majority of the respondents say that break time for advertisement, if not welcome, is useful for self and family. "Does advertisement corrupts the young generation?" In response to the question, majority of the respondents say 'No'. The survey analysis shows that, irrespective of age, sex, education, occupation and income almost all the respondents support celebrity endorsement of products. The survey analysis shows that a thumping majority of the respondents support strongly for the role of media as an influencing force, which ultimately leads the people for adoption of modern lifestyle.

Consumer behaviour models help in understanding the behaviour of the consumers in buying situations in the environment of external and internal influences. The findings about the media ad impact on the consumers of Berhampur from Chapter VII and the knowledge on consumer behaviour models from the Chapter V of this report have led the researcher to design and develop a consumer behaviour model to observe the impact of television ad on the individual consumers. The models also show the flow path of the impact and the interactions, through feedback channels, between the central control units of the consumers and the various steps on the path.

Chapter 8 LIFESTYLE COMMUNICATIONS THROUGH PRINT AND ELECTRONIC ADVERTISEMENTS

PART–A

PRINT PRESENTATION OF LIFESTYLE

8.1 INTRODUCTION

The present chapter explains print presentation of lifestyle advertisements. Twenty-five print advertisements were collected and analysed from different magazines. For advertisement copy, please see Appendix I.

Gone are those days, when goods and services were advertised in terms of their quality only. There is a sea change in the present day advertising market scenario. Most of the present day advertisements, besides communicating product quality, disseminate lifestyle elements.

Advertisements are an integral part of the commodity culture, which in turn has become an important sign of modernity. They signify for the viewer a 'modern' self marked by consumerism, such that the purchase and consumption of commodities constitute in itself a value. This is what Stuart Ewen in all-consuming images calls the "commodity self", a selfhood or identity mediated and constructed through the use of consumption of commodities. This is how advertisements succeed in producing or at least influencing changes in lifestyle, so much so that cultural theorists have argued that they promote not products but lifestyles. The advertisements below clearly demonstrate this through the human subjects that they present.

Advertisement No. 1 and 2

Product: Cigarette

Brand name: India Kings and Wills Navy Cut

What is immediately apparent in the two ads is the set of differences between the human figures depicted. First, the Navy Cut ad shows a young couple while the India Kings ad shows a single man, who is also evidently older than them. The couple has just moved into a new house - they are moving furniture—and are therefore presumably recently married. Their youth, casual dress and gay abandon connote an informal style that is in marked contrast to the very formal appearance of the India Kings man. The latter is shown as a person who stands apart from the rest, ruling over others like a true "king", suggest visually by depicting him in sharp focus against a background that is blurred. The visual technique of foregrounding here signifies differences of power and status. (Compare this with the Navy Cut ad, which uses a deep focus shot to produce both foreground and background as equally sharp.) This is a very good instance of how slogan, brand name and a superbly coded visual work together in producing the ad's meaning. By showing the two packets of India Kings in the same ground, the ad produces a relation of equivalence between the cigarette and this very self-assured and powerful individual—with the implication that if you smoke India Kings you will acquire the same self-assurance and power. In contrast to this, the Navy Cut ad promotes an image of young lovers who are, like the perfectly blended tobacco, "made for each other." In other words, while the India Kings ad prefigures control over both self and the world as important and valuable in one's self-definition, the Navy Cut ad prefigures youth, mutual love and togetherness. Clearly the two ads interpellate different identities and are therefore targeted at two different kings of consumers, two distinct lifestyles.

An important point in both the ads—the fact in all cigarette ads—is the obvious contradiction between the images of healthy and happy individuals who are in control of their lives and the statutory caption at the bottom, "cigarette smoking is injurious to health". The images clearly work to erase the meaning of the caption, which is always set apart from the visual field of the ad to signify its irrelevance to the world that the ad represents, a world of fantasy and wishful thinking, a world that is shown as possible and realizable yet never real.

Advertisement No. 3 and 4

Product: The Apparel/Fashion Accessory

Brand name: Wills Lifestyle and Liberty

Like the Navy Cut and India Kings ads, the Lifestyle and Liberty ads constitute their viewing subjects through contrasting differences. The Liberty ad shows pairs of young boys and girls in a fashionable and 'hip' setting, perhaps a disco club, asserting their "liberty" from social conventions. This image of youth subculture opposed to 'Establishment' values is supported by the charmingly irreverent slogan, "*Hum duniya se nahin, yeh duniya khudko humse jaane!!!*" The slogan locates the image and the values appropriate in the ideological space of the Hindi film genre that glorifies modern youth rebelling against the values of an outdated and constricting tradition. The use of Hindi words in English script refers to a particular class of elite, English-educated urban youngsters who use such a mixture of Hindi and English as a way of being 'cool'. The ad promotes a self that is young, liberated, pleasure-seeking and free of the responsibilities of the adult world. The Wills Lifestyle ad, in contrast, promotes an image of youthfulness combined with formality, responsibility and a restrained pleasure in the good things. The young man and woman are in clothes that are formal without being conventional, and they appear 'cool' but not too much so. They represent the new class of young entrepreneurs and professionals - "new age leaders" - who are both a part of the Establishment and opposed to it, "breaking down the shackles of hierarchy and domination" from within rather than outside. As in the India Kings ad, the use of sharp focus and foreground sets them apart from the world that serves as their background, functioning as a visual index of power and status. Finally, the 'Western' look of the two models and the references to European fashion houses in the ad copy promote an image of global leadership that has become valuable in the age of multinational capitalism.

Advertisement No. 5

Product: Ladies vanity bag

Brand name: Louis Vuitton

The Louis Vuitton ad promotes fashion products specifically for women, offers highly erotic images of the female body within a semiotic context in which sexual desire acts as a stand-in for consumerist desire. In the Louis Vuitton ad, the woman looks seductively into the eyes of the viewer as she sits by the swimming pool on a full moon night—all elements of a setting that connotes romance. By placing the bag in the field of this image and making its handle resemble the pool's handrail, the ad establishes it in a relation of equivalence to the valuable of wealth, romance and leisure that the image connotes. The sensual facial appearance appears to the viewers a lot.

Advertisement No. 6

Product: Cotton bra

Brand name: Loveable

The Loveable ad promotes high-class fashion and stylish product specifically targeted for women, offers highly erotic and sensual images of the female body within a semiotic context in which sexual desire acts as a stand-in for consumerist desire. The completely uncovered breasts comparatively connote two cold soft drinks. The naval portion of the naked lady appeals sexual desire to a greater extent. The Loveable ad establishes an equivalence between the undergarment it promotes and 'cool' sensuality. The ad promotes an image of woman as erotic and desirable, coded within vales that are clearly western and modern lifestyles.

Advertisement No. 7

Product: Washbasin

Brand name: Hindware

It displays high-class quality washbasins. Three curvaceous women, two in vertical pose, one in reclining pose, are made to stress the shapes of three commodes or hindwares. Sexual allusion is obvious. This is the type of ad, which reduces women to the level of urinals/latrines/washbasins equipment depiction. Women with fairly prominent hips and protruding breasts are not presented in a dignified manner. They are commodified, cheapened. The purpose of the advertisers seems to hog the attention of their male clients by arousing their libidinal passions/dreams. The words such as great shapes, fascinating, and the pictures of scantily-dressed feminine shapes, they all present a scene of sexual gratification meant for the male customers. The swimming pool and the swim costume of the three young ladies again projects sexual appeal, high-class lifestyle and western modernity.

Advertisement No. 8

Product: Lady undergarment

Brand name: Sloggi

This ad shows two young women revealing their lower zones of pleasure. These cotton briefs are no more undergarments. The posture of the women is provocative, not because they put on the briefs, but because they unbutton their jeans trousers to give an idea of concealment of privacy. Erotic quality of this ad is heightened by the women's willingness to undress. The presentation of two women in such physical closeness is also suggestive of lesbian love, for one woman directs her finger to the briefs-covered area of the other woman; and the words "And so much more" make this reading rather explicit. Although this ad is meant for female customers, it does not lose sight of male customers. Such ads show women in a poor light. The purpose of our ad man is to attract attention to its brand name 'Sloggi'. They do not perhaps care much for their customers' appreciation or depreciation of such ads. The ad projecting 'Sloggi' undergarments is highly stylised, westernised and modern lifestyle pattern.

Advertisement No. 9

Product: Wristwatch

Brand name: Longines

This ad to promote Longines' watches shows a refinement of taste and subtleness of sensibility which most of the Indian ad agencies lack. A woman of real elegance and substance sits in a posture reflecting on something more important than the goodness or preciousness or the brand of her watch. The watch is visible to us, but the wearer does not consciously want to show it. The worthiness of the charming wearer is transferred to the watch. The elegance we find in the lady is a by-product of her attitude to life, her inner make-up. The watch is honoured to be worn by her. Not the other way round. Dolce Vita, meaning pleasant life, is in sine with the soft smile, which shows itself on the reflective face of the lady. There is an air of romantic melancholy about the wearer of the Longines' watch The customer/the viewer of this tasteful ad may feel tempted to buy this watch hoping to elevate himself/herself to the pleasant reflectiveness of the wearer of this watch.

Advertisement No. 10

Product: Face cream

Brand name: New Ever Youth

Women are the most potential sources of any advertisement campaign. Their look, their gesture, their glaze and their mute expressions can cause a spell on every individual. In the present context, the advertisement of 'Ever Youth', connotes the cool and serene feeling, symbolically represented by the smiling lady with an impressive look, glorious texture of her face and the finger of the lady pointing out her youthfulness. The flakes of cucumber, a piece of lemon, leaf of neem and mint in the advertisement suggest their importance in protecting the human skin from the sun damage, as prescribed in Ayurveda. With the applications of these, in an advanced form will keep one as pristine as the pristine beauty of the coy and demure lady as projected in the present advertisement. The ad signifies high-class lifestyle that promotes fashion products specifically targeted for female segments. The dazzling eyes connote young and beautiful charming lady. The smile appeals utmost satisfaction.

Advertisement No. 11

Product: Cell Phone

Brand Name: Samsung T 500

The advertisement projects Samsung T 500 cell phone accompanied by a young beautiful expressive woman. The crystal embedded Samsung T 500, is not the less resisting than the soliciting eyes of the lady-campaigner. That the compact and trendy cell comes in all shades, is evident from the various nuances of her complexion, her overpowering eyes, luscious lips, inviting looks, inscrutable waist. The gradient and changing hues of the countenance is sure to cast a spell on the onlooker, the jewel that she could be one's precious possession, if one wanted. The curvature of her body-line, the sheen, the shade and her inscrutable waist gives a stunt to the product as the prime object of desire.

Advertisement No. 12

Product: Cool Mint

Brand name: Listerine

The advertisement postures Listerine cool mint, along with two funny young models. Funny, though it may seem the couple with their nostrils shut with a pair of clips, highlight that bad breathes no longer need to be 'masked'. With Listerine, now they can ooze out love, even though they exhale through the mouth. No bad breath, no putrid smell, the freshness of love puts the lovers in a trance. The glow in their faces, representing the power of the elixir *i.e.,* Listerine. Listerine mouthwash does not guard their breath, it mixes their breaths in perfect unison of love and harmony. Thus the ad aptly represents both the human and alchemic dimensions of love. The use of Listerine to avoid bad breath is a symbol of modern lifestyle and high-class attitude.

Advertisement No. 13

Product: Wristwatch

Brand name: Omega

The advertisement pictures a wristwatch with superb sports celebrity Anna Kournikouva. An elegant watch, with superb artistry and impeccable design cannot be better advertised without stardom, and especially an immaculate tennis player like Anna Kournikouva. Anna Kournikouva being the model for the ad, it not only lends the product an impression of being the elite among the coterie of watch making companies, but also adds a new glamour to it. Besides the glamour of the star model, the product calibrates itself on her gracefulness, her acute sense of timeliness, cute looks and intrinsic merit. The diamond set bezel she wears is a lavish proof of its grand merit. The star-lady simply seems to reach the message of the merits of the product by her lucid gestures. In this advertisement, there is a perfectly blend of enchanting smile, glittering eyes, high-class life profile and quality.

Advertisement No. 14

Product: Home Appliances

Brand name: Jagdish Store

The advertisement that shows a cosy home with fine tapestries, gaudy fabrics, lavish door hangings, and precise blinds for room decoration is a dream of every housewife. Nobody in the country, however, choose to be outlandish for the sake of cosy-comfort in export-oriented markets, when there is an abundance of such finery and tapestry for their home décor. The housewife seems to be delighting herself on her overwhelming range of finery, starting from upholstery covered with floral designs, cheek patterns, contrasting stripes, the feathery rounded pillows, the exquisite patterns on them, the exotic range of colours and of course the matchless blinds that set the foreground of the picture. The advertisement with bedroom designed material signifies rich lifestyle.

Advertisement No. 15

Product: Male Undergarment

Brand name: Rupa Euro

The advertisement shows the man standing akimbo with her dear lady reclining on his strong right arm sets the foreground of the ad. More to be probed in the advertisement is the ease at which the man cradles the lady, without flexing even an extra muscle. The lady seems to be dangling from her arms in the most natural manner. The shape and size of the body of the man is in perfectly matched with the lady. The cut, the design and the feel is what is emphasised in the intimate moments of the loving pair. The stylish presentation of the undergarment appeals viewer attention.

Advertisement No. 16

Product: T-Shirt

Brand name: Provogue

The man in the ad is a perfect example of a sportsman sitting relaxed after a gruelling session of football. The ruddy on his face, the indomitable stamina in his eyes, the strength in his build and the attire he wears are lavish overtones of his prowess and sportsmanship. The brands of his T-Shirt at the frills of his hands and collarbone seem to be giving him an extra grip to his personality and thereby adding an extra fillip to his sportsmanship. The advertisement communicates the high-class lifestyle by projecting the film star.

Advertisement No. 17

Product: Shirt

Brand name: Color Plus

The advertisement that speaks of a spick and span gentleman, clad in delicate cotton shirts seems to be ideal for the gentleman of the by-gone days. Today's macho man is represented by his rugged, tough, flanky Teflon attire. Be it smeared while gulping his 'Tandoor Dal' at the Dhaba or greased with the lubricants of his bike, every stain that will create its image on his shirt, will wash off as presented in several advertisements of the older days. The status as shown are vacillating and will not stick to the fabric, a speciality of the shirt 'Color Plus' as shown in the advertisement.

Advertisement No. 18

Product: Air Journey

Brand name: Indian Airlines

The advertisement portrays a young gentleman with a smiling face and executive dress-up stretching his hands into the sky. The hands represent the wings of Indian Airlines flight inviting the people to fly in it. The background cloud indicates that even in clouds (difficult climatological position) the IA is safe on board. In addition, the more one avails air journey in IA, the more mileage points are assured in return, the ad promises. The structuring of the IA ad is a good example of attracting more and more people to avail of IA flights. The advertisement portrays high-class lifestyle and targets rich section of the society.

Advertisement No. 19

Product: Women's Wear

Brand name: Allen Solley

In this modern age of competition for the sale of products in the markets, Allen Solley has made a good piece of advertisement to popularise its women's wear, particularly the Agile Trousers. The lady, in the picture, seems to be very jolly and contented while riding the bicycle putting on the Agile Trousers manufactured by Allen Solley, which is indeed the oldest company established in 1744 A.D. at Nottingham in England. Frankly speaking, the lady in action, probably proceeding to a destination, attracts the attention of the onlookers as it (the picture) gives a message to all concerned that ladies can freely and independently without any escort and support can travel to far off places. The small bag which she has hung at the handle, the wrist watch of the right hand, the *kankan* of the left hand, the dress, appearance, bodily posture and, above all, the very smile on the lips with a loud laughter are the things worthy to watch. For wide pushing sale of the articles manufactured by Allen Solley, this photograph is certainly a good selection, for the lady who is quite young enough to her age seems to be touched much by modernity and she also possesses a sophisticated style and gentle appearance.

Advertisement No. 20

Product: Body Perfume

Brand name: Jadore

Impression of the First Eye: The lady in the picture seems to be in a melancholy mood possessing much mental agonies. She is depressed for some reasons and her angry look conveys the feeling that she has either some unpardonable grievances against somebody or a deep grudge against some one who had betrayed her aspiration. From her facial expression one can assume that probably the so-called traitor (the enemy) is approaching to her side and therefore she is gazing at him with full mental alertness as if she is even in a mood to kill him as a matter of revenge.

Impression of the Second Eye: From another angle if somebody looks at this picture, he will find that the lady is drowned with heavy sex-urges. She is totally unsatisfied; and her eyes, lips and the total facial expression and bodily behaviour explains the point that she is too much sexy and as if she is waiting for her partner with much hope amidst frustrations.

Advertisement No. 21

Product: Club Wear

Brand name: Wills

Party and clubs are the destinations of new age Indian women, who have come a long way from the *pallu* of a *saree*. But there is no grace in the looks of the princess. She appears scared, for glamour is a burden under the glitter and glare.

Happenings happen at the hips
hip-hip-hurray for the hips
club at the hips which provokingly protrudes under the
impact of club wear.

The advertisement connotes modern aged young generation who prefers to visit club with suitable club wear. Clublife is a concept associated with high-class lifestyle and rich society. This ad communicates high-class lifestyle of the richer section, for whom, club attending is an important part of life. The dress style is highly modern. The posture of sitting is executive. The eyes and facial appearance signify looking for something special.

Advertisement No. 22

Product: Car

Brand name: Maruti Zen

The motorcar with a lady in front talk about, that the ladies are no less than a Zen motorcar. As a lady brings new vision, new thinking, new challenges in the life of a man, so also the Zen motorcar brings hopes, prosperity and new vistas in the life of an owner. The mission of life is to bring meanings in one's life-path, and to own it one has to be there at the driving seat rather than in any other seat. To win, one has to occupy the driving seat. This attitude would certainly help the human being to reach the goals and to achieve the mission of life. The eyes are bit expressive. The facial appearance connotes that the young modern lady is quite confident. Mesmerist looks are more deceptive. The mesmerising looks and winning attitude of the young lady adds extra quality to the Zen brand. The ad is targeted for the rich segment. The caption 'Just add Zen to your life' signifies high-class lifestyle.

Advertisement No. 23

Product: Wine

Brand name: Aristocrat

The advertisement belongs to business aristocrat cocktail snacks. The ad distinguishes good looks that complements high-class lifestyle, enhanced with quality well-healed features. The picture shows a dreadful nighttime, where there are many secrets waiting to be unravelled and that is the irregular, riotous beat of the two hearts. Both the young couple are ready to rumble in the thrill of things with aristocrat wine.

Happiness is unbound by time or by reason.
All it requires is the right mood; the
right thing and a spontaneous expression.

The ad connotes two young couple enjoying their togetherness with aristocrat wine. It signifies a classic example of high and rich lifestyle. The cocktail party is completely associated with high profile rich society. Wine glass in the hands of the woman connotes modernity. The facial expression of both the young men and women shows that, they are desperate to enjoy the cocktail party. The background scene portrays a vehicle, which adds extra quality to their lifestyle.

Advertisement No. 24

Product: Aftershave Lotion

Brand name: Old Spice

Advertisement has become a subtle business attempt, which exerts profound impact on human psychology. While witnessing an ad for Old Spice aftershave lotion (musk), one can see how two youngsters of opposite sex are knit together closely exhibiting infatuation for its odour, giving vent to sensuality. The sensuality is so explicit that the semi-blooming rosy lips with her pretty closed eyes of the young lady earnestly in quest of satiating her inner sensual urge. On the other hand the young man while embraced by the excited young lady lost himself in lust through her expressive eyes and facial postures. Such ads certainly change the mode of life in the present day but how far they act upon the growth of society towards betterment is an issue left to the posterity to decide.

Enhancing consumers' commonality presence, it endeavours to be the ultimate masculine sensation. It is created to reflect customers' kind of personality as defined by his character. The ad communicates high-class lifestyle through projecting Old Spice aftershave lotion.

Advertisement No. 25

Product: Cotton Shirt

Brand name: Cliff

The advertisement shows shirts and trousers depicting a young lady with sensual outlook. The facial appearance expresses deep sense of sexual arousal. The eyes are in search of somebody. The wayward hairstyle signifies over excitement towards sex. The lips connote desperate search for male touch.

The slogan "Give me a man who can change his shirt as often as I change my mind" is largely appealing. The sexual appeal in the ad signifies high-class and western lifestyle of women. The ambience, the mood and the company… all the ingredients are inviting. The erotic presentation through depicting a young model adds extra value and appealing to the product quality.

SUMMARY

The summarised picture of the above analysis is outlined in the following. The Western outlook of the models and the references to European fashion houses in the ad copy promote an image of global leadership that has become valuable in the age of multinational capitalism.

The swimming pool, a full moon light connotes romance. The sensual facial appearance appeals to the viewers a lot. The sensual images of the female body within a semiotic context in which sexual desire acts as a stand-in for consumerist desire. In some advertisements, women with fairly prominent hips and protruding breasts are not presented in a dignified manner. They are commodified and cheapened. They all present a scene of sexual gratification meant for the male customers. Women are the most potential sources of any advertisement campaign. Their look, their gesture, their glaze and their mute expressions can cause a spell on every individual.

From the above analysis it may be concluded that the present trend of advertisement is towards modernity, western culture, high-class lifestyle and fashion. Uncovered female body hardly matters. People hardly take serious note of this nakedness. Almost it became a part and parcel of modern lifestyle.

PART–B

ELECTRONIC PRESENTATION OF LIFESTYLE

8.2 INTRODUCTION

Part—B of this chapter discusses electronic presentation of advertisements. Twenty-five different types of television advertisements are analysed below. The electronic ads have been collected and recorded in a compact disc (CD), which has been placed in Appendix II. Out of 70 TV commercials, the selected 25 have been placed almost in chronological order.

Advertisement No. 1

Product: Pan Masala

Brand name: Pan Parag

Ashok Kumar in 'Pan Parag': The purpose is obviously to reach people and create a lasting impression in the mind of the targeted audience. The ad creates an admirable dramatic suspense with the important event of matrimonial negotiation. That too is portrayed by a heavyweight champion of cinema world—Ashok Kumar who is well known for his nuance in serio-comedy. The climax of the suspense comes when the groom's father tells "*one thing I forgot to tell you*". This statement clearly brings anxiety and seriousness. But when the groom's father tells to arrange for 'Pan Parag' the whole situation changes with the punch-line by Ashok Kumar uttering with his usual comical simplicity, "I was not aware that you also like Pan Parag". It indicates that Ashok Kumar liked Pan Parag and the people coming to make relations with him also like Pan Parag. To greet the groom's party with Pan Parag shows its popularity.

In short, the message reaches the mind of the audience. The ad is quite successful due to the amiable character of Ashok Kumar and his natural action. The lifestyle portrayal of Ashok Kumar appeals the viewers to a greater extent.

Advertisement No. 2

Product: Soft Drink

Brand name: Coca Cola

In the recent ad of 'Coca Cola' we find the emphasis on reduction of the price and quality of the product. Though popular the product reduced to almost half of its price. This message should not go negatively to the consumers. Hence the theme communicating the message of reduction of price gains importance.

The character in a robust rustic appearance reflects two things: resemblance with Pandavas and the Pandav like truthfulness with simplicity. The whole thing is short but the message is clear that the rate of a bottle of Coca Cola is five and '*thanda matlab Coca Cola*', which speaks of quality and popularity as well. The tall, robust, dark coloured character does not resemble a Dracula or a monster, but gives the air of Bhim, which comes after hearing about Pandavas. The forceful answer and making the silly mistake by the central character creates seriousness as well as fun when the message is well received. The addition of the two girls was necessary to mellow down the macho feeling and speak on behalf of public.

The ad is a success. The celebrity lifestyle significantly adds value to the quality of the product.

Advertisement No. 3

Product: Hair Oil

Brand name: Navaratna

The ad of 'Navratna Tel' is a piece of normal one enriched by Govinda's presence and handling the matter. Govinda is a lively hero with smile all the way. His telling about the product casts a sway on the audience. Further, his calling the name of Chandramukhi gives an odour. It reminds of the scene Govinda had with Chandramukhi character earlier in a cinema, which was made in a hilarious backdrop. The ad gains importance for its jovial sequences of Govinda.

The punch-line '*Thanda Thanda Cool Cool*' is having wider appeal. The ad communicates lifestyle of Govinda, which ultimately adds value to the quality of the product. The audio-visual presentation is eye catching.

Advertisement No. 4

Product: Bath Soap

Brand name: Jeeva

The advertisement projects bath soap through a beautiful half-naked young female model. The damsel is bathing. "*Purchase 'Jeeva' and get gold worth five crores*"—the message attempts to capitalise on the greed of the consumer. The herbal elements add extra value to the product. It doesn't bother to highlight on the effectiveness of the product nor on its being used by beautiful girls. Women who generally like gold may be tempted not for the soap but for the offer of gold. This advertisement may not appeal because nowhere the quality of the gold is declared. It can be a gold plated bracelet.

Advertisement No. 5

Product: Cool Drink

Brand name: Thums Up

The advertisement shows a well-built hero and a heroine with dashing dress. A very unusual *Mantrik, Tantrik* setting all over. Thums Up bottle in hand, tries to take out one old precious thing from its place in a cave. Tremors shake. The hero Akshay Kumar snatches the 'precious thing' substituting it with the bottle of the 'Thums Up'. The damsel runs away with the precious thing. The hero snatches the bottle and feels the thunder of the shaking and breaking cave in a cinematic style with the heroine in the embrace. The ad portrays a number of filmy scenes with the celebrity.

Advertisement No. 6

Product: Motor Bike

Brand name: Kinetic Boss

The advertisement shows a boy who is a hero worshipper of Kapil Dev the cricketer. He gets a ride with a helmet worn person while he was going for a cricket selection to which he would have been late. The boy expresses his wish to be a cricketer of Kapil's stature and on inquiry says, he prefers Kapil for his speed and fast bowling. Suddenly few young school going boys are crossing the road. The boy exclaims, as the vehicle was likely to dash into the boys. The person riding the two-wheeler applies brake and the vehicle abruptly stops. The rider removes his helmet and the boy to his pleasant surprise finds Kapil. Kapil reflects as the speed of the vehicle. Hidden message is its good brakes. Price is displayed with an offer by Kapil that "*Purchase Kinetic and play cricket with me*".

This is a good advertisement for its high motivational value and the value for the product. Use of women is totally avoided. The audio-visual presentation is highly appealing. The lifestyle portrayal of Kapil Dev adds value to the product.

Advertisement No. 7

Product: Mobile Phone

Brand name: Samsung Digital

The value addition of a product is highlighted exploring the tendency of consumer for something extra. In a mobile phone, if a digital mobile camera is fit that adds value. This is an advertisement that appeals to the human tendency but prize display would have helped to promote the product better. Unrealistic reeling of a stick falling at the footsteps of the holder of the instrument makes it appear as a realistic happening. The ad does not associate the product with any hero, rather projects the intrinsic worth of the product.

Advertisement No. 8

Product: Sauce

Brand name: Kissan Ketchup

Children distaste food even if it is prepared out of ingredients taken from nature like fresh cucumber stuffed in toasts. The young boy expresses this clearly to the mother. Daughter gives no such expression, perhaps not allowed to. May be she is little elder, yet it is the son who expresses displeasure. Both mother and sister are found in the kitchen picking up a bottle of Kissan Ketchup. Mother makes funny movements and places a 'N' mark on the prepared toast. The boy relishes with delight the toast. It promotes a popular food culture in which our youth is caught. The boy is pampered. Both mother and daughter work hard and make funny movements to win over the boy. This is reflective of Indian household and lifestyle, but wrong values indeed!

Advertisement No. 9

Product/Services: Modern Restaurant

Brand name: Pizza Hut

The advertisement shows a middle-class family intended for watching a movie but unfortunately fails to get the ticket, as it becomes houseful. However, to kill time they go to a nearby 'Pizza Hut' and delight themselves and others by dancing and tapping the plates.

It shows the lifestyle of the city dwellers. They are bored of regular cooking at home and sometimes enjoy themselves by going to a movie, restaurants etc. Pizza Hut is an American Chain Hotel with reasonable prices in India. So, the Indian family finds the restaurant affordable. The ad also portrays the delicious foods that attract the viewers.

Going to restaurants, dancing with porters signifies Western lifestyle and the ad particularly influences the middle class Indian family as it serves with affordable price.

Advertisement No. 10

Product: Cold Drinks

Brand name: Pepsi

The new television advertisement on Pepsi (a cold drink) depicts a complete ultramodern lifestyle. Featuring Bollywood stars Saif Ali Khan, Fardeen Khan, Preety Zinta and Kareena Kapoor, it shows the actors talk about open out their undergarments for the sake of a Pepsi. Once upon a time this type of ad were considered vulgar and unethical, but now it is widely acceptable and even popular among the viewers. They do not hesitate to talk about sex and other related things. The world is now completely open for boys and girls to talk freely about sex.

The punch-line used by the celebrity '*Garmi ka mausam hai, Pepsi ke liye hum besharam hai*' appeals viewers attention. The ad is highly modern and portrays high-class lifestyles.

Advertisement No. 11

Product: Cell Phone

Brand name: Nokia

The advertisement on Nokia Cell Phone shows the effect of cricket on Indian families. Created by Bomman Irani, a famous advertising icon, the ad shows a family, watching cricket match on TV while the boyfriend of their daughter paid a visit to them. The father is not happy to see him, but suddenly the other family members are shown an inclination towards him as the TV fails at an eagerly watching movement. But the message in the Nokia mobile shows a sixer by an Indian batsman. The father asks his father (the photographed picture acts as a third umpire) and the green light is signalled.

This ad seems to have an impact on the Indian lifestyle, because it depicts the effect of cricket on every family. The ad is also appreciated by number of well-known world level ad gurus.

Advertisement No. 12

Product: Television

Brand name: Samsung

The advertisement shows a family, which have changed their lifestyle completely by purchasing a Samsung television. They have purchased a series of Samsung products and realised an enormous change in their attitude, attire and lifestyle. The punch-line '*Samsung badalde aapki duniyaa*' appeals viewers' interest. The advertisement again proves that, when the visitor paid a visit to the concerned family, he himself is surprised by seeing the sudden change in their lifestyle. Their child who was calling his father '*pitajee*' now calls 'dad'.

This particular advertisement depicts the change of lifestyle of a middle class family.

Advertisement No. 13

Product: Squash

Brand name: Brahmi Sudha and Shanti Sudha

The advertisement shows a number of young female models with half covered body, old man and kids for displaying the *Sharbat* (squash). A well-furnished swimming pool is shown, where an old man jumped into it and started swimming accompanying with a small kid. On the other hand a young man seen in the ad is having fear for swimming. The punch-line '*buddhe ban gayee jawan, aur bachae ho gayen balwaan*' sounds interesting.

The ad wants to disseminate the message that Shanti Sudha squash makes an old man young and makes the kids energetic. It is an instant source of supplementing energy. It makes people free from tension. The young women prefer to talk with the old but neglect the young man. It shows masculinity and energy power inclination. Overall picture shows that besides the product, the ad communicates a rich lifestyle such as swimming pool, young women and their provocative style.

Advertisement No. 14

Product: Car

Brand name: Maruti Suzuki Waganor

The advertisement shows two beautiful young male and female models, a group of Doberman hunter, a high-class quality car. The car is shown with driving condition accompanied by two young beautiful models. The lady wore half covered dress with smiling face. The car started running followed by a group of Doberman hunters. After a lay while, the car stopped and both the young male and female got down from the car and allowed the Doberman to get an entry inside the vehicle.

The ad projects two beautiful male and female models as well as the Doberman hunter. On the other hand, the energy, running power of the vehicle has been compared with the Doberman hunter.

The facial appearance of the male model shows courage and confidence, while the lady's overpowering eyes, luscious lips and inviting looks appeal viewers' attention. The half-naked body shows something erotic.

In fine, the ad communicates high-class lifestyle with executive attitude of the models for displaying the car.

Advertisement No. 15

Product: Butter

Brand name: Amul

The theme is simple– every one irrespective of caste and creed, young and old, everybody relishes Amul butter. The concept of universal brotherhood is seen in the ad. The characters hail from all the backgrounds—many religions. All of them are in love with the product. The unique combination of people from different set up is the striking point. Being a food product, the children of vegetarian families like Punjabis, South Indians have special fascination for the food. Even a child refers to cricket and a snap reminds of the bat. This speaks of energy. For hard work energy is needed and that energy is derived from the product. The only demerit in the ad is showing unapproved overweight, which is injurious to health.

Advertisement No. 16

Product: Car

Brand name: Opel Corsa

Two young couple are portrayed with the Corsa Sail Car with driving position. The ad shows the young man kissing a beautiful young lady inside the car.

The kissing style, embracing position, dress style and above all the sensual look of the woman appeal viewers' attention. With the help of these lifestyles of young men and women, the ad intends to project Corsa Car. The visual presentation, musical background and attractive slogan appeal viewers' attention.

Advertisement No. 17

Product: Gel Pen

Brand name: Add Gel

The ad is a small chip—a real fabric of life woven to the pattern of daily needs. The main theme is on purchasing a pen. The shopkeeper is natural and the boy is quite natural in emphatically demanding for a better product as a customer. He wants good quality not an ordinary pen, which also writes. The dialogue is touching and the attraction is natural—spontaneous. The special appearance—body language of the boy with his extraordinary eyes makes the episode memorable. The natural, boyish but quality consciousness of the boy who has appeared in such aggressive roles gives an impact to the product selling. The role of the shopkeeper is also impressive as he tries to push through his product. As a whole, the ad is successful in popularising the product.

Advertisement No. 18

Product: Scooter

Brand name: Honda Eterno

The advertisement shows Honda Eterno accompanied by a father and his son in a driving position. Both father and his son reached their home point. The mother of the boy asked for some gift if they brought for her. But the small boy with smiling face says 'No'. The lady with an angry face shows something disinteresting for the new scooter. But at the same time her husband shows some interesting gift, which is lying inside the scooter and that suddenly appeal the attention of his wife.

The advertisement communicates the stylish life pattern of the family in order to project the new Honda Eterno scooter. The smile of the boy, his father and mother sketches attention. The boy shouts, the punch line '*I got Honda*' appeals a lot.

Advertisement No. 19

Product: Toothpaste

Brand name: Close up

Without telling much in wordy jargon, the ad leaves a lasting impression in all segments of the customers and fulfils the purpose of reaching the twin messages (*a*) Close up is not costly - it sells at Rs.25/- for 80gm and (*b*) it is admittedly superior to others or even it is the only material in the market.

Starting with a college background a boy is seen with a jovial mood keeping a "Physical Chemistry book close to his chest, which is indicative of "Physical Chemistry" of Close up or the girl or even the boy himself. The boy's uttering the words in a subdued manner looking to the front physique of the girl and chuckling words with usual tremor due to nervousness owing mainly to the closeness of the body of the girl is supreme. He casts a charm perfectly coaxing the girl for his product. Since he is not a salesman the matter assumes more importance.

Coming to the girl, she has an imposing personality in the sequence. After talking to the boy triumphantly, she realises about his facial expression seen during conversation. He finds that she is having bad breathe. At this the boy sends a body language reminding her of his suggestion.

The message is couched in a good vehicle to reach the target and make the mark.

Advertisement No. 20

Product: Club Soda

Brand name: Bag Piper

It combines two poles—two contrasts–two forces *Purush* and *Prakriti* in the classical background. Erotic passion subdued by the background song. The desire to fly and dance on arid land. Macho action with feminine submission.

India is the land of religion, spirituality. Hence going away, flying away is the escape root from reality and that is the effect of the product. It charms like a piper-bags the attention takes to dizzy heights like the captains bringing an air of higher echelon of the society. It gives imagination, strength for fighting or *Tandav* and insight to enjoy *lasya*. The intoxicating effect is balanced by singing to God for union with love of immorality.

Advertisement No. 21

Product: Toilet Soap

Brand name: Rexona

The ad conveys that Rexona makes the body silky. A lady takes bath with Rexona. When she puts the *Bindi* it does not stick to her forehead. It falls down once and again. Rs. 2/- is written on the *Bindi* indicating the reduction amount at which the ad is also aimed. The brightest skin among women is capitalised. The *Bindi* does not stick to her forehead because of extreme smoothness of the skin and it is due to the touch of new Rexona. The ad gives an extra benefit of Lux doodh malai and a discount of Rs. 2/- per cake to the consumers. The ad harps at both product quality and price.

The glamour of the lady is noticeable. However, as per Hindu custom *Bindi* is the sign of a married woman and its disappearance indicates a bad omen. Its falling down will not be taken easily by the women folk, particularly in rural India, for which the ad is meant. The ad tries to appeal viewers' attention through projection of silky skin and celebrity lifestyle.

Advertisement No. 22

Product: Edible Oil

Brand name: Tirupati

The advertisement shows a beautiful Indian dressed housewife busy in cooking. The lady and food are displayed simultaneously so that we can infer that every item is cooked by the lady. The lady seems talking over telephone to the person in office eating food from a tiffin carrier happily expresses the mood of a good quality recipe. The display of Tirupati brand of edible oil makes us to infer that the good food; the creditworthy woman and happy husband are all due to this brand. With minimum of verbal message excepting some musical presentation, the advertisement has driven home the message. The enchanting smile, pleasant eyes and above all the funny movement of the lady draws attention.

Advertisement No. 23

Product: Fairness Cream

Brand name: Fair & Lovely

The advertisement projects two middle aged husband and wife, a young bride and a groom and a *lagna mandap* for Fair and Lovely small pack fairness cream presentation.

1st Scene: Husband is very much depressed about his daughter's ugly face. But his wife is bit confident as she is frequently showing her five fingers towards her husband. This connotes the price of Fair and Lovely face cream. The lady intends to speak that, ugliness of her daughter does not matter because of the presence of low priced Fair and Lovely.

2nd Scene: A '*lagna mandap*' is shown where the groom is highly surprised by seeing the new face of the bride. The punch line used by the groom '*kya baat hai, din ba din nikharte ja rahe ho*' is highly popular and eye catching. The next scene portrays the bride using Fair & Lovely cream.

The ad communicates the product on one hand and presents a stylish presentation of family lifestyle on the other.

Advertisement No. 24

Product: Glucose

Brand name: Glucon-D

The advertisement shows Glucon-D accompanied by two small kids, a middle-aged man and woman. In the first part of the ad the father of the kids denied of dancing with his son due to his hectic tiredness.

Taking advantage of this situation, his wife gave a glass of Glucon-D. The energy supplementation helped him to say 'Yes' for dance with his kids. The background music and dialogue presentation makes the ad attractive. The slogan '*Naa ko haan karde*' delivered by the lady is bit mind blowing. The smiling face of the lady, her glittering eyes show immense satisfaction. The facial appearance of the middle-aged man was very much depressed at the first glance, but got handsome energy after taking a Glucon drink. The facial appearance of the two kids connotes complete confidence.

Advertisement No. 25

Product: Toilet Soap

Brand name: Nirma

This advertisement shows the portrayal of beauty Nirma bath soap.The celebrity star Sonali Bendre, with half uncovered body displays the usefulness of Nirma soap. The smiling face, attractive young outlook, uncovered body, bathe scene, and sensual look of Sonali appeal viewers' attention to a greater extent. The waterfall and natural background scene, and above all the audio-visual presentation of the ad draws attention. The advertisement communicates Sonali's lifestyle, which ultimately adds extra value to the quality of the soap.

SUMMARY

The summary of the above analysis is presented in the following. The first ad creates an admirable dramatic suspense with the important event of matrimonial negotiation. The ad is quite successful due to the amiable character of noted film star Ashok Kumar. The theme of the second is to communicate the message of price reduction. The celebrity lifestyle significantly adds value to the quality of the product. The third ad gains importance for its jovial sequences of Govinda, the celebrity star of Bollywood. The Thums up ad in a cinematic style, accompanied by noted film star adds extra value to the product. 'Kinetic Boss' is a good advertisement for its high motivational value and the value for the product. The Samsung ad with its dramatic presentation projects the intrinsic worth of the product. The 'Kissan Ketchup' ad is reflective of Indian household and lifestyle, whereas 'Pizza Hut' ad shows the lifestyle of the city dwellers. The ad particularly influences the middle class Indian family as it serves with affordable price. A completely ultramodern lifestyles of the young film stars are projected to popularise Pepsi brand soft drink. The Nokia advertisement depicts the effect of cricket on every Indian family, whereas the Samsung television portrays the change of lifestyle of a middle class family. In Maruti Suzuki ad the lady's overpowering eyes, luscious lips and inviting looks appeal viewers' attention. The Bagpiper ad gives imagination, strength for fighting and the insight to enjoy lasya. The intoxicating effect is balanced by singing to God for union with love of immorality. The message from the Close-up is couched in a good vehicle to reach the target and make the mark.

Thus to conclude, most of the above advertisements on television presents a rich and fashionable culture with Western outlook.

Chapter 9 ADVERTISING IN THE AGE OF ECONOMIC LIBERALIZATION

9.1 INTRODUCTION

Economic Liberalization is a broad term that usually refers to fewer government regulations and restrictions in the economy in exchange for greater participation of private parties. The arguments for economic liberalization include greater efficiency and effectiveness that would translate to a bigger pie for everybody.

Liberalization is a concept with many differing definitions. It is a process which entails the free movement of capital, goods, services and labor around the world. Economic Liberalization is the massive control of the world's economy by big business, this control transcends the boundaries of state and country.

At political and economic level, liberalization is the process of denationalization of markets, politics and legal systems, it is the rise of global economy. Many international organizations, governmental institutions and the whole academic world discuss the consequences of this political and economic restructuring on local economies, human welfare and environment. It is one of the most important features of present world. At a business level, the process of globalization is when companies decide to take part in the emerging global economy and establish themselves in foreign markets. They adapt their products or services to the linguistic and cultural requirements of different nations. Then, they might take advantage of the Internet revolution and establish a virtual presence on the international marketplace. More and more companies do their business online. E-commerce has changed traditional business practices by providing direct international access to information and products.

Some scientists agree that globalization has also cultural and ecological connotations, and that it is not only political or economic phenomenon. It means that countries all over the world become interdependent in many possible ways. There is probably no area of human activities left that is not affected by globalization. We listen to the same music, eat the same food, wear the same clothes, and decide ecological and war and peace issues together.

The process of globalization has been an integral part of the recent economic progress made by India. Globalization has played a major role in export-led growth, leading to the enlargement of the job market in India.

One of the major forces of globalization in India has been in the growth of outsourced IT and Business Process Outsourcing (BPO) services. The last few years have seen an increase in the number of skilled professionals in India employed by both local and foreign companies to service customers in the US and Europe in particular. Taking advantage of India's lower cost but educated and English-speaking work force, and utilizing global communications technologies such as Voice-Over IP (VOIP), e-mail and the internet, international enterprises have been able to lower their cost base by establishing outsourced knowledge-worker operations in India.

As a new Indian middle class has developed around the wealth that the IT and BPO industries have brought to the country, a new consumer base has developed. International companies are also expanding their operations in India to service this massive growth opportunity.

Notable examples of international companies that have done well in India in the recent years include Pepsi, Coca-Cola, McDonald's, and Kentucky Fried Chicken, whose products have been well accepted by Indians at large.

Globalization in India has been advantageous for companies that have ventured in the Indian market. By simply increasing their base of operations, expanding their workforce with minimal investments, and providing services to a broad range of consumers, large companies entering the Indian market have opened up many profitable opportunities.

Indian companies are rapidly gaining confidence and are themselves now major players in globalization through international expansion. From steel to Bollywood, from cars to IT, Indian companies are setting themselves up as powerhouses of tomorrow's global economy.

In Literal meaning, globalization means worldwide or pertaining to or embracing the total. In market terms, it would mean interdependence of the world based on demand and supply phenomenon. In the Indian context, globalization came with the implementation of liberalization in the early 1990's. The pre-liberalization era In India was referred to as the 'license raj, which meant that during the period one needed to obtain licenses for everything before initiating business. When India opted for a mixed economy after independence in 1947, the stress was more on a socialistic pattern of economy.

After more than 45 years of independence, some political parties began to seriously consider opening the Indian economy to international investment. Serious thought was also given to disinvesting the government's shares in public sector undertakings, many of which had become perennial loss makers and a liability for the public exchequer. The Congress party led by Prime Minister P.V. Narashimha Rao, after winning the elections in 1992, became the architect of liberalization in India. There were doubts about its success and criticism from many quarters, especially from the left parties and Swadeshi lobbies.

Globally, the disintegration of the USSR, the merging of East and West Germany, the creation of the European Union, the softening of the socialist economy of China, the role of the World Bank, and the growing need of the developing nations to borrow money and technology from the developed countries were some of the factors that contributed greatly to globalization. Some analysts in India relate globalization to the old philosophy of 'Vasudhaiv Kutumbakam' , while others believe that it will lead to economic imperialism of the worst kind. Whatever the reasons or effects of the phenomenon, never since the coming of the East India Company has India been thrown open to overseas bidding on as big a scale as now. In fact, there are two schools of thought in the country, one that believes that liberalization is irreversible and another that believes that the current phenomenon is not liberalization in the true sense of the term. Hey feel that the current system is a total sellout. It is one way traffic opening the Indian economy to foreigners, while suffocating Indian industry.

Globalisation, feel some analysts, has become a favourite catch phrase with journalists and politicians. It has become a key idea for business theory and practice, and has entered academic debates. However, what various people understand by the term globalization is often confusing.

Globalization is often used as an omnibus term to describe the connectedness of markets, communication through free access and technology across the world. To others, globalization is synonymous with exploitation- the rich nations entering unexploited markets in the developing world and buying cheap labour. Globalization has strong socio-economic, cultural, and geopolitical dimensions. Companies such as Nike, Adidas, and Ralph Lauren have come under sharp criticism for paying a pittance to workers in developing countries- as little as 13 cents per hour against $10 for similar work in the USA. Global companies are criticized for venturing into markets that may not need their commodities. With their smart marketing techniques and persuasive communication they are able to hook millions of people, especially the youth and children in poor countries, on to products they would be better off without, such as lifestyle products like liquor and tobacco. Klien argues that the concept of branding was brought in by some management theorists in the mid 1950', who believed that successful corporations must produce brands and not products .

Many believe that globalization has widened the gap between the rich and the poor. However, Nobel laureate Amartya Sen argues that to look at globalization as merely western imperialism of ideas and beliefs would be a serious and costly error. Globalization, he feels, is much more than that, the emergence of institutions like the World bank and the European Central bank has brought new constraints and imperatives.

Globalization may be about connectivity-but more through wires and Internet than through interpersonal interactions with various constituencies. Online banking and retailing have enabled companies to connect with people and communities living in various continents and speaking different languages in a short time. The interconnectivity provided by the web and the live chat look at the various consumer sectors that have truly tasted globalization before we look at its impact on advertising.

9.2 BRANDING STRATEGIES IN INDIA

The Economic Liberalization impact on some consumer durable sectors has been analyzed in the following section.

Soft Drinks

Coca-Cola left India in 1977 when a non- Congress government was voted to power for the first time in the post -emergency election. After 12 years, rival Pepsi was allowed entry, masquerading as a processed -food venture. It did not receive much favourable media support initially. Coca-Cola reentered the Indian market in 1993 at a time when Pepsi was doing fairly well. Thums Up, which emerged as the answer to Coke after Coke left in the late 1970's, had become the undisputed leader in the Indian market. It was bought over by coca-cola as a strategy. Over the years, comments a survey, the perception of being aliens has faded away. Coke-Pepsi advertising bouts have become agreat source of entertainment to many urbanites. The per capita consumption has gone up from three to four bottles.

Toothpaste

The toothpaste market was always open with many global brands jostling with each other. The entry of the American giant Procter & Gamble (P&G) has been significant as its marketing strategies are said to have textbook precision.

Detergents

According to analysis, in 1990, long after the Nirma magic faded in marketing circles, few could have foreseen the technology wave that was headed towards Indian shores. The early phase of liberalization brought with it a player, P&G launched Ariel, a compact detergent that forced Lever to come out with an improved product, surf Ultra, and ten Surf International with its Anglo-Dutch technology. Both brands have since been fighting for the unban housewife's attention. In 1994, P&g launched its Ariel Super Soaker, a high tech product aimed at Nirma users at the low end. The Product, according to market analysis , became a super success. The last few years have seen the market value of this brand going up and the excise duty going down. Many other brands such as fena, Tide, and locally manufactured Ghadi have joined the fray. Price cuts have been the foremost strategy with most of the competitive brands. The advertising campaigns are also designed towards sales promotion activities. The leader Surf took an interesting route in 2005 by involving cine actress and social activist Shabana Azmi, who ex horted that people suse Surf as it required less water to wash clothes. Coming at a time when there was water scarcity everywhere, the TVC seemed to touch a chord with its tagline, "Do bucketpaani hai abb bachchana". However, the Surf advertising campaign that remains the most memorable is the 1980's campaign featuring Lalitaji with the inimitable tagline, Surf ki khariddari mein hi samajdhari hai against Nirma's *'sabki pasand Nirma'* with a little girl as its mascot. (Jaishri, 2006)

Soaps

In 1991, the restrictions on the import of raw material for soap, except coconut oil and pal, kernel oil, were removed. Unilever, a multinational, hiked its stake in Hindustan lever. Proctor & gamble, America's largest soap player, came in forming an alliance with Godrej soaps, Lever's main rival at that point. Procter & gamble introduced Camay at a competitive price. Many others soaps such as premium Dove also entered the market.

Cosmetics

Cosmetics attracted120% excise duty till 1991. Herbal offerings, which tend to be more expensive than synthetic ones, constituted about a third of the Rs. 650 crore market. Since then, excise duty has been skashed in stages. Some sought after international brands, which up-market Indian women have craved for, are now available at the international price. Global cosmetic players such as Revlon, Avon, Oriflame,, and L'Oreal have swept the market. There is a plethora of cosmetic products such as fairness creams, anti-wrinkle creams, hair colours, gels, etc.,each more alluring than the other. Overall, the Indian cosmetic market is placed at more than Rs. 1,500 crore, with a growth rate of a frenetic 18–20% per annum. With the coming of a variety of brands carrying international equity with them, analysts feel that the share of herbal products is dwindling. Lakme, a tata brand, was a pioneer in the cosmetic industry in post independence India. Somewhere along the way, it lost its premium position. The brand has repositioned itself in the last few years with a plethora of new products for beauty conscious young women.

Colour Television

The booming TV market is considered among the most happening in the past one decade. Brand proliferation has put the consumer in the driver's seat, especially as no foreign brand was allowed till 1992. Excise duties were cut drastically and import tariff on kits was reduced. Local brands have virtually been driven out of the market, with the exception of one or two brands. The coming of Sony and some Asian giants such as Akai, LG, and Samsung has changed the market scenario like nothing before. Attractive trade offs and the availability of combinations of a variety of products of the same brand and now of other companies also have given the average consumer a wider choice.

Audio Equipments

The audio equipment segment has seen a product range explosion like probably no other sector. Ill 1991, Philips had the monopoly in the audio market with its power house brand which had virtually no competition in the product category. The rest were cheap two in one cassette recorders or top end hi-fi systems. With many international players such as Sony, Samsung, LG, and Akai entering the market, the growth has been phenomenal.

Washing Machines

Before liberalization, low end tubs with motors were considered washing machines accounted for 30%, while fully automatic machines constituted a 10% share of the market. The R & D departments of various companies took into account Indian conditions such as scarcity of running water, and voltage fluctuation, to provide a suitable product.

Cars

The car market has seen phenomenal change. Successive government have undertaken a number of projects on flyovers in urban India, along with the task of improving highways. Though the process of improvement has been gradual and a lot more needs to be done, this has not deterred the best brands from entering the Indian market, be it Mercedes Benz, BMW, Ford, Toyota, Peugeot, Mitsubishi, or Hyundai. The entire market is brimming with excitement.

For decades after independence , there were only two brands on Indian roads, viz. Ambassador and fiat. Maruti changed it all the mid -eighties when it launched its Maruti 800 in exciting colours. The car attracted more premium than its original cost of about Rs. 60,000 a unit. It proved to be not only sleek and stylish, but a great petrol saver at a time when the world was going through a petrol crisis. There has been no looking back. Apart from maruti, which has a partnership with Suzuki of Japan, the South Korean brand Hyundai and many others have invaded the market. The going has been easier as easy finance is available from banks.

There seems to a place for every brand. Tata's entry into the passenger car segment at the turn of the century proved that despite many foreign brands , when it came to goodwill., it scored over everyone else. Before launching its passenger car Indica, it was able to mop up amount 1,500 crore as advance booking from purchasers. (Jaishri, 2006)

Air Conditioners and Refrigerators

Surprisingly, the air-conditioning market, though expanding, has not attracted many foreign bidders. In the area of refrigeration, some Indian companies have technical collaborations, such as BPL- Sanyo, Videocon-Matsushita, general Electric in alliance with Godrej, Electrolux, Whirpool, Modi Hoover and Samsung. A mild degree of protectionism still persists in this segment. The government allows marketers to import fully built refrigerators only if they have a capacity of 300 litre or more.

Ice Cream

The ice cream segment is another product category that has not been able to cut much ice in multinationals.

In the over Rs.850 crore ice cream market in India, not a single multinational brand has been able to make headway. Indian tastes seem to be ruled by Amul, Mother airy, and some regional brands such as Vadilal, Dinshaw, and Arun. Mc Donald's also offers ice cream at its outlet that is probably the most economical.

Swiss brand Movenpick parted way its local franchisee Ravi Jaipuria in 2002, because of steep pricing. The brand is now marketed through third party arrangement, though its brand visibility is very low.

Amul ice cream , which is 50% cheaper than Kwality Walls that is owned by the Lever group, is many notches ahead of its competitors and has plans of reaching the Rs. 1,000 crores mark by 2010.

An interesting phenomenon witnessed the world over, especially after the expansion of markets globally, is that old players are either relegated to the background or have a negligible presence. Critic s and market analysts ascribe this to the growing use of persuasive communication and fierce marketing strategies that include sales promotion, etc. For instance, pioneering companies that were synonymous with their products, such as Xerox for copiers, IBM for PCs, and Ford for cars, are no longer the market leaders. Canon has overtaken Xerox in the copier and office document management business, car pioneers Ford and GM are facing tough competition from Japanese car companies, especially Toyota. Low-cost manufacturing companies, especially from China and Korea, have taken over a sizable share of the electronic and automobile market globally. Similarly, carrier, once the largest manufacturer of air air conditioners, has been overtaken by South Korean giant LG. The rise of LG in the global AC industry , according media reports, mirrors its strong growth in India where it virtually ousted Carrier to take the number one position in the segment. In the field of mobile phones, Motorala's visibility was blurred the moment. Nokia came on the scene. Motorola was the undisputed leader in the 1990's.

Kelvinator has been in India for a long time. The brand belonged to a company by the same name, a pioneer in the field of mechanical refrigerators for home use. The company is now with Videocon, an Indian multinational company. Maytag pioneered washing machines in the world. The company that also owned Hoover, the first electronic vacuum cleaner , has now been acquired by Whirlpool.

The global marketplace has created new paradigms of success. With the availability of many brands and the severe competition, there have been price cuts and better and better offers on all kinds of goods, from automobiles to electronic items, detergents to chocolates. The consumer could not have asked for more. (Jaishri, 2006)

9.3 ADVERTISING MANAGEMENT IN A GLOBAL SCENE

This is one area in which the Indian advertising industry has seen mind boggling changes in the last one and a half decades. In India, there is a mixed bag of agencies- some are proprietary in nature, some a re private limited, while others have transnational affiliations. With the opening up of the economy, there has been a tremendous spurt in agency affiliations and tie ups. As the marketplace turned global with multinational companies selling products globally, various international mega brands began to look for partners across Europe and America. Some potential areas included Africa, Asia, Eastern Europe and the Soviet Union. According to industry analysts, Asian Markets are highly valued for their growth potential. Major transnational advertising giants such as Mc Cann Erickson, O&M, JWT and Baker have fairly strong presence in the region.

Though a late entrant, Dentsu is trying to make its presence felt in the Indian market. Agencies world over generally do not handle competing brands. In Japan, the reverse is true. Both Dentsu and the second largest agency, Hakuhodo, that has a turnover of over $6 billion, control 45% of the advertising pie in Japan and handle many competing brands. Similarly, the advertising of global brands is generally handled by the same agencies in various countries to ensure energy in communication in a seamless world. How ever, in the case of the Japanese behemoths, this is not the case. Japanese clients often use a different agency in the different countries in which their products are marketed.

Awards in the field of Advertising

International awards in advertising have been in existence for many years, but it is only in the last decade or so that advertising communities, especially from the developing world, have begun taking an interest in showcasing their work. Some prestigious awards include the following:

The Cannes Lions International advertising festival is the annual get together of the world's advertising, creative, direct marketing , interactive, film, radio, media, sales promotion, and marketing communication fraternities. More than 20,000 entries are received at Cannes from 75 countries. The Cannes festival is a huge event that attracts thousands of people from the advertising fraternity all over the globe. The Indian government's representatives from the Ministry of Information and Broadcasting are also usually present at the event. Media partners create a lot of hype to get entries from within the country.

The Cresta Awards were launched in 1993 by Creative Standards International in partnership with the International Advertising Association. They are open to advertising agencies , advertisers and studio production companies worldwide. The entries have to be original and should not have been sent for any other award consideration. International pre selection juries in USA, Europe and other selected countries determine the short list of finalists that is then submitted to an international grand jury experts for final evaluation.

The John Vaples Awards were established in the memory of the late John Caples whose professional life spanned 58 years, during which he worked for BBDO for 56 years. He is credited to have established the theory method and mathematical principles of response measurement. Until the time he passed away in 1990, he proclaimed the need to recognize creative individuals included in direct response.

Concluding Remarks

In this chapter we looked at the liberalization of markets, the pace of globalization, the reasons for it, and the fact that there is no possibiity of a reversal of the process. Even traditional economies such as India and socialist economies such as China have embraced globalization in the last couple of decades. We looked at advertising in a global world. Should agencies opt for a central advertising campaign, as the consumer is also increasingly becoming a global citizen or adopt a localized approach in advertising to suit the local milieu? The chapter addressed the issue of culture, which is very important when reaching out to disparate communities. We also looked at the emergence of distinct styles of advertising in various countries. Advertising on the internet to reach out to a young audience was analyzed, comparing the target market in India and the US. Management of advertising has probably seen the maximum number of changes in the globalized world. Some agencies that were traditionally rivals have found themselves together in global groupings. Independent media buying outfits have emerged as important entities. Clients often ask for media presentations by these companies, which are also known as the Agencies Of Record(AORs), before deciding on an agency for creative work.

Advertising, which was earlier confirmed to particular countries, now has various for a to showcase its work globally. The chapter looked at some prestigious international awards that have provided advertisers of various countries with the opportunity to meet in one place and appreciate the work of various agencies. They could probably walk away with some recognition and awards. In the case study segment we have looked at how an Indian company, Videocon, has acquired some global companies to become a multinational in its own right.

Chapter 10 CONCLUSIONS, MAJOR FINDINGS AND RECOMMENDATIONS

10.1 INTRODUCTION

The present study titled "Advertising and Lifestyle Communication: An Assessment of Media Impact on Consumer Behaviour" is an attempt to explore the usefulness of advertising, measure the effectiveness of various media of advertising, show the lifestyle communication through advertisement and specially to assess the impact of advertising on consumer behaviour. The summary of the findings of the study is presented in the following paragraphs.

10.2 MAJOR FINDINGS OF THE STUDY

It has been observed from the analysis undertaken in the earlier chapter that advertising as such is found to be quite useful for all the respondents while buying products/services in the modern day competitive market. A preponderant majority of the respondents in fact, accepted advertising as an important tool in guiding and helping the prospective buyers in the market place while choosing product/service.

Though advertisement is commercial in nature, it is supposed to present a true and fair picture of the products or services. This enables to earn the consumers' confidence with the advertised product/service. In the present survey it is surprising to see that more than half of the respondents have agreed that advertising presents a true picture of the product/service in spite of its dramatised presentation. This proves product credibility and its truthful presentation.

In the modern competitive society with the existence of buyers market, the options before the consumers are wide open with the availability of a wide range of products and services. In making a choice regarding the needed product/service, advertising provides the necessary clues to the consumers. As a matter of fact, every consumer depends upon advertising for gathering all possible information about the product/service, which helps in making intelligent and judicious purchase decisions. However, a very few majority of the sample indicate that advertising is manipulative in nature. It attempts to generate favourable opinion towards the advertised products/services through all possible means. Therefore, exclusive dependence on advertisements for selecting products/ services may lead to gullibility of the buyers, they opine.

A thumping majority opined that advertising always leads to the cost enhancement of products and services. But the rest feel that the public service ads that enhance quality of life are distributed free of cost to the consumers.

As far as the impact of advertisement is concerned, the respondents are considerably influenced by advertisements in a positive manner. The exposure of all respondents to advertising clearly establishes the all-pervasive influence of advertising on the socio-economic environment.

Brands will only succeed in as much as they build relationships with the consumers. It is no longer a question of functional or even emotional relation with the brand. It has to be a more comprehensive relationship, which will have to be based on an understanding of the way consumers behave. In our survey about 90 per cent respondents have agreed that advertising really helps the company in building brand image of the products/services whereas the rest disagree with such a view. This is a pointer of the fact that dependence of modern business on advertising is a judicious and economy-driven decision.

Sample opinion is almost unanimous as far as ranking of all the media is concerned. It is observed from the foregoing analysis that television emerges as the clear choice of the respondents as the first favourite medium followed by newspaper. Therefore, it is clear that the electronic media particularly television as a medium of advertising dominates all other media due to its exceptional feature of audio and vision in one cell. With the combination of audio and vision, colour, movement, sound, timing, repetition and presentation at a considerable cost, television is considered to be the most popular advertising medium than any other media.

Television programmes and advertisements are both sides of the same coin. Television programmes are usually sponsored by advertisers who always search for programmes, which are watched by a majority of the viewers. The programmes on TV considered to be most popular are film-based events and mega serials. Such an opinion provides the most appropriate cue to the prospective advertiser/ businessmen who are always looking for popular programmes to insert television commercials.

Out of the various categories of products advertised, the convenience goods are said to be given top priority followed by soft and durable goods.

Almost half of the sample feel that brand switching is more due to the TV commercials than any other media or means.

The mega serials and film-based programmes on TV show the neo culture of social drinks during various parties, which seem to influence viewers especially the younger generation. Although consumption of liquor is a social taboo and is considered to be unethical, it is surprising to find out that all the male members as well as one-third of the female members go for social drinks either regularly or occasionally.

In this study the respondents are found to be greatly influenced by the lifestyles of the celebrities such as film stars, sports stars and top-class models. They are adopting quickly the changing lifestyles and new varieties of fashionable goods endorsed by these celebrities. As much as eighty-three per cent respondents are influenced by the portrayed lifestyles of celebrities.

The semiotic analysis of both print and electronic ads show certain distinct trends of modern lifestyles.

It is remarkable to notice that skimpily dressed young girls are featured in ads of products not necessarily meant for women. It seems as if nudity is on sale in the name of modern lifestyle. The copywriters or creative artists use all types of expressions in the ads - the smiles, the sensual look, the hairstyle, the provocative exposure of various sensitive parts of the body. This is obviously an attention-drawing technique employed by the advertisers.

The advertisers portray the celebrities from film, sports and modelling in order to cash in on their popularity.

The ads are invariably designed to cater to the whims and pleasures of the affluent class of consumers neglecting the very interests of the common mass.

From the semiotic analysis it is noticed that a type of neo culture imitating the Western lifestyle is engulfing the media world.

10.3 TESTING OF HYPOTHESES

The hypotheses formulated in the first chapter are tested on the basis of analysis of data collected from the survey and semiotic analysis.

(*i*) Advertising has significant impact on choice of brand. An overwhelming majority of 89 per cent support the above claim. On change of brand 40.50 per cent of the sample have switched their loyalty in the convenience goods, 27 per cent changed their loyalty in case of soft goods, and 21 per cent of the sample agreed that advertising has altered their choice in the durable goods category. Advertising influences buying decisions as it ranks number one in the list having 55 per cent (Table 7.11). Thus, this hypothesis is found to be true.

(*ii*) A preponderant majority of the sample accepted television as the most preferred medium of advertising having the highest weighted average ranking of 62.04 among all the respondents. Thus, the second hypothesis is also found to be true (Table 7.13).

(*iii*) In our study a significant percentage of respondents use Internet occasionally or frequently, but the majority (72 per cent) of them are not interested to go to pornography website and they are also not interested in pornography magazine (Table 7.30). But in case of drinking wine (social drink) cent per cent male enjoy drink - regularly (9.87 per cent), occasionally (41.98 per cent) and sometimes (48.15 per cent) whereas, these figures for female are regularly (nil), occasionally (23.33 per cent) and sometimes (6.67 per cent). From semiotic analysis it is revealed that the creative artists have taken the liberty of featuring young girls in various provocative poses probably considering the indifferent attitudes of the viewers. Hence the third hypothesis can be taken as partially true.

(*iv*) The modern lifestyle has been greatly influenced by celebrity. A majority of the total respondents (83 per cent) support the claim as the celebrity endorsement of product appeals the viewers' attention to the maximum possible extent. This indicates that the fourth hypothesis is true (Table 7.56).

10.4 PRACTICAL UTILITY OF THE RESEARCH STUDY

1. The present study can assure the advertisers to invest without fear in advertising as the findings of the study obtained through empirical research points towards that.
2. The findings of the present study take out a lot of burden from the shoulders of the managements for which media selection is a predicament while launching the advertising campaign.
3. The research study helps the ad agency people especially of the creative departments to properly conceive and design the storyboard for the commercials.
4. The study also includes the analysis of the types of programmes on the TV, which are crowd-pullers. This helps the sponsors and the agency people to select the time slots to insert the commercials for proper impact and research within the constraints of the funds allocated for the purpose.

10.5 FUTURE EXTENSION OF THE STUDY

To the best of the knowledge of the researcher, the present study is a virgin one. Despite hard efforts and detailed probing, lack of precedence has rendered it with some unforeseen weaknesses. That apart, the lack of proper resources and enough time for a behavioural research study of this dimension has led to the creeping in of some of the snags.

The sample size chosen for the study appears to be quite sizable considering that the study is only an academic one. But considering the importance of the findings and their bearings on subsequent practical applications, the size of the sample can easily be extended so that representative aspect of the same can be taken care of. A limitation of the study has been the sample being confined to Berhampur city only. After analysing the data collected through the administration of a structured questionnaire survey, it has been found that more objectivity could have been incorporated in the questions and the same could have been set more scientifically to elicit more appropriate and accurate information from the respondents for the purpose of analysis and interpretation.

The above limitation of the study pave the way for further extension of the present endeavour in more than one way. The study can be undertaken on national level or even in the state of Orissa on a large scale maintaining sample representatives. A direct interview method can also be adopted to elicit more accurate information from the respondents to make the response, analysis and interpretation of the collected data more scientific and empirical. However, the analysis presented in this study does help in not only understanding consumers of Berhampur, but also does the spade work for further research in this area.

CASE STUDIES

1. LAKME GIRL

Revlon—the cosmetic giant in the West created a breakthrough in advertising by featuring Revlon girl. Cindy Crawford, the well-known super model, is now te Revlon girl. The face for many years was of a model, Lauren Hutton. In 1987, thcy created a new campaign titled" the most Unforgettable Women in the World. Renowned beauties like Imam were featured with Jerry Hall.

Lakme in India has also featured versatile as well as saleable faces—yasmin (Miss India-1966), Purnima Dixit, Maureen Keelan. Lakme's search for a model gave them a sophisticated face of shyamolie verma in 1981. Shyamolie became a corporate model for all their products for three years. Then followed an assortment of faces, some known, some unknown. However none of these faces could take on the whole gamut of products. Shymalie surprisingly has surpassed all her successors. Once again the search for a Lakme girl is on. Lakme Lever never took an Unknown face. Besides, Lakme as a brand is bigger than the face. Bipasha Basu was their change in the mid 90's. To be Lakme face today, you do not have just to look good, you have to feel good. (Jaishri, 2006)

Problems:

a. What is the logic behind a Lakme girl versatile enough for the entire range of products?

b. What is the difference between a Lux model recommending the soap and a Lakme model?

c. What do you think are the reasons for the success of Shyamolie Verma as lakme's model for all their products for three years?

2. ALEMBIC CHEMICAL WORKS LTD.

Direct Mailings of Alcephin: The legend among Antibiotics.

The pharmaceutical companies have to do direct marketing by necessity as they cannot advertise ethical products in layman's media for him, but are required to promote only to the medical profession. They produce fine visual aids and products literature which could either be sent as direct mailings to the medical profession or can be delivered to them through medical representatives. The most important thing to make the mundane promotion out standing by creative ideas. Promotions of S.S. Oberoi came out with a set of 10 four-page folders for Alcephin based on the theme' the Living legends'.

The folders are extremely well executed-well designed and printed. The graphics and typography and illustrations are appealing. The idea is outstanding, ten living legends are chosen and include names like Satyajit Ray, Mother TERESA, Baba Amte, Lata Mangeshkar, Sunil Gavaskar, R.K. Laxman, Abdul Kalam, and Shivram Karanth. Each folder deals exclusively with one legend. The selection covers a wide cross section of interests. Each folder is well researched. it brings out the circumstances that inspired the magic in each of them. It becomes a collector's series. The centre spread has the manufacturer's plur. A short write-up on the characteristics of alcephin and the line The legend among antibiotics. It is not intrusive at all. Yet it is effective. (Jaishri and Jain, 2006)

Problems:

a. Which other business/products can be suitable candidates for direct marketing? What promotional techniques can be employed.?

b. Please do some research of your own on direct mailings of pharmaceutical companies. What are your reactions?

c. Put on your thinking cap. Identify a theme for a campaign of one general tonic.

3. SOCIAL AWARENESS ADVERTISING

Social awareness advertising promotes ideas. But for these ideas, creativity will be of a different kind. A product is out there in a shop. A bar of soap is an investment of small consequences. Trying to sell an idea—like a free cancer check-up, the need to keep the Ganga clean, the importance of family planning, is altogether a different proposition. It needs more care, more study, more perception, more inspiration and above all, more sensitivity—not in the good- table—manners sense but as honesty as it is possible for a human being to speak like a person and not an ad man.

Tara Sinha wants advertising to become an instrument to accelerate the process of change in the urban and rural society. Social awareness advertising, according to her, should be much more than tokenism with a potential to do PR job. It should have a better fate than being hung in galleries or occasionally released in media. Public Service Adveritisng or Social Awareness Advertising must bear a stamp of professional excellence that moves people to action-especially the voluntary organizations who together with the makers of advertising and planners of media form a part of the team. She emphasizes that it is important to ensure that there is an agreed statement on the specific and if possible measurable action which the advertising must generate among groups of people. It is also necessary that public service advertising be viewed on a campaign basis: adequate time must be given for a advertising to work.

It is desirable to have an agency like the Ad council of the USA which makes use of the team work of the agencies., the corporate entities and the media. The agency created for this purpose brings together cause and resources. There are areas of exception like the IOC educating the consumers on the do's and do not's of cooking with packaged gas, the campaigns designed to show car owners how they could get the most mileage out of their vehicles. (Jaishri, 2006)

Problems:

a. Think of the social obligations of business. Then think of social obligations of advertising agencies. What socially relevant causes can be taken up for this genre of advertising?

b. What is the similarity of this kind of ads? How do they distinct them?

c. Contemplate how breast-feeding can be promoted amongst Indian women?

4. COMPLAN

Formulated by Glaxo, UK as "complete planned food. Found its way into emergency rations for British soldiers during the Second World War. First positioning 'meal in a tea cup' for famished men in the army.' 'Complete meal for soldiers. Glaxo India's largest brand . Sales touching Rs. 60 crore. Launched in 1967 in India. Milk beverage market, currently estimated as Rs. 300 crore. 705 of the market is of white beverages. Complan's share is a third of this market. Market has stagnated in the last four years. Complan has however managed a 10% annual growth rate. First positioning in India; ideal food supplement for aged and recuperating promotion: ethical.

Larger targeting: Growing children. Make it tastier and appeal to kids. Chocolate variant made its entry. Tasty nutrition drink. Another flavor—cardamom saffron. Mass media campaigning while continuing ethical promotion through chemists and doctors.

Communication Strategy:

To create a personality for the brand: 'I am the complan boy; I am the complan girl.'

Sales Promotion schemes to keep excitement alive.

Problems:

a. Discuss whether Complan can be targeted both to the children and the aged.

b. Discuss how Complan can best meet the competition.

c. Can Complan think of relationship marketing ? How?

d. What role SP: sales Promotion, can play in effecting sales of Complan?

5. LINTAS

Prakash Tandon, the ex-chief of Lever had remarked that LEVER was a creative experience. Padamsee, the ex-chief of Lintas was greatly influenced by this, and decided to make Lintas a creative organizations in the best sense. But that did not mean that he wanted accountants to become creative. However, he did emphasise innovative accountants who could find new and better ways to do their tasks. Lintas was made new. The salary structure including the year end gifts also evolved to keep pace with this new Lintas. The organization must break off the old JWT syndrome. When Padamsee took over, the copy and the art departments were separated. He paird them up. Creative teams were constituted. Copywriters and visualizers were made to work in close co-operation. It sparked off excellent creativity. Padamsee formed mini-agencies, instead managing one huge one. He introduced a managing committee of eight to nine well informed, dedicated and intelligent people to run Lintas. They throw in ideas.

Many new ideas emerge in the meeting of the managing committee, *e.g.* small is beautiful. Lintas, Bombay was divided into Lintas Bombay 1 and Lintas Bombay 2. Two MD's were appointed to head these. Padamsee became the chairman of the BOD, rather than MD. The MD's set objectives, and MBO was introduced. Padamsee was left free to conceptualize by these arrangements. At the lowest rug, jobs are managed . Up scale, people are to be managed. At the top, concepts are to be managed. They put down a Lintas code. The code read, 1. We believe there is always a better way of doing things. 2. We believe in completing everything we start. To complete an idea, you must have an author or father of that idea or else the idea becomes a step child. 3. We believe tht we should treat our colleagues as our friends, and not rivals. (Jaishri, 2006)

Problems:

a. Discuss the challenges involved in managing an ad agency.

b. Is it correct for an agency to position itself, say as a creative agency?

6. TELEVISION COMMERCIAL

A tanned young man skiing effortlessly through a meadow of flowers and grass. Despite the clouds of possen all about, he does not even wrinkle his nose. That is because he takes Allegra, Hoechst marion rousell's anti allergic medicine. Ads on prescription drugs in the US are estimated to be US $3 billion in 2009. This exceeds ad expenditure on beer. Ads on TV alone exceeded US $70 million in the four months of 2009. A Celebrity has been endorsing Claritin and anti allergy prescription drug. People tend to see their doctors after seeing a drug ad. These doctors then prescribe a drug. TV ads of Valtrex, treatment for genital herpes, made Glaxo to receive 6 lakh calls. Direct advertising help people about their treatment for common ailments. In some cases , patients learn more about rapidly treatments than doctors do *e.g.* HIV infection.

Lifestyle drugs are better sold through ads. Self medication and over prescription are two danger areas of direct advertising. Expensive new drugs are promoted in place of low cost simple molecules. Disease management through advertising is the next step. Such infomercials can be developed for chronic diseases like diabetes and arthritis.

Problem:

Examine a lifestyle drug's advertising campaign.

7. THUMPS UP

2009: Sales promotion campaign. A crown redemption scheme. Later, two under the crown schemes. Now a scratch card game.

2010: The ad line is back to 'Taste the thunder' which focuses on flavor differentiation. 'I want my thunder' served its purpose by instilling a pride of usership. Research has shown that a user chooses Thumps Up for taste, which is uniquely Indian. It helps washing down of spicy food of tikka type.

Thums Up personality continues to be blend of brain and brawn. In the commercial, Akshya Kumar retrieves a Thumps Up bottle from underwater for a girl.

Akshay Kumar , the teen-ager's idol is brought back as endorser.

Problem:

Akshay Kumar derides the other drink as kids drinks, whereas for Thumps Up you have to grow up. Comment to this.

8. THE TAJ GROUP OF HOTELS

In the beginning of the 90's, Taj undertook a formal marketing research exercise to understand the furrent lifestyles. Formerly, it relied upon research inputs from the air line and travel industry. The research attempted to discover what would appeal to the future customer. The top ranking was received by exclusivity. The findings also revealed that the company's existing customer base of traditionalists who liked the classy under stated Taj was shirnking. Taj is a powerful brand name, with a high degree of unaided recall. The recent corporate campaign strengthens this strong identity of the Taj. The Taj is symbolized by an enigmatic woman who is known for hospitality and efficiency. This is the new identity developed after consumer attitude study towards the Taj. In-depth interviews were conducted. The research was qualitative. The parameters examined were doing the right things, the quality of check-in, the smile, the greeting or the welcome drink. The Taj has been given a distinct personality of being caring, efficient and enigmatic. It is an emotional slot. The line goes on' She is the Taj.' The base line is 'Nobody cares as much. (Jaishri, 2006)

Problem:

A new hotel at a tourist spot, say a hill station is trying to create its identity. How can it be done? What is the role of relationship marketing in marketing a hotel chain?

9. LIRIL AD

Years ago, when Padamsee first proposed to Gian Bahl, the advertising manager of Lever, an advertising idea for Rexona Soap which featured a girl bathing under a waterfall, he rejected it on the ground that it would outrage the modesty of woman hood. Later the same idea was used for Liril soap.

Liril positioned asfreshness soap is in the midst of another relaunch, though it has already witnessed several relaunches in past 23 years of its existence. The package has been redesigned , the shape changed and the fragrance too. It also promises new freshness. The relaunch promotion concentrated on the youthful segment, especially the teenagers,. The classic waterfall, girl and jingle ad was modified to meet the needs of the relaunch. The youthification has been intensified. Communication a la MTV and channel V style was developed to address the youth. The commercials for the first time omitted the waterfall and the girl. Liril of late has not been doing well. Perhaps, the lime factor no more matters most for the consumers. It is a testing time for the soap advertisers.

The latest Liril campaign features skimpily clad tara harma braving sub-zero temperatures to sella cake of Icy Cool mint soap atop a glacier in Iceland. The ad had been conceptualized by R. Balakrishnan, the creative head of Lowe.

Problem:

Is it right for the company to emphasise youth? What are your suggestions?

10. DABUR CHYAVANPRASH

Introduced in 1970. The brand name itself had become problematic later. It would have been better if a non-generic brand name had been chosen. Others were free to adopt this brand name and reap the benefits of promotional efforts of Dabur.

First Positioning: A tried and tested natural health tonic for the family. Rishi was chosen to propagate its benefits. The authenticity and continued tradition of centuries was conveyed by this ad. The ad ran for a decade. Dabur then decides to contemporize the brand. The plastic package was introduced. In 1984, the brand appeared on TV. Time tested caption was retained, twin benefits of health and vitality were offered. Endorsed by actor Shriram Lago. Commercial ran till 1989. Zandu and Baidyanath introduce their versions. Corporate brand name Dabur which was not so far been stressed was now highlighted. The name was repeated in a 20 second film for at least 7 times. In1991, again benefit route was chosen. The commercials were focused on various user groups.

Target audience

Middle-class scooter owning households, in the social economic class B. Spill over expected from A and C classes.

Positioning

The tonic to develop and strengthen the body's immune systems which helps the body fight infections/diseases.

Problem:

What can the company do to distinguish its product from those of the Competitors ?

APPENDIX–I

BIBLIOGRAPHY

Aaker, David A. and Myers, John G., *Advertising Management*, Prentice Hall of India Pvt. Ltd., New Delhi, 1996.

Alderson, W., *Dynamic Marketing Behaviour*, Homewood III, Irwin, 1965.

Alderson, W., *Marketing Behaviour and Executive Action*, Homewood III, Irwin, 1957.

Alderson, Wroe, *The Productivity of Advertising*, 1960.

Alexander, R.S., *Marketing Definitions: A Glossary of Marketing Terms*, Chicago, American Marketing Association, 1980.

Alexander, Ralph S. (ed.), *Marketing Definitions*, American Marketing Association, Chicago, 1964.

Allport, G., "Attitudes", C. Murchison (ed.), *Handbook of Social Psychology*, Worcester, Mass., Clark University Press, 1935.

Anderson, Clinton, P., *The New York Times*, July 13, 1955.

Barden, Neil H. and Marshall, Martin V., *Advertising Management—Text and Cases*, Taraporevala, Bombay, 1972.

Barton, R., *Advertising Media*, New York, McGraw Hill, 1984.

Bauer, R.A., "Consumer Behaviour as Risk Taking", Robert S. Hancock (ed.), *Dynamic Marketing for a Changing World*, Chicago, American Marketing Association, 1960.

Bellur, V.V., *Marketing Research: Theory and Practice*, Himalaya Publishing House, Bombay, 1987.

Birn, Robin, *Effective Use of Market Research*, Kegan Page, London, 1992.

Blackwell, R.D., Hensel, J.S., Philips, M.D. and Sternthal, B. *Laboratory Equipment for Marketing Research*, Dubuque, Iowa, Kendal Hunt Pub. Co., 1970.

Blake, Reed H. and Maroldson, Edwin O., *A Taxonomy of Concepts in Communication*, Hastings House Publishers, New York.

Bolen, William H., *Advertising*, John Wiley and Sons, 1984.

Book, A.C. and Lary, N.D., *The Television Commercial: Creativity and Craftsmanship*, New York, Decker Communication, 1970.

Brehm, J.W., *A Theory of Psychological Reactance*, New York, Academic Press, 1966.

Brewster, Judson A., Palmer, Herbert A. and Ingrahama, Robert G., *Introduction to Advertising*, McGraw Hill, 1947.

Broadbent, Simon, *The Advertising Budget*, NTC, Henley, 1989.

Burton, Graene, *More than Meets the Eye—An Introduction to Media Studies*, Edward Arnold, London, 1990.

Burton, Philip W., *Principles of Advertising*, Prentice Hall Inc., New York, 1955.

Chandan, J.S., Singh J., and Malhan, P.N., *Essentials of Advertising*, Oxford and IBH Publishing Co. Pvt. Ltd., New Delhi, 1990.

Chunawalla, S.A. and Sethia, K.C., *Foundations of Advertising: Theory and Practice*, Himalaya Publishing House, New Delhi, 1995.

Churchill, Gilbert A. Jr., *Marketing Research: Methodological Foundations*, The Dryden Press, Hinsdale, Illinois, 1976.

Claude, Hopkins, *Scientific Advertising*, Mac Gibbon & Kee, London.

Committee on Definitions, *Marketing Definitions: A Glossary of Marketing Terms*, American Marketing Association, Chicago, 1985.

Connor, Williams and Thomas A. Wilson, *Advertising and Market Power*, Harvard University Press, 1974.

Cummins, Jullian, *Sales Promotion*, 2nd Edition, Kegan Page, London, 1993.

Dalens, A.H.R., *Principles of Market Research*, B.I. Publications, Bombay, 1964.

Daver, S.R. and Daver, R.S., *Business Organisation and Industrial Management*, Progressive, Bombay, 1966.

Driver, John C. and Gordon, R. Faxall, *Advertising Policy and Practices*, Halt, Rinehart and Winston, East Bourne, East Sussex, 1984.

Dunn, Watson, *Advertising: Its Role in Modern Marketing*, 2nd ed., Holt, Rinehart and Winston Inc., London, 1969.

Dunn, Watson, S., *Advertising: Its Role in Modern Marketing*, Holt, Rinehart and Winston, New York, 1961.

Edwards, Allen L., *Techniques of Attitude Scale Construction*, Appleton-Century Crafts Inc., New York, 1957.

Engel, J.F., Kollat, D.T. and Blackwell, R.D., *Consumer Behaviour*, Second Edition, Holt, Rinehart and Winston, Inc., New York.

Engel, J.F., Wales, H.G. and Warshaw, M.R., *Mass Communication, Promotional Strategy*, Revised Edition, Homewood, Irwin, 1971.

Evans, Robin B., *Production and Creativity in Advertising*, Pitman, London.

Fadil H. Zuwaylif, *Applied Business Statistics*, California, Adison-Wessley Publishing Company, Inc., 1970.

Goode, William J. and Hatt, Paul K., *Methods in Social Research*, McGraw Hill Book Company Inc., New York, 1952.

Greyser, Stephen A., "Advertising: Attacks and Counters", *Harvard Business Review*, March-April, 1972.

Gupta, R.S., Sharma, B.D. and Bhalla, N.S., *Business Management*, Kalyani Publishers, New Delhi.

Hall, C., *A Primer of Freudian Psychology*, New York, Mentor, 1954.

Hepher, Harry W., *Modern Advertising Practices and Principles*, McGraw Hill, 1956.

Hopkins, C.C., *My Life in Advertising*, Chicago, Advertising Publications, Inc., 1966.

Hotchkiss, George B., *An Outline of Advertising; Its Philosophy, Science, Art and Strategy*, The Macmillan Company, New York, 1955.

Hovland, C.I., Janis, I.L. and Kelley, H.H., *Communication and Persuasion*, New Haven, Conn., Yale University Press, 1953.

Howard, J.A. and Sheth, J.N., *Simplified Description of the Howard-Sheth Model of Buyer Behaviour, The Theory of Buyer Behaviour,* New York, Wiley, 1969.

Ind, Nicolas, *Great Advertising Companies*, Kegan Page, London, 1993.

India, 1995, *A Reference Manual*, Ministry of Information and Broadcasting, Government of India, New Delhi.

ITC Code of Advertising Standards and Practice, The Independent Television Commission.

Jefkins, F., *Advertising Made Simple*, Heinemann, London, 1986.

Jefkins, Frank and Daniel Yadin (eds.), *Advertising*, Prentice Hall, Fourth Edition, 2000.

Jefkins, Frank., *Dictionary of Advertising*, Pitman, London, 1990.

Jefkins, Frank, *Modern Marketing*, Pitman, London.

Jethwaney,Jaishri.,*Advertising Management*, Oxford University Press,2006, New delhi.

Jha, B.N., *Modern Educational Psychology*, The Indian Press Limited, Allahabad, 1946.

Jha, S.M. and Singh, L.P., *Marketing Management in Indian Perspective*, Himalaya Publishing House, Bombay, 1988.

John R. Webb., *Understanding and Designing Marketing Research*, Academic Press, London, 1993.

Katma, G., *The Powerful Consumer*, New York, McGraw-Hill, 1960.

Kleppner, Otto, *Advertising Procedure*, Prentice Hall Inc., New York, 1945.

Knight, Frank H., *The Ethics of Competition*, Harper Bros, New York, 1935.

Kohler, W., *Gestalt Psychology*, New York, Liveright, 1947.

Kothari, C.R., *Research Methodology: Methods and Techniques*, Wiley Eastern Ltd., New Delhi, 1988.

Kotler, P., *Marketing Management Analysis, Planning and Control*, Tenth Edition, Prentice Hall of India, New Delhi, 1996.

Krech, D., Crutchfield, R.S. and Ballachey, E.L., *Individual in Society*, McGraw Hill, New York, 1962.

Lasker, A., *The Lasker Story*, Chicago, Advertising Publications, Inc., 1963.

Laskin, D., *Getting into Advertising*, Ballantine Books, New York, 1986.

Lewin, K., *Principles of Topological Psychology,* New York, McGraw-Hill, 1936.

Lifestyle Pocket Book, NTC, Henley.

Lolley, R.H. (ed.), *Practical Guides and Modern Practices for Better Advertising Management: Evaluative Advertising Effectiveness*, New York, Association of National Advertisers Inc., 1959, VII.

Longman, K.A., *Advertising*, New York, Harcourt Brace, Jovanovich, 1991.

Lyman, R., *Attention, Arousal and the Orientation Reaction*, Oxford, Pergamon, 1966.

Lynn, R. Kable, Basin Poulos and Ajay Sukhdial, "Changes in Social Values in the United States During the Past Decade", *Journal of Advertising Research* February/March, 1988.

Mandell, M.I., *Advertising*, Second Edition, Englewood Cliffs, N.J., Prentice Hall, 1968.

Maslow, A.H., *Motivation and Personality*, Harper & Row, Inc., New York, 1954.

Mathur, Navin, *Advertising and Consumer Reaction in India: A Case Study*, Printwell Publishers, Jaipur, 1986.

Mathur, Navin, *Press Advertising*, Himalaya Publishing House, Bombay, 1987.

Mc V. Hunt, J., "Motivation Inherent in Information Processing and Action", O.J. Harvey (ed.), *Motivation and Social Interaction*, New York, Ronald, 1963.

McCarthy, E.J., *Basic Marketing: A Managerial Approach*, 6th Edition, Richard D. Irwin Inc., Homewood, Illinois, 1978.

McDougall, William, *An Outline of Psychology*, Methuen and Co. Ltd., London, 1928.

Miller, Clyde R., *The Process of Persuasion*, Crown Publishers Inc., New York, 1964.

Mishra, M.N., *Sales Promotion and Advertising Management,* Himalaya Publishing House, Bombay, 1995.

Mohan, Manendra, *Advertising Management*, Tata McGraw-Hill Publishing Co. Ltd., New Delhi, 2001.

Murray, H.A., *Explorations in Personality*, New York, Oxford University Press, 1938.

Neidle, Andrea, *How to Get into Advertising*, Cassell, 1999.

Nicosia, F.M., *Summary Flow Chart of the Nicosia Model of Buyer Behaviour, Consumer Decision Process: Marketing and Advertising Implications*, Englewood Cliffs, N.J., Prentice-Hall, 1966.

Obermeyer, H., *Successful Advertising Management*, McGraw-Hill Book Company, 1969.

Ogilvy, D., *Confessions of an Advertising Man*, New York, Atheneum, 1964.

Ogilvy, David, *Confessions of an Advertising Man*, Atheneum, New York, 1998.

Osborne, A.F., *Applied Imagination*, 3rd Revised Edition, New York, Scribner's, 1963.

Porter, Mildred, *Survey, Poll and Samples: Practical Procedures*, Harper and Row, New York, John Weatherhill Inc., Tokyo, 1950.

Potter, David M., *Advertising Age*, October 4, 1954.

Potter, David M., *People of Plenty*, University of Chicago Press, Chicago, 1954.

Prasad, L.M., *Principles and Practices of Management*, Sultan Chand & Sons, New Delhi.

Ramesh Kumar, S., *Marketing Inertia*, Indian Management, February 1988.

Rathore, B.S., *Advertising Management*, Himalaya Publishing House, Bombay, 1996.

Report of the Definitions Committee, *Journal of Marketing*, 12(2), 1994.

Sahu, P.K. and Raut, K.C., *Salesmanship and Sales Management*, Vikas Publishing House, 1993.

Schudson, m., *Advertising: The Uneasy Persuasion*, Basic Books, Inc., New York, 1986.

Sengupta, Subrota, *Cases in Advertising and Communication Management in India*, Indian Institute of Management, Ahmedabad, 1976.

Shanton, William J., *Fundamentals of Marketing*, McGraw Hill, New Delhi.

Sharma, R.D., *Research Methods in Social Sciences*, National Book Organisation, New Delhi, 1988.

Sherlekar and Sherlekar, *Principles of Business Management*, Himalaya Publishing House, Bombay.

Sheth, J.N., *A Theory of Family Buying Decisions, Models of Buyer Behaviour*, Harper & Row, New York.

Simon Julian A., *The Management of Advertising*, Prentice Hall Inc., New Jersey, 1971.

Simon, J.L., *Issues in the Economics of Advertising*, University of Illinois Press, 1970.

Singh, Kanwar Deep, "Individual Brand versus Clubbed Advertising", *The Economic Times*, New Delhi, September 24, 1984.

Sissor, Jack Z., "Another Look at the Question: Does Advertising Affect Values", *Journal of Advertising*, Summer, 1978.

Thorson, E., *Advertising Age: The Principles of Advertising at Work*, NTC Business Books, Lincolnwood, Illinois, USA.

Warner, W.L., "Classes Are Real", Gerald W. Thielbar and Saul Feldman (eds.), *Issues in Social Inequality*, Boston: Littlebrown.

Watson, J.B., *Behaviourism*, The People's Institute Publ. Co., New York, 1925.

Webb, John R., *Understanding and Designing Marketing Research*, Harcourt Brace, Academic Press, 1993.

William, Raymond, *Advertising: The Magic System,* Problems in Materialism and Culture, Verso, London, 1980.

Wilmshurst, John, *The Fundamentals of Advertising*, William Heinemann Ltd., London, 1985.

Wright, John S., Winter, Willis L. and Zeigler, Sherlyn K., *Advertising*, Tata McGraw Hill Publishing Co. Ltd., New Delhi, 1982.

Yadin, Daniel, *Creative Marketing Communications*, Kegan Page, 1998.

Zaveri, Bhawna, *Effects of the Use of Women in Advertising*, IIM, Ahmedabad, 1982.

Journals and Periodicals

Advertising Age, March 15, 1999 and April 30, 1990.

Advertising and Marketing, 28 February 1999, 31 March 2000.

Anster, H., "Semantic Satiation and Generation: Learning? Adaptation?" *Psychological Bulletin*, Vol. 62, 1964.

Barksdale, H.C. and Darden, B., "Marketer's Attitudes Toward the Marketing Concept", *Journal of Marketing*, October, 1971.

Beckhell, J.C. and McIsaac, R.W., "Test Marketing Cookware Coated with Teflon", *Journal of Advertising Research*, Vol. 3, 1973.

Bell, M.L. and Emory, W., "The Faltering Marketing Concept", *Journal of Marketing*, October 1991.

Caffyn, J.M., "Psychological Laboratory Techniques in Copy Research", *Advertising Research*, Vol. 4, 1986.

Colley, Russel H., "Defining Advertising Goals for Measured Advertising Results", *Association of National Advertisers Inc.*, New York, 1961, pp. 62-69.

Dean Joes, "Does advertising Belong in the Capital Budget?" *Journal of Marketing*, October 1966, pp. 15–21.

Engel, J.F., "Psychology and the Business Sciences", *Quarterly J. Economics and Business*, 1989, Vol. I.

Facts for You, March 2000.

Faison, E.W., "Effectiveness of One-sided and Two-sided Mass Communication in Advertising", *Public Opinion Quarterly*, Vol. 25, 2001.

"Frequency in Broadcast Advertising: 1", *Media/Scope*, Feb. 2002.

Gross, I., "The Creative Aspects of Advertising", *Sloan Management Review*, Fall, 2000.

Indian Journal of Commerce, November 2000.

Indian Journal of Economics, November-December 2000.

Indian Journal of Marketing, December 2000.

Journal of IIMC, April 1999.

Kelley, Richard J., "The Advertising Budget", *Association of National Advertisers Inc.*, New York, 1967, p. 19.

Kotler, P., "Megamarketing", *Harvard Business Review*, March-April 1999.

Kotler, P and Zaltman, G., "Social Marketing: An Approach to Planned Social Change", *Journal of Marketing*, July 2000.

"More Exposure Means More Effectiveness", NBC Research Bulletin, 1990.

Patti, Charles H. and Vincent Blasko, "Budgeting Practices of Big Advertisers", *Journal of Advertising Research*, 21 (6), December 1981, pp. 23–28.

Sales Management, April 2000.

"What Stirs the Newspaper Reader?", Printers Ink, June 21, 1993.

Wittink, Dick R., "Advertising Increases Sensitivity to Price", *Journal of Advertising Research*, 17 (2), April 1977, pp. 39-42.

Newspapers

Business Line, "Catalyst", 1st Jan. 1998; 22nd Jan. 1998, 29th Jan. 2000, 12th March 2001, 31st March 2002, 24th April 2003 and 29th April 2003.

Financial Express, "Brand Wagon", 24th December 2002.

The Economic Times, "Brand Equity", 5th November 2002 and 6th April 2003.

APPENDIX–II

PRODUCT AND SERVICE ADVERTISEMENTS

Fig. 1. Product: Bodywear

Fig. 2. Product: Longines Wristwatch

Fig. 3. Services: Air India Airservices

Fig. 4. Product: Undergarments

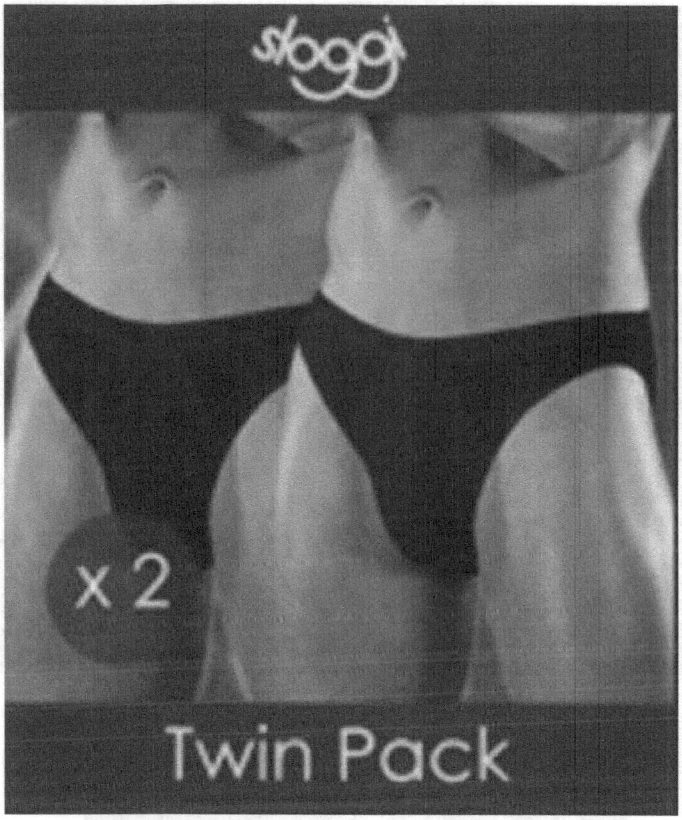

Fig. 5. Product: Sloggi Men's Undergarments

Fig. 6. Product: LG Kitchen Appliances

Fig. 7. Product: Aristocrat Wine

Fig. 8. Product: Sloggi Undergarments

Fig. 9. Product: Lovable Personal Garments

Fig. 10. Product: Colourplus Garments

Fig. 11. Product: Jadore Perfume

Fig. 12. Product: Longines Watch

Fig. 13. Brand Product: Hindware Bathroom Appliances

Fig. 14. Everyuth Face Cream

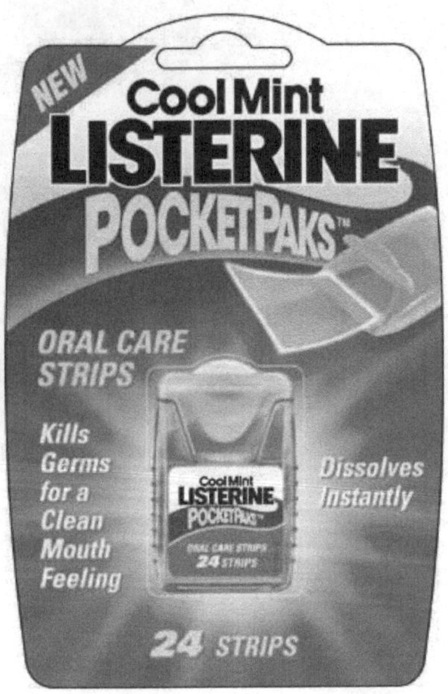

Fig. 15. Product: Cool Mint

Fig. 16. Product: Dior Perfume

Fig. 17. Product: Louis Vuitton Variety

Fig. 18. Product: Longines Ladies Wristwatch

Fig. 19

Fig. 19.1. Product: Maruti Zen Car

Fig. 20. Product: Provogue Dress Materials

Fig. 21. Product: Omega Wristwatch

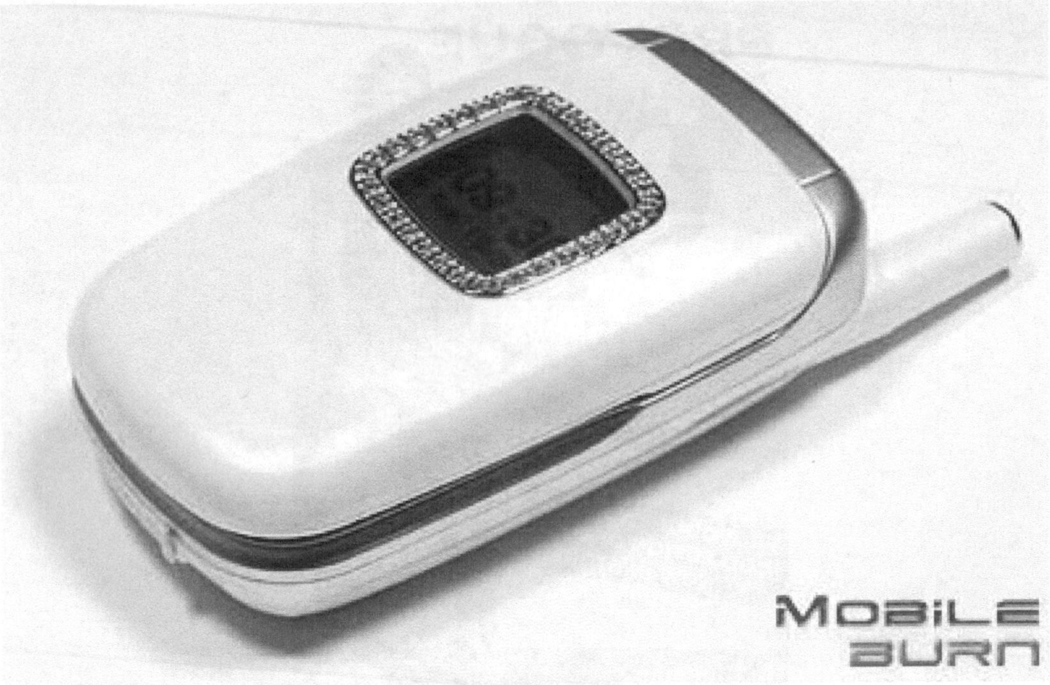

Fig. 22. Product: Mobile Phone

Fig. 23. Product: Allen Solly

Fig. 24. Product: Old Spice Shaving Lotion

Fig. 25. Product: Wills Lifestyle Cigarette

Fig. 26. Product: Wills Cigarette

APPENDIX–III

QUESTIONNAIRE

Dear Respondent

I have undertaken a research study titled "Advertising and Lifestyle Communication: An Assessment of Media Impact on Consumer Behaviour", as part of my Ph.D. degree examination of Berhampur University. The following questionnaire is intended to elicit consumer opinions towards media advertising. I solicit your kind cooperation in providing frank responses to the questionnaire enclosed herewith. Please feel free to give honest information to enable the project to take a correct shape. I assure you that the information so collected will be used for my research work and your identity will be kept strictly confidential.

Soliciting your kind cooperation.

Thanking you

Sincerely yours,

Mahendra Kumar Padhy
Junior Research Fellow(JRF)
Department of Journalism
and Mass Communication
Berhampur University.

RESPONSE SHEET

(Please tick wherever required)

PART ONE

1. Do you read Newspaper/Magazines? Yes/No

   If yes, please specify:

   (*a*) More often ☐ (*b*) Sometimes ☐

   (*c*) Seldom ☐ (*d*) Always ☐

2. (A) Do you watch Television? Yes/No

   If yes, how much time you devote for TV viewing in a day?

   (*a*) Less than 2 hours ☐ (*b*) 2 hours to 4 hours ☐

   (*c*) More than 4 hours ☐

   (B) Please specify the programmes which you watch most.

   (*i*) ____

   (*ii*) ____

   (*iii*) ____

3. (*a*) While watching TV or reading magazines/newspapers, do you look at advertisements? Yes/No

   (*b*) If yes,

   (*i*) You simply ignore them ☐ (*ii*) Watch/read them ☐

   (*iii*) Watch/read them carefully and Analyse the message content ☐

   (*iv*) Non-response ☐

4. As a consumer, do you feel advertising is useful? Yes/No

   If yes, please specify:
   To some extent/Very much

5. Advertising gives:

   (*a*) A true picture of the product/services ☐

   (*b*) An exaggerated picture of product/services ☐

   (*c*) Both facts and fantasies ☐ (*d*) None of the above ☐

   (Please rank the responses in order of preference)

6. Who influences your buying decisions?

   (*a*) Advertisements ☐ (*b*) Friends and neighbours ☐

   (*c*) Family and relatives ☐ (*d*) The reference group ☐

   (Please rank the responses in order of preference)

7. Advertising is -

   (*a*) Informative ☐ (*b*) Entertaining ☐

   (*c*) Educative ☐ (*d*) Manipulative ☐

   (Please rank the responses in order of preference)

8. Rank the following on the basis of suitability as a medium for advertising.

   (*a*) Magazine ☐ (*b*) Newspaper ☐

   (*c*) Television ☐ (*d*) Radio ☐

   (*e*) Hoardings ☐ (*f*) Billboards ☐

   (*g*) Wall-writing ☐

9. Advertisement helps the company in building brand image as well as brand loyalty of products/services.

   (*a*) Agree ☐ (*b*) Disagree ☐

   (*c*) Can't say ☐

10. Are you of the opinion that advertisement increases the cost of the products/services? Yes/No

11. (A) Do you think that TV advertisements are more informative than others like radio, newspaper or magazine? Yes/No

    (B) If yes, to what extent

    (*a*) Very much ☐ (*b*) Moderately ☐

    (*c*) Not so much ☐

12. Television has revolutionised the consumer behaviour and mostly influences consumer needs and choices.

Agree/Disagree

13. (A) Have you experienced any major attitudinal change in your purchasing behaviour after the advent of television advertisements on a large scale? Yes/No

    (B) If yes, please specify the products/services, which you have opted for after watching television advertisements.

    (*a*) ______________________________

    (*b*) ______________________________

    (*c*) ______________________________

    (*d*) ______________________________

PART TWO

1. (A) Do you use a cell phone? Yes/No

   (B) If no, why?

   (*a*) It is unnecessary ☐ (*b*) You cannot afford it ☐

(*c*) Both (*a*) and (*b*) ☐

2. The use of cell phone is a -
   (*a*) Fashion/style ☐ (*b*) Need ☐
   (*c*) Status symbol ☐
3. How often do you chat on Internet?
   (*a*) Frequently ☐ (*b*) Occasionally ☐
   (*c*) Rarely ☐ (*d*) Never ☐
4. Chatting on Internet is:
   (*a*) Interesting and relaxing ☐ (*b*) Wastage of time ☐
   (*c*) Need of the hour ☐ (*d*) A way of acquiring friendship ☐
5. Do you think that browsing porno websites on the Internet and reading pornographic magazine is permissible?
   (*a*) Strongly Agree ☐ (*b*) Agree ☐
   (*c*) Neither agree nor disagree ☐ (*d*) Disagree ☐
   (*e*) Strongly disagree ☐
6. A. Do you use a computer? Yes/No
   B. If yes, please specify the location:
   (*a*) At home ☐ (*b*) In cyber café ☐
   (*c*) In office ☐
7. Do you do tele-shopping/sky shopping/online shopping? Yes/No
8. You buy readymade dresses because
   (*a*) They have a brand image ☐ (*b*) They have a style ☐
   (*c*) They are convenient to purchase ☐ (*d*) They combine all the above ☐
9. With sufficient money available, what brand of car, motorbike would you like to purchase?
   (*a*) Car ______________________________
   (*b*) Motorbike ______________________________
   (*c*) I am not interested in either
10. If your response is (*a*) or (*b*) of the above, why should you buy them?
    (*a*) They are fuel efficient ☐ (*b*) They are costly ☐
    (*c*) They are the latest in style ☐ (*d*) They combine all ☐
11. Do you take cold drinks and fast food?
    (*a*) Almost regularly ☐ (*b*) Sometimes ☐
    (c) Occasionally ☐ (*d*) Not at all ☐

12. You prefer to drink
    (a) Mineral water ☐ (b) Filtered water ☐
    (c) Tap water ☐
13. How often do you participate in social drinking?
    (*a*) Regularly ☐ (*b*) Occasionally ☐
    (*c*) Sometimes ☐ (*d*) Not at all ☐
14. How often do you invite any one for drink?
    (*a*) Regularly ☐ (*b*) Occasionally ☐
    (*c*) Sometimes ☐ (*d*) Not at all ☐
15. How often do you participate in disco dancing?
    (*a*) Whenever opportunity comes ☐ (*b*) Almost regularly ☐
    (*c*) Occasionally ☐ (*d*) Not at all ☐
16. Name the TV channels you watch?
    1. ______________________________
    2. ______________________________
    3. ______________________________
    4. ______________________________
17. The girls in tight jeans and skimpy dresses, who appear on TV are:
    (*a*) Modern and up-to-date ☐ (*b*) Lacking in traditional Indian values ☐
    (*c*) Immoral and promiscuous ☐
18. What aspects of beauty contests do you like the most?
    (*a*) Pleasing figure ☐ (*b*) Dressing style ☐
    (*c*) Message ☐ (*d*) None ☐
19. Use of condom in advertisements on AIDS gives a message of:
    (*a*) Multiple sex ☐ (*b*) Safe sex ☐
20. Advertisement of sanitary napkins
    (*a*) Offends the viewers ☐ (*b*) Informs the target group ☐
    (*c*) Contributes to health awareness ☐
21. If things are not advertised
    (*a*) The lifestyle will be narrowed ☐ (*b*) Life will be rather dull ☐
    (*c*) Progress will be in jeopardy ☐ (*d*) Nothing will happen ☐
22. (A) Do you think advertisement corrupts the young generation? Yes/No
    (B) If yes, please specify why?

(*a*) It sells dreams ☐ (*b*) It commodifies life ☐
(*c*) It creates unnecessary desires/false needs ☐
(*d*) It makes them extravagant ☐

23. When you watch your favourite serial, music movie or sports, do you consider the break for advertisement is:
(*a*) A hindrance and disturbance ☐
(*b*) If not welcome, useful for self and family ☐
(*c*) Sometimes tolerable ☐

24. Do you enjoy advertisements in which you find celebrities endorsing the products/services?
(*a*) Yes, very much ☐ (*b*) No, not at all ☐
(*c*) To some extent ☐ (*d*) Makes no difference ☐

25. Who helps you to lead a modern lifestyle?
(*a*) Friends only ☐ (*b*) Family and relatives ☐
(*c*) Media only ☐ (*d*) All of them ☐

26. What is your goal in life?
(*a*) To be a perfect human being ☐ (*b*) To excel in the field of work ☐
(*c*) To have a modern lifestyle ☐
(*d*) If any other, please mention ____________________

PERSONAL PROFILE

1. Name:
2. Age:
(*a*) Up to 19 years ☐ (*b*) 20–35 years ☐
(*c*) 36–60 years ☐ (*d*) Above 60 years ☐
3. Sex:
Male ☐ Female ☐
4. Educational qualification:
(*a*) Under-graduate ☐ (*b*) Graduate ☐
(*c*) Post-graduate ☐ (*d*) Professional degree holder ☐
5. Your occupation:
(*a*) Service ☐ (*b*) Business ☐
(*c*) Professional ☐ (*d*) Student ☐
6. Monthly total income of the household:
(*a*) Up to Rs. 5,000/- ☐ (*b*) Rs. 5,001–10,000/- ☐
(*c*) Rs. 10,001–15,000/- ☐ (*d*) Rs. 15,001–20,000/- ☐
(*e*) Above Rs. 20,000/- ☐

Abbreviations

AAAA: American Association of Advertising Agencies
ABC: Audit Bureau of Circulations
Ad: Advertisement
Ads: Advertisements
AIDA: Attention, Interest, Desire, Action
AIOs: Activities, Interest and Opinions
AMA: American Marketing Association
ANA: Association of National Advertisers
ARF: Advertising Research Foundation
CCU: Central Control Unit
DAGMAR: Defining Advertising Goals for Measured Advertising Results
DAR: Day after recall
DM Direct Advertising and Direct Marketing.
EPS: Extended Problem Solving
GSR: Galvanic Skin Response
IQ: Intelligence Quotient
ISA: Indian Society of Advertisers
LPS: Limited Problem Solving
MIS: Management Information System
MR: Marketing Research
ORG: Operation Research Group
OTS: Opportunity to see
PDR: Pupil Dilation Response
PDR: Pupil Dilation Response (PDR)
PIP: Picture-in-Picture
POP: Point of purchase
4Ps: Product, Price, Place and Promotion
RR: Routinised Response
R-R: Response-Response
SMART: Stop Merchandising Alcohol on Radio and Television
S-R: Stimulus-Response
SRI: Stanford Research Institution
TOI: Times of India
TV: Television
USP: Unique Selling Proposition
VALS: Values and Lifestyle Survey

Index

Symbols

(AIOs) 113
4Ps 20

A

A study by Steiner 64
Above-the-line Media 43, 58
Ad agencies 40
Ad Message 41
Advantages of Segmentation 32
Advertising 21
Advertising Age 22
Advertising agency 36
Advertising and Lifestyle Communication 216
Advertising and Psychology 33
Advertising Appeals 50
Advertising Campaigns 23
Advertising Communication 34
Advertising Creativity 49
Advertising Expenditures 41
Advertising Exposure 45
Advertising Exposure Model 140
Advertising for Mass Consumption 66
Advertising Goals 26
Advertising in Shaping Brand Image 156
Advertising Management 23
Advertising Messages 22
Affective Activity 39
Agencies of Record (AORs) 215
Aggressive Promotional 5
AIDA Model of Hierarchy of Effects 37
American Marketing Association 23
Applications of Lifestyle Marketing 119
Attitude-oriented Appeals 52
Audience 34
Augmenting of Resources 60

B

Barriers to Communication 132
Basic Model for Human Behaviour 101
Below-the-line Media 43, 58
Binocular Rivalry 142
Borden Points Out 62
Boredom Barrier 80
Brand Awareness 32
Brand Opinion 32
Brand Policy 30
Brand Switching 160
Broadcast Media 44, 47
Business Cycles 65
Business Process Outsourcing (BPO) 208

C

Capital Formation 66
CCU 106
Celebrity Endorsement 180
Cell Phone User 160
Choice and Competition 35
Clinical or Psychological Theory 103
Cognitive Activity 39
Cognitive Stages 37
Cognitive Theory 103
Communication Models 36
Compensatory Consumption 88
Competitors' Strategies 31
Component of the Economic Systems 19
Comprehension and Recall Tests 144
Conative Activity 39
Concept of REACH 34

Conscious and Dormant Motives 99
Conspicuous Consumption 87
Consumer Analysis 81
Consumer Behaviour 79
Consumer Behaviour and Lifestyle 159
Consumer Behaviour Research 78
Consumer Goods 80
Consumer Profiles 41
Consumer Research 82
Consumer Research Process 83
Consumer-oriented Advertising 58
Controlled Advertising 33
Conventional Demand Theory 61
Copy Design 48
Copywriting 55
Coverage 42
Coverage' and 'Reach' 42
Creation Stage 54
Creative Imagination 73
Creative Process 54
Creative Styles 56
Creativity 49
Creativity in Advertising 48
Creativity in Communication 49
Criticised Advertising 8
Criticism 26
Customer Loyalty 30
Customer Self-selection 33
Cycle of Communication 36

D

DAGMAR 26
DAGMAR's Approach 27
Deception 67
Deceptive Advertising 75
Decision Process Approach 79
Demand Curve 62
Demographic Data 41
Denationalization of Markets 207
Determining the Positioning Strategy 57
Detrimental Force 5
Dialogue and Monologue Copy 56
Direct Advertising 44
Direct and Indirect Appeals 52
Direct Mail 44, 47
Direct Mail Advertising 47
Direct Mail Purchases 47
Direct Marketing (DM) 44
Distribution Channels 31
Distributive Approach 81
Downward Communication 131
Drucker's Philosophy 20

E

Economic Activity and Employment 65
Economic Benefits 5
Economic Effects of Advertising 59
Economic Growth 60
Economic Imperialism 209
Economic Implications of Advertising 59
Economic Liberalization 207
Economic Systems 60
Effect of Urban Growth 25
Effective Advertising 42
Emotional Appeals 51
EPS (Extended Problem Solving) Behaviour 91
Equity and Debenture Capital 66
Esteem Needs 50
Ethical Advertising 72
Ethics and Morality 71
Experiences of the Investigator 15
Explicit Role of Advertising 59
Export-led Growth 207

F

Fact-finding 55
Factors Influencing the Marketing Mix 31

Fear Appeal 51
Feature-oriented Appeals 52
Federal Trade Commission 69
Final Consumer 3
Fixed Deposits 66
Flow Process 29
Formulation of Hypotheses 6
Frequency of Internet Chatting 163

G

Galvanic Skin Response (GSR) 142
Gestalt Model 103
Gimmick Copy 56
Global Communications Technologies 208
Global Economy 207
Goods and Services 23
Guide to Prospective Buyers 61

H

Hierarchy of Effects 37
Hierarchy of Response 80
High Attention-getting Value 31
Historical Perspective 24
Howard-Sheth Model 92
Human Behaviour 50
Hypotheses 13

I

Idea Development 55
Idea-finding 55
Idea-production 55
Identified Sponsor 2
Illusions and Glorifying Sex 5
'Image' studies 45
Image-oriented Appeals 52
Impersonal Means of Communication 20
Incremental Cost of Products 157
Indian Council of Applied Economic Research 41
Indirect Appeals 52
Inelastic Demand 62
Inescapable Part 1
Informative Value of Television Advertising 158
Innovation 63
Innovation Adoption Model 38
Institute of Practitioners in Advertising 36
IQ 49

L

Lambin's Study 64
Lavidge and Steiner Model 37
Layout 48
Learning Theory 102
Liberalization 207
Lifestyle 11
Lifestyle Advertising 120
Lifestyle and Communication 114
Lifestyle Communication 148
Lifestyle Marketing 118
Lifestyle Research 113
Lifestyle Segmentation 122
Lifestyles-oriented Appeals 52
Limitations of the Study 17
Linear Communication Model 37
Local Economies 207
Long-run Market Trend 60
Long-term vs. Short-term Business Trends 61
Love Needs 50
LPS (limited problem solving) Behaviour 91

M

Magazine Advertising 46
Management Information System (MIS) 95
Manipulation 68
Marginal Role of Substitution 61
Market Expansion 60
Market Segmentation 32

Market Share 36
Marketing 28
Marketing Management 25
Marketing Mix 20, 21, 28
Marketing Research 94
Marketing Research Process 96
Marketing Strategy 40
Mass Media in the US 21
Matching Message 35
Materialism 69
McGee of Pfizer India 6
Meaning of Money 88
Media Advertising Expenditures 60
Media Costs 42
Media Department 40
Media Mix 41
Media Plan 40
Media Planning 39
Media Planning and Scheduling 58
Media Planning Process 44
Media Research 40
Media Research Departments 40
Media Selection 39, 42
Media Selection for Advertising 39
Media Strategy 40
Medium-long-term Gains 32
Message Content 44
Model of Buyer Behaviour 91
Model of the Advertising Communication System 139
Model of the Creation and Production Process 54
Monopolies and Restrictive Trade Practices Act 29
Monopoly 5
Moral Appeals 51
Morphological Approach 81
Motivation 84
Motivation of the Trade 31
Multidimensional Activity 19
Multimediation Model for Consumer Behaviour 106

N

Narrative Copy 55
Narrow-cost-Media 44
National Income 61
Need for Marketing Research 96
Needless Purchases 5
New Market Segment 36
Nobel laureate Amartya Sen 209
Non-commercial Marketing 29
Non-personal Presentation 23

O

Operational Model 38
OTS 35
Outdoor Media 44, 47
Outsourced IT 208

P

Packaging 31
Patronage Motive 98
PDR (Pupil Dilation Response) 148
Personal Selling 21, 30
Persuasive Communication 80
Persuasive Role of Advertising 68
Picture and Caption Copy 56
Planning in the Modern Marketing 29
Point of Sale 31
Point of Purchase Display 25
Popular Culture 21
Popular Programmes in Television 151
Positioning by Competitor 57
Positioning by Price-Quality 57
Positioning by Product Class 57
Positioning by Product Use 57

Positioning by Use 57
Positioning Strategies 56
Positive and Negative Motivation 85
Positive Appeals 51
Post-purchase Behaviour 93
Potential Audience 1
Potential Consumers 19, 31
Pre-test 142
Preferable Medium of Advertising 155
Primary and Selective Demand 62
Primary and Selective Motives 98
Primary Demand 62
Process of Persuasion 9
Product Planning 30
Product Proliferation 65
Product-comparison Appeals 52
Product-oriented Indirect Appeals 52
Promotion Mix 21
Promotion of Ideas 23
Psychographic Data 41
Psychographic Segmentation 120
Psychological Needs 50
Public Mode of Communication 2
Public Opinion 21
Publicity 21
Pull Effect 31
Pupil Dilation Response (PDR) 142
Purchase Behaviour 159

Q

Qualitative Research 14
Quality-conscious Consumers 30

R

Rational and Emotional Motives 98
Rational Appeals 51
Recommendations of Sachar Committee 76
Refinements of DAGMAR 28
Regional Magazines 46
Research Problem 12
Review of Literature 7
Rival Advertising 64
Roger's Model 38
Role and Importance in the Modern Business World 25
RR (Routinised Response) Behaviour 91

S

S-R (Stimulus-Response) Model 102
Sales Promotion 21
Salient Points of Marketing Research 95
Sample Design 13
Sample Size 14, 219
Satellite Channels 44
Scathing Criticism 5
Segment Profile 124
Segmentation 40
Selective Demand 62
Self-actualisation Needs 50
Sex and Advertising 74
Short-term Gains 32
short-term Trends 60
Significant Group-oriented Appeals 52
Situational Setting 36
Social Class Lifestyle 86
Social Class Profiles 123
Social Drink 170
Social Issues in Advertising 66
Special Interest Magazines 46
Statistical Techniques Used 16
Step in the Media Plan 41
Straight-line Copy 55
Strategic Planning Institute 60
Study of Wittink 69
Subconscious-oriented Appeals 52
Subliminal Advertising 80

T

Target Audience 41
Target Market Selection 110
Target Segment 33
Techniques of Lifestyle Segmentation 121
Tele Shopping/Online Shopping 167
Television Viewing Pattern 150
Testing of Hypotheses 218
The AIDA Model 37
The Black Box Model 100
The Eye Movement of Camera 142
The Federal Trade Commission of the USA 67
The Goliath of Advertising 50
The Lavidge and Steiner Model 38
The Nicosia Model 104
The Press Council of India 74
The Rational Consumer 97
The Study of Lambin 63
The Tachistoscope 142, 143
Third World countries 3
Time and Place Decisions 43
Tips for Advertisements to Avoid Dissatisfaction 94
Total Advertising 41
Trademarks 76
Transit Advertising Media 44
Triangle of Communication 34, 35
Truthfulness in Advertising 153
Types of Media 43
Types of Purchase Decision Behaviour 91

U

Unethical Advertising 72
Unique Sales Propositions (USP) 19
User-oriented Appeals 52

V

VALS 115
VALS2 115
Values and Lifestyle Classification (VALS) 147
Values and Lifestyle Survey 115
Vasudhaiv Kutumbakam 209
Vehicle Mix 45
Voice-Over IP (VOIP) 208

W

Western Imperialism 209
Word-of-mouth Communication 38